MAD HOUSE

HOW
DONALD TRUMP,
MAGA MEAN GIRLS,
A FORMER USED
CAR SALESMAN,
A FLORIDA NEPO BABY,
AND A MAN WITH
RATS IN HIS WALLS
BROKE CONGRESS

MAD HOUSE

ANNIE KARNI and LUKE BROADWATER

RANDOM HOUSE

NEW YORK

Random House
An imprint and division of Penguin Random House LLC
1745 Broadway, New York, NY 10019
randomhousebooks.com
penguinrandomhouse.com

Hardback ISBN 9780593731260
Ebook ISBN 9780593731277

Printed in the United States of America on acid-free paper

2 4 6 8 9 7 5 3 1

FIRST EDITION

Book design by Barbara M. Bachman

The authorized representative in the EU for product safety and
compliance is Penguin Random House Ireland, Morrison Chambers,
32 Nassau Street, Dublin D02 YH68, Ireland,
https://eu-contact.penguin.ie.

To the leakers, gossips, and busybodies
who populate the halls of Congress

CONTENTS

———

———

We're electing idiots.

—LIZ CHENEY

I F THERE WAS ONE THING POLITICIANS OF EVERY ILK SERVING IN THE 118th session of Congress could agree on, it was that they were members of a dysfunctional legislative body populated by a bunch of clowns.

Those were their words, not ours.

"It's just going to be the same stupid clown car with a different driver," vented Rep. Dusty Johnson of South Dakota, the chairman of the Republican Main Street Caucus, as House Republicans struggled to elect a new leader following the ouster of House Speaker Kevin McCarthy in October 2023.

Rep. Chip Roy, the goateed Texan grandstander from the far right, ranted on the House floor on one of many gray afternoons in the winter of 2024 as his colleagues labored to pass spending bills, "Nobody in this country looks at Congress and says, 'Wow, heck of a job, guys and gals, well done.' Who would do that?"

When we told Rep. Don Bacon, a Republican from Omaha, Nebraska, who represented a district that Joe Biden won in 2020 by seven points, that we were writing a book about this Congress, he immediately offered us a succinct title: *Shitshow*. (Alas, it's tricky to promote a book with a curse word in the title.)

Everyone agreed it was a clown parade—the differences of opinion lay only in whom one considered to be the clowns.

To progressives, the gradations between far right and middle-of-the-road right were imperceptible—the entire GOP had become an interchangeable circus of Trump-enabling, election-overturning, abortion-outlawing extremists.

To the retiring breed of old-fashioned conservatives, the problem was Donald J. Trump and his mimicking minions, who had adopted his brand of theatrical, racist, isolationist, democracy-threatening politics and made it all their own. Liz Cheney, the departed Republican representative from Wyoming who had become a pariah in her party and a hero to "the resistance" for breaking so forcefully with Trump, summed it up at a June 2023 event at the 92nd Street Y in New York: "What we've done in our politics is create a situation where we're electing idiots," she said. Or, in at least one case, an actual con man. (More on George Santos later.)

To members of the hard right, the clowns were the leaders of their own party, whom they tortured if those leaders ever made a responsible decision to team with Democrats in an attempt to actually pass important laws, like avoiding catastrophic debt default or sending military aid to a democratic ally getting trampled by a murderous dictator. The hard right wanted to overturn the system, and their bozo leaders were trying to work within it. They believed an establishment-controlled Congress deserved to be broken.

Whomever you blamed, and however far back you wanted to trace the problem, the reality was that the long-simmering dysfunction of Congress reached its boiling point in 2023 and 2024, when House Republicans, divided against themselves, made all kinds of embarrassing history—ousting their own Speaker and then, seven months later, trying to oust his replacement; promising and failing to come up with any plausible reason to impeach Joe Biden; unapologetically allowing Trump to dictate policy from the campaign trail and acting as his first line of defense against a court system closing in on him; and regularly blocking their own party's bills from coming to the floor for a vote.

These years in Congress were so chaotic that, at various points, six different men could lay a claim to the title of Speaker of the House: On different days, there were two different Speakers, a Speaker pro tempore, and three other men who became Speaker-designates.

It had been clear since the night of November 8, 2022, at the world's saddest political victory party in a basement ballroom at a bland Westin Hotel in Northwest Washington, that this was not going to be a normal

Congress. After months of predicting a "red tsunami" in the midterm elections that would win Republicans some 40 additional seats in the House, Rep. Kevin McCarthy, then the Republican minority leader, was still watching the disappointing results trickle in from a conference room upstairs well after midnight.

In almost every midterm election since the Civil War, the party out of power had made considerable gains in Congress, and 2022 was expected to be a prime example of this historical trend. The highest inflation rate in decades, rising gas prices, and concerns about crime were supposed to carry the night for Republicans. "Strong. Safe. Secure," read the signs the khakied crowd was expecting to wave in front of the stage when McCarthy gave his victory speech.

They never waved them, and McCarthy never gave a speech. He stayed hidden in his conference room until 2 A.M., when, with the thrumming dejection of a bombing stand-up comedian, he finally addressed an empty ballroom to tell the handful of reporters who had stuck it out that Republicans would eventually win. The results of the House elections would not be finalized for more than a week.

McCarthy was right, barely. But barely right is still right, and Republicans eventually eked out a victory, gaining control of the chamber by a margin of 4 measly votes that set the stage for the massive dysfunction that followed. And the players in Congress delivered, giving hard-right nihilists in the House outsize power over their leaders and making one branch of government work reliably only sometimes, like an Amtrak train running along the Northeast Corridor.

How disruptors like Reps. Matt Gaetz and Marjorie Taylor Greene came to be national political power players with the ability to dictate how Capitol Hill functions (or doesn't) is a story of the slimmest majority in history; a changing electorate that threatened white voters, particularly men, with losing power; a media environment that prioritizes the most extreme voices and those who treat the job like a role on a reality show; a financial incentive structure for candidates that brings out their worst; a weakened party establishment; and the accelerant fuel that was and still is Donald J. Trump.

What follows is the inside story of the first MAGA-controlled Congress, one that fully adopted the extremism and stagecraft of Trumpism and then made it all its own. This group of lawmakers repeatedly ground the federal legislature to a standstill through a combination of half-baked ideology and full-blown theatrics, humiliating the United States at a heavy time when the Israel-Hamas conflict and the war in Ukraine were both raging abroad.

The rabble-rousers of the House, propped up and egged on by right-wing influencers, often pretended to be motivated by passionately held beliefs and to act on principle. But you didn't have to be Columbo to discover that what really motivated them were petty personal disputes and a need for attention as deep as the bottomless margaritas they once drank at Tortilla Coast.

Dysfunction bred dysfunction: With a Republican majority that was unable to do much more than the bare minimum of keeping the lights on and avoiding the perpetually looming government shutdown, it was easy for lawmakers to adopt the mindset that playing games *was* the job.

This Congress didn't invent unproductive and chaotic. The pre–Civil War era was marked by several lengthy speakership battles. In 1856, Rep. Preston Brooks, a South Carolina Democrat, assaulted Sen. Charles Sumner, an anti-slavery Republican from Massachusetts, with a cane, bloodying him on the Senate floor. But in modern times, there has been nothing close to the chaos we have witnessed over the past two years. This rowdy band of lawmakers forgot to make laws, passing the smallest number of bills since the Great Depression.

These years of peak chaos saw many of those politicians with a responsible streak sprinting for the exits. Some of them were so miserable that they couldn't even hang on until the end of their terms, choosing instead to leave early and bringing the Republican majority down, at one point, to one sad, lonely vote.

Throughout it all, Democrats tried to stay united and above the fray, positioning themselves as the stalwart saviors of democracy who could be turned to when the grown-ups needed to take over and steer the careening ship away from the rocks. This worked until it was their own ship, captained by an aged president, that was heading for the rocks, and they had to quickly figure out how a united party could force out its own leader. Their willingness to ultimately do so distinguished them from Republicans, who were incapable of doing the same to Trump.

The moments Congress worked felt like brief interruptions of a long
fall down a rabbit hole. There's not too much you can say in defense of the
history-making 118th Congress, the one that finally broke, but there is
one undeniable truth everyone can agree on: It may have been depressing,
but it wasn't boring.

We asked Lawrence Lessig, a Harvard law professor who studies institutional corruption, for his thoughts on exactly how Congress broke. He
answered by quoting Ernest Hemingway's famous line on how one goes
bankrupt: "gradually, then suddenly."

This book is about what suddenly looks like.

MAD HOUSE

1

Now we learned how to govern.

—KEVIN McCARTHY

O N JANUARY 6, 2023, DAY FOUR OF A SENSATIONAL POLITICAL FIGHT, with the nation wondering when and even whether House Republicans could elect a Speaker of the House, Rep. Matt Gaetz, the wolfish MAGA congressman from Florida, had what he thought was a brilliantly devilish idea for humiliating the party's nominee, Kevin McCarthy: He would nominate the woman once widely rumored to be McCarthy's mistress for the job McCarthy was trying desperately to get.

That woman, Renee Ellmers, a nurse turned Republican congresswoman from North Carolina, hadn't served in Congress since 2017. But at the Capitol, the name "Renee Ellmers" was often invoked as shorthand for one of the chief reasons McCarthy blew his shot at the speakership when he first hoped to win it in 2015. Ellmers and McCarthy, both married, denied the affair rumors at the time, but the chatter was pervasive enough that it was referenced by Republican lawmakers as a reason McCarthy should be prevented from holding the post of Speaker.

In that less jaded, pre-Trump political environment, extramarital affairs were seen as damaging for politicians who talked up family values. And Ellmers didn't behave in a way that tamped down the rampant speculation. "I can't vote for someone who doesn't ask for my vote. I'm apparently not high on his priority list," she told reporters at the time, sounding like a spurned lover and making the process feel more like a student council race than one about choosing the most powerful person in Congress, who is also second in line to the presidency.

But that was all ancient Capitol Hill lore by 2023. Despite the bally-hooed "red tsunami" failing to crest in the previous year's midterm elections, Republicans were back in power in the House with an excruciatingly slim majority, thrusting Washington back into a moment of divided government and placing McCarthy, eight years later, once again within spitting distance of the speakership. And that's when the specter of Ellmers threatened to rise and re-humiliate him.

McCarthy arrived in Washington ahead of the long week with the shorn-sheep look of a man with a too-fresh haircut, smiling big even as he anticipated a rocky path ahead. The sunny demeanor was the Kevin McCarthy way—over the past two decades, the California Republican who used to flip used cars in the small city of Bakersfield had worked his way to the pinnacle of politics by smiling, glad-handing, raising heaps of money, and recruiting candidates constantly, all with a single-minded goal of one day becoming Speaker of the House. McCarthy was not shy about how much he wanted it, which gave his members great power over him.

Before Trump, McCarthy had been more of a stock Chamber of Commerce Republican character in Washington. He was once hailed as the new fresh face of the GOP, alongside Reps. Paul Ryan and Eric Cantor. (The trio even wrote a book together in 2010, billing themselves as "the Young Guns," despite Cantor's being forty-seven years old.) But ever since the 2016 campaign, McCarthy had worked hard to ingratiate himself with Trump and the hard right of his party, often shrugging off their worst behavior by saying that they accurately represented the voters who had sent them to Washington. "If you think Marjorie Taylor Greene is crazy," he would tell skeptical donors, "just go to her district and have a look at the voters who elected her."

McCarthy often described his job of party leader as that of a thermostat: controlling the temperature. But the truth was he often acted more like a thermometer: simply measuring the political temperature and then adjusting himself to be comfortable in it.

Following and tolerating was a weak way to lead, and it explained the position McCarthy found himself in when Congress convened at the beginning of 2023 and he decided to take his shot. Since the disappointing midterm elections, when Republicans won control of the House by just

4 seats, McCarthy and his closest allies had been convinced he would not have the votes to win the speakership on the first round of voting. That, in and of itself, was historically embarrassing—since 1923, no Speaker had needed more than one ballot to be elected. McCarthy, an optimist by nature, was deeply uncertain he would ever have the votes.

The drawn-out, once-in-a-century floor fight that followed acted as a civics lesson, as dysfunctional government situations often do. The American people learned how the process of electing a Speaker actually works: Bizarrely, House members just keep voting, over and over, until someone emerges with the outright majority. The process is low-tech and transparent: Reporters sit in the chamber to witness it, the House clerk marks down the vote with pencil and paper, and it's all carried live on C-SPAN. And this time, the whole world was watching: During his later international travels, McCarthy would be told by the president of Egypt, Abdel Fattah el-Sisi, and by Pope Francis's chief assistant that they had been glued to the television for all fifteen rounds.

For a good vote counter, there should be few surprises. Holdouts would have been identified and negotiated with beforehand, deals cut, and one would've known exactly how every member of one's caucus planned to vote before any votes were recorded on the House clerk's tally sheet.

The job of House Speaker is, after president, the hardest job in electoral politics. In the modern-day Congress, where both parties have governed with narrow margins, the job is fundamentally about math: How do you get to 218, the number of votes needed for a bill to pass with all members present? That task needs constant, careful calibration to appeal to all the various flanks of the party and an encyclopedic knowledge of members' districts, their committees, their priorities, and their vulnerabilities. It requires the Speaker to already know what those members want so they can start negotiations with them on the smallest minutiae. Former Democratic Speaker Nancy Pelosi would often refer to each bill as a kaleidoscope: You rotate it to reveal a new combination of members that will get you to 218. And with every bill, it will be a different coalition.

Lawmakers who have served in leadership often talk about how important it is to understand that "no" doesn't always mean no and "yes" doesn't always mean yes. They learn how to read the difference between a "hell, no" and a "convince-me-otherwise no." Perhaps more important, they know when an assurance that "you have my vote" is wobbly. They know when to call a vote to lock in the wobbly ones and when to pull a vote from the floor because the support is not there. "You must act without hesitation," Pelosi wrote in her book about the job of Speaker. "The minute you hesitate, your options are diminished."

Add to the difficulties of the Speaker's job the reality that the House is massive and fast-paced, and a stray comment in the hallway from a member can have massive downstream consequences. The most successful leaders move quickly and decisively—call the play, build consensus, count the votes, and go to the floor.

McCarthy had counted the votes, and they weren't there—but he went to the floor anyway.

That January, the American people also learned that you don't have to be a member of the House to be nominated for Speaker. (In one of the fifteen rounds, Gaetz nominated Donald Trump.) They also learned that you don't even have to *know* you are being nominated for Speaker to be nominated for Speaker—which is how Gaetz came up with the cruel ploy of bringing up Renee Ellmers at a moment when McCarthy looked like he was going to flop again.

Gaetz, a political nepo baby from Florida—his father is the former Florida state Senate president and political power broker Don Gaetz—arrived in Congress in 2017 as an unknown on the national stage. But he was a good fit for the political moment in which he landed: A sound-bite machine and a natural on television, he fed on conflict and, more quickly than any other Republican in office, took to Trump's brand of scorched-earth politics. By 2023, Gaetz was a bona fide MAGA celebrity, viewed by many of his colleagues in Washington as cunning and immoral—"a textbook sociopath," a colleague of his said—and the Speaker's race was going to be his Super Bowl.

The too-slim majority meant that, for months, McCarthy had been anticipating making major concessions to the hard-right faction of his party and to people like Gaetz, who had the ability to deprive him of the speakership. A group of twenty far-right Republicans, who branded themselves with the rather disappointingly straightforward name "the Twenty," were staunchly anti-McCarthy and recognized that he needed them far more than they needed him. And they weren't shy about making the dynamic clear to him.

On January 2, the day before the first vote, Gaetz texted McCarthy an appeal that made the Speaker-in-waiting realize the holdouts were going to wring him dry like a washcloth for every concession he was worth. "I had a great night's rest," Gaetz texted. The day before, the two had discussed what McCarthy could give Gaetz to win his support. "As we discussed, my creative mind thought of several other things that can conclude our negotiations one way or another." McCarthy had no interest in Gaetz's creative machinations, but he was in a bind.

Working against McCarthy were not only the nihilism of his political detractors and the weakness of his own position, but also a difficult institutional reality. Historically, it's been challenging for a Republican majority leader to rise to become Speaker. Republicans are known for their tendency to cannibalize their own, to demand someone different for different's sake. Republican Speakers just didn't last long, and McCarthy had unhelpfully served in leadership since 2009, something he and his advisers knew would count against him.

But McCarthy was more than fine with concessions. He would put members of the Twenty on powerful committees, he would allow them to change the House rules so that any one person could trigger a snap vote to try to oust him from the speakership (known, in Hill parlance, as the "motion to vacate," or even more gratingly, the "MTV"). Ultimately, McCarthy would go on to justify that a lot of the changes he had once described as "non-negotiables" were actually good for the institution of the House, good for the Republican conference, and even good for his position as Speaker.

Dealing with the consequences of his concessions, he figured, was a problem for his future self to contend with. The only thing that mattered to him on that unseasonably warm January morning was that he was on the precipice of the job he had long dreamed of holding, and there was no serious challenger, or even a half-decent fallback option, standing in his way.

What followed over the course of five *Groundhog Day* days was worse than anything he or his most pessimistic allies had anticipated, as it became clear that the hard right actually enjoyed the spectacle of torturing

McCarthy and that he would continue to take the punishment by trying to placate them.

Later, when all was said and done, McCarthy tried to spin his mortification into a strength. "Because it took this long, now we learned how to govern," he would tell reporters. "So now we'll be able to get the job done."

2

You'll get the portrait.

McCARTHY KNEW THAT WHAT HE WAS DOING WAS AKIN TO NEGOTIAT-ing with terrorists—whatever he gave them, they wanted more. But his hands were tied. Matt Gaetz and Rep. Bob Good, a far-right lawmaker from Virginia, had been stirring "anti-Kevin" sentiment for months and trying to get their colleagues to sign a pledge that they would never support McCarthy as Speaker.

One day ahead of the first vote, McCarthy and Pelosi ran into each other near the Rayburn Room, an ornate event space off the House floor where members of leadership often hold press conferences.

"Do you have the votes?" Pelosi, famous for her ability to twist votes out of her members, asked McCarthy.

Pelosi and McCarthy loathed each other. When McCarthy served as minority leader and Pelosi as Speaker of the House, McCarthy would dread any meeting of the so-called "Big Four"—the top two Democrats and top two Republicans from the House and the Senate—which he grumbled would inevitably begin with a ten-minute diatribe from Pelosi detailing all his weaknesses. "I don't know what the hell he's doing here. Why is he even here?" she would say in front of him. This about summed up her view of McCarthy: He was a waste of space, and it was a waste of her time to have to talk to such an idiot.

But for all their animosity, Pelosi was concerned about the House's ability to function.

"Not yet," McCarthy told her, conceding that a faction of his members was making demands on him, including the one-vote motion to vacate. Pelosi's advice to McCarthy was straightforward: "Just get the votes," she told him. "Democrats will always preserve the institution."

Her words would ring in McCarthy's ears for months, transforming into a more concrete promise than she had intended them to be. McCarthy would tell anyone who listened that Pelosi had promised him that if anyone from his own party tried to remove him from the speakership, Democrats would come to his rescue.

The night before McCarthy was planning to go to the floor for the first vote—which he knew he would lose because the "Never Kevins" were not yet ready to get on board—Trump phoned to tell him that Gaetz and his band of holdouts had a plan to present to him. "They're going to come to you with something," Trump said. The former president didn't know the details and wasn't particularly invested in the situation at that point. But he had a decent-enough relationship with McCarthy and wanted to help if it was no skin off his back. Gaetz, along with colleagues that included Rep. Lauren Boebert, the child-size, gun-toting rabble-rouser from Colorado, came to the Speaker's office to meet with McCarthy, who had already moved into an office he had yet to win.

Gaetz, the skillful manipulator of a handful of members whom he used to try to control McCarthy, did all the talking, waving around a ten-page list of demands he said were his new preconditions to the negotiations. "The motion to vacate is necessary but not sufficient," he told McCarthy, referring to what he needed to give up for the gavel.

McCarthy leaned back in his chair to listen. "Okay," he responded.

"Lauren needs to chair the Subcommittee on Resources," Gaetz said, pointing at Boebert, a high school dropout who, before she was elected to Congress, had owned a bar called Shooters Grill and who was taking her cues from Gaetz.

Rep. Scott Perry of Pennsylvania, the chairman of the House Freedom Caucus, needed to chair a new committee aimed at amplifying Republican critiques of the Biden administration, Gaetz added. That committee, he said, "needs a budget equal to that of the January 6th Select Committee."

For himself, Gaetz had picked out the leadership of a key panel on the

Armed Services Committee. (His district in Florida's Panhandle included three major strategic military installations.)

Gaetz rattled off his demands from a sheet of paper, which McCarthy asked to see. "I can't give you one," Gaetz said, "because I only have one hard copy."

The Speaker-in-waiting finally reached his limit for abuse and laughed. "Matt, it sounds like you want to be Speaker," he said.

"You'll get the portrait," Gaetz fired back. It was a nasty dig at McCarthy that cut to the unflattering caricature of the Republican leader: that he wasn't interested in policy or legislating, that he just wanted the job for the power trip and the gold-framed oil portrait that would one day hang in the ornate Speaker's Lobby outside the House Chamber.

"I've got a lot of pictures of myself; I don't need a fucking portrait," McCarthy said before tossing Gaetz and his friends out of his office. It was a low moment: His aides had rarely seen the preternaturally sunny Californian so grim. McCarthy and his top advisers at that point thought they would never have the votes to prevail.

At least Gaetz had actual demands. For McCarthy, there was the compounding issue of members who seemed simply to relish the spotlight that came with being a "Never Kevin" and didn't want anything more than that. These were people who simply wanted to overturn the system he represented.

Boebert, who had squeaked by in her re-election campaign, winning her seat by just 546 votes, basked in her role at the center of that action. In her five-inch Lucite heels and skintight dresses, she would parade up and down the halls of Congress, refusing to speak to reporters except to proclaim "I love President Trump!" when asked why she was standing in the way of his preferred candidate.

If her too-close-for-comfort re-election campaign meant that Colorado voters didn't like her brand of disruptive politics, she didn't care to receive that message. Boebert, a backbencher who had never wielded any real power apart from her fame, was milking the moment. At one point, she even claimed that God Himself was instructing her to oppose McCarthy. "Maybe He'll have you ball up your fists and have you stand in front of some demons, maybe a Speaker of the House," she said of . . . the Almighty.

Her opposition to McCarthy was driven in part by her ongoing feud with Rep. Marjorie Taylor Greene of Georgia. The two women, competing for the position of queen MAGA bee of the House, had long despised each other. After Republicans won back the House, McCarthy told people that Boebert had assured him she would be with him, but when she watched Greene craft a similar alliance, she tacked in the other direction. (Boebert denies this.)

And then there were the types like Rep. Eli Crane, a forty-three-year-old former Navy SEAL from a rural district in northeastern Arizona who had just arrived in Washington. After thirteen years in the military and five wartime deployments, Crane started Bottle Breacher, a company that makes bottle openers out of fired ammunition. He got a taste for public life as a contender on the reality show *Shark Tank,* where he hawked his signature product, a .50-caliber bullet fashioned into a bottle opener, which he marketed as the perfect gift for a certain kind of groomsman.

Now he was in Congress, arriving on Capitol Hill by making a bit of a splash: He was the sole freshman lawmaker in his party to withhold his support for McCarthy until the bitter end. "What's it going to take?" Crane was asked by McCarthy allies throughout the week. But it proved impossible for them to negotiate with a guy who didn't seem to want anything—not a seat on a particular committee, not a change to House rules, not even media notoriety. Crane simply felt that he had been elected to stand in opposition to "the Swamp" and it was a point of pride merely not to cave to the "pressure" of Washington. "I didn't want anything, other than to do what I was sent here to do," he said. He shrugged at the price he might pay for his intransigence. "I might wind up in the broom closet."

The only thing that gave McCarthy allies some confidence they might prevail was that some 200 members were steadfastly with them and getting increasingly furious at the holdouts for standing in the way for no apparent reason.

Ahead of the first floor vote, McCarthy's staff reached out to Vin Weber, a former congressman from Minnesota and a longtime friend with experience running nominating conventions. Weber told them to rethink their original plan of having McCarthy sit in the cloakroom and have members come in, one by one, to meet with him. McCarthy needed to stay on the floor, no matter how embarrassing it all was to bear witness to,

Weber advised. "It's really hard to fuck someone when they're sitting right there," he told them.

He advised them to assign seats on the House floor to McCarthy's top allies. "Put them in strategic places," he said, "so there's no place on the floor that doesn't have a committed organizer for Kevin." It was a convention strategy: surrounding people who were not on board and not allowing a dissonant coalition to appear larger or infect others. The most important thing to do, Weber said, was to make sure another serious contender did not emerge.

There were colleagues circling McCarthy like vultures eyeing a wounded animal. Rep. Steve Scalise of Louisiana, who for years had been McCarthy's number two, if only on paper, was a longtime rival and didn't lift a finger throughout the process to help McCarthy.

Instead, Scalise had spent the week quietly making phone calls, sussing out whether there might be enough defections for him to step into the breach. Calling members to sniff around, he alluded to the fact that McCarthy was trading away committee assignments and gathered intel on how it was all playing.

A quieter vulture surveying the landscape was the little-known, mild-mannered Louisiana congressman Mike Johnson. Johnson had only a low-level leadership position and had no chance of rising to become the Speaker in January 2023—many of his colleagues wouldn't have been able to pick him out of a police lineup. But throughout the week, he planted himself next to John Leganski, McCarthy's young floor director, and gave off the distinct impression he was listening to everything play out and taking mental notes.

One of the worst parts of all of the machinations was that, under normal circumstances, your friends, colleagues, loved ones, hated ones, frenemies, and outright enemies can't watch your humiliation unfold on C-SPAN. "The preference in politics is to always suffer your indignities in private, not in public," Rep. Patrick McHenry, the bow-tied, bespectacled congressman from North Carolina, who played a key role in the negotiations, said at the time. "That was the goal. It was evident that we would have to suffer this in public."

C-SPAN, the wonky cable network that broadcasts live all the daily congressional roll calls on the House and Senate floors, had unique access to the drama during the Speaker's race. Its cameras followed the main players around the floor as if they were at a sporting event. This was all unprecedented: Typically, C-SPAN's access to the floor is overseen by the party in control of the chamber, which decides what portions of the floor action viewers can see and hear. The network's cameras are usually allowed to broadcast either a view of the lectern from which a member is speaking or a bird's-eye shot of the entire floor. In other words, it broadcasts the votes, not the drama happening in between them. But with no Speaker elected, there was no party in charge to set the rules, and C-SPAN was left to roam the floor freely, as if shooting a Bravo reality show. The cameras were rolling on Gaetz and Rep. Alexandria Ocasio-Cortez, the progressive star from New York, for example, when this odd couple huddled together in tense conversation.

Gaetz told her that McCarthy was telling Republicans he could get Democrats to vote "present," thus lowering the threshold and allowing him to win the speakership.

"Absolutely not," Ocasio-Cortez told him. There was no such deal in the works.

The cameras also zoomed in to show which members were sitting together and what they were reading. For the first time, maybe (certainly) ever, C-SPAN was producing content that appealed to an audience wider than congressional wonks.

The press hailed it as a win for transparency, while Republican members grumbled that it only added to the chaos: Members began acting out specifically *because* there were cameras there to catch it.

IT WAS THE OPENING DAY of the new Congress, the first time members of the entire House of Representatives were all in the same room at the same time, and the place buzzed with first-day-of-school energy as they took three rounds of roll call votes and McCarthy lost all three. Ahead of the first vote, members were working the floor, networking and trying to figure out on which committees they might want to serve.

Pelosi, dressed in a hot-pink pantsuit, took a seat in the back half of the chamber, a physical demonstration of how she was passing the torch to a new generation of Democratic leaders up front. So did Rep. George Santos, the con man from New York: He sat conspicuously alone, shunned by members of his own party, and buried himself in his phone.

The reading clerk took her place at the front of the chamber and began reading from the top of her alphabetical list. By the time it got to the *B*s, the roll call vote had gone off the rails. Rep. Andy Biggs of Arizona was the first defector, standing up to yell out his own name when he was called on, and things somehow devolved further from there. Rep. Dan Bishop of North Carolina followed suit with a vote for Biggs, and when Boebert stood up, she said, "I rise to cast my vote for the honorable Jim Jordan."

McCarthy could afford to lose just 4 votes, and he had already lost the first round by the time the clerk got to the letter *C*. But they continued through the exercise anyway. Gaetz voted for Biggs. By the end, 19 members had defected, and McCarthy came in a whopping 15 votes short of the 218 he needed to become Speaker.

More milling around the floor ensued, as Gaetz and his crew of hard-right "Never Kevins" huddled together and McCarthy tried to look like things were going just as he wanted them to, even stopping to kiss a baby.

The House clerk finally called the members to order and read out the historical precedent for the once-in-a-century situation in which the House had found itself. "Following the procedure used by the House in 1923, and recorded in *Cannon's Precedents,* volume six, section twenty-four," she said, "the clerk is prepared to direct the reading clerk to call the roll anew."

And with that, Rep. Jim Jordan of Ohio rose to nominate McCarthy, and they started the entire process again, from the top.

By the end of the long day, the House had taken three votes and the number of Republicans voting against McCarthy had actually grown. "I'm staying until we win," McCarthy said, undeterred. "I know the path."

If there was one, it was covered in brambles. Republicans were deadlocked as members of the hard right relished their open revolt against the party leader.

Ahead of that day of failure, McCarthy had already started moving his things into the Speaker's office, but there was not yet a sign over the door with his name on it. Gaetz immediately wrote a letter to the Architect of the Capitol asking if there was "precedent" for a three-vote loser to occupy the ornate office of the Speaker. For two years, his colleagues had been referring to McCarthy as the "Speaker-in-waiting." Was he going to become some sort of Sisyphean character whose political fate in life was to come so close to what everyone knew he wanted so badly but never actually make it?

Rep. Tom Emmer, the hockey-loving, back-slapping majority whip from Minnesota, tried to play the role of convener in his large suite of offices in the Capitol. He had watched the first day of failed votes with concern. So, that night, Emmer summoned anyone who was around the Capitol to come by to try to hash things out like adults.

It was almost 11 P.M., and they were all calmly talking through the issues when Scott Perry, the chairman of the Freedom Caucus and a Gaetz ally, received a call from Trump. McCarthy was also on the line, from his office down the hall. Perry excused himself and took the call privately in Emmer's office. When he returned, he looked ashen. "He told me to get it done," Perry told the group. "These guys don't listen to me!"

It would come to be a common line for Perry. "I've got real mercurial guys," he would often tell leadership, throwing up his hands at his inability to control a group of members aligned only in their desire to disrupt. "I'm just telling you what they're telling me."

Democrats, meanwhile, were united in a view that Republicans needed to fix their own mess and couldn't count on them for help. Not that anyone had ever seriously reached out to ask them for it. The only real conversation that was ever held between Democratic and Republican leaders that week was about the need to preserve the discharge petition, a motion that gave Democrats the option to bypass House Republican leadership and pass legislation on their own.

Rep. Hakeem Jeffries, the new Democratic leader from New York who was following in Pelosi's hard-to-fill footsteps, was concerned that without it, Republicans might actually drive the country into economic default by refusing to raise the debt ceiling. "Their willingness to default on our debt because they believed it may benefit them politically was something that we understood early on," Jeffries said. "We needed every available tool to prevent that from occurring."

Aware that the cameras were always panning to him for a reaction shot on the floor, Jeffries sat as still as a statue, with no expression to decipher.

For five repetitive days, he did not read, he did not look at his phone, he did not even talk to the people sitting next to him. His goal was to demonstrate that he took no joy in the disarray on the other side of the chamber and to project that what was happening was serious and sad business for the country.

It was classic Jeffries—unemotional and overly controlled. Not everyone took that approach. Rep. Katie Porter, a progressive from California, was hamming it up, prominently reading *The Subtle Art of Not Giving a F*ck* as she sat through the repetitive votes. Pelosi was photographed reading a *New Yorker* article, "What Kevin McCarthy Will Do to Gain Power" (pretty much anything, was its thesis).

Pelosi, who had been given the honorific "Speaker emerita" when she stepped down from leadership, was horrified by the spectacle and embarrassed for the institution of the House. "You know, Hakeem, you may be Speaker sooner than you think, as a result of death, dishonor, and defeat," she told Jeffries at one point during the week.

The impasse on the floor prompted some panicked ideas among Republicans about how they might be able to win over some Democrats to help them out of the mess. One night, Rep. Abigail Spanberger, a moderate Virginia Democrat, was in the locker room of the members-only gym at 10 P.M., changing for a quick workout after another long day of failed votes.

"When are you guys going to end this?" a Republican colleague said to her. "You could stop this in a minute."

"Are you serious right now?" Spanberger shot back. "This is not us. This is you guys being crazy." She was appalled by the assumption that it was Democrats' fault the GOP was ungovernable. "I'm never going to vote for Kevin McCarthy," she said.

After three days of chaos, even key concessions from McCarthy had failed to get him the majority of votes he needed, and the exercise was beginning to look like McCarthy was acting out that old definition of insanity: doing the same thing over and over again and expecting a different result. But McCarthy and his team had decided early on that there was no way out but through. They would stick it out, no matter how many rounds of voting it took, no matter how embarrassing it looked, no matter how much power they had to trade away.

There were few limits to the humiliation McCarthy was willing to endure in public. But appearing on Tucker Carlson's show on Fox News opposite Gaetz was one of them. Carlson pitched the idea of brokering a deal live on television. Leganski, McCarthy's lanky floor director, who had worked for him since graduating from Stanford, was opposed, and the team politely declined the offer on McCarthy's behalf.

As he stalked back and forth through the Capitol from the House floor to his office, McCarthy stuck to inspirational bromides. "It just reminds me of what my father always told me: It's not how you start, it's how you finish," he told the horde of reporters following him. He sounded like a Little League coach bucking up a pack of middle schoolers who were having their clocks cleaned. Except he was both the coach and the team.

Meanwhile, the ugly Ellmers rumor had reached McCarthy's inner circle, who blanched at the prospect of Gaetz going through with nominating her for Speaker and pictured complete chaos breaking out on the House floor if he did. So sure were they that Gaetz was serious about it that a close McCarthy ally placed an uncomfortable phone call to Judy, McCarthy's wife, to let her know to brace herself for what was likely to transpire on the floor.

SUCH A STUNT WOULD have put a fine point on what was ultimately driving Matt Gaetz, beyond trying to dictate committee appointments: a cruel and personal animus toward Kevin McCarthy that went far beyond any policy disagreement. Even Gaetz ultimately got cold feet about such a brazen act. (He now denies that he ever considered it.)

On the seventh round of votes, instead of Renee Ellmers, Gaetz nominated Donald Trump. Trump was supporting McCarthy but also enjoying the made-for-television action of it all. Steve Bannon, the Trump adviser turned podcast host, had long pushed the idea that Trump should become Speaker for one hundred days, if for nothing else than the *Apprentice*-like theatrics of his sitting on the dais banging an oversize mallet and yelling, "Order!" Nothing about Congress had ever appealed to Trump until the week of the Speaker's race, when he saw just how riveting the floor action could be. The former president received only one vote for the speakership in the seventh, eighth, *and* eleventh rounds, which was mocked in television coverage, enraging him. Gaetz didn't try the stunt again.

Behind the scenes, McCarthy allies were quietly trying to leave Gaetz on an island and make appeals to the rest of the holdouts through respectful discussions. One late night, deep into the dysfunction, two groups were meeting separately in different wings of Emmer's offices. About an hour into what was shaping up to be a productive discussion, Gaetz arrived, dramatically bursting through the door, disrupting one of the groups. "What the fuck is going on here?" he asked. Even the most hardcore "Never Kevins" appeared to be involved in a calm discussion. Gaetz didn't like the looks of what he saw in front of him and became peeved.

"Let me be crystal clear," he said. "If anyone thinks there is some pathway to electing McCarthy Speaker, they're fucking crazy." He signaled to his faction that it was time to leave the negotiations, believing they'd follow his direction. But he had misread the room. Like Jerry Maguire, fired and flailing, leaving his office with a loyal goldfish in tow, Gaetz dramatically left the meeting alone, slamming the door behind him. Everyone sat there silently and watched him go.

After endless hours of meetings in the Capitol, the tide finally turned for McCarthy on the twelfth vote, when 14 of the holdouts called out his name, leaving just 7 opponents to win over. He picked up one more detractor, Rep. Andy Harris of Maryland, on the thirteenth vote, before the House adjourned until ten o'clock that night. He was getting closer, but he still needed a few more votes to get over the finish line.

By that evening, McCarthy's team had made an informal agreement with Gaetz: Stand down and look like the final dealmaker. Gaetz went on Fox News and indicated that his opposition was waning, and he crowed about his success: "I'm running out of things to ask for," he said.

McCarthy's allies had tried appealing to the human in Gaetz, telling him that one Texas member's wife had suffered a stroke and yet he couldn't be at her bedside because Gaetz was prolonging the vote. "I don't think you understand," Gaetz told them coldly, according to someone who heard the conversation. "The personal appeals have no effect on me."

The McCarthy allies thought they could get Boebert and two others simply to vote "present" and that would make the math work, but Gaetz wasn't finished yet.

As the House gaveled back into session at 10 P.M., Gaetz asked McCarthy's top aide if they could adjourn until Monday, a sign that his antics were not over. The answer was no.

Ahead of what was expected to be the final vote, McCarthy called McHenry, an ally who had been at his side throughout the Speaker fight, and asked him to give what he hoped would be the final nominating speech on the fourteenth vote for Speaker. The Speaker-in-waiting had corralled supportive members who had left Washington to deal with serious personal issues back to the Capitol for the late vote—including another Texas congressman, whose wife was in the hospital suffering from complications after the premature birth of their son—to fly back for the late vote. McCarthy's family was gathered in the Speaker's suite, popping champagne and celebrating.

When McHenry approached the microphone that night to nominate McCarthy, his presence was interpreted all over Washington as a sign that the deal was finally done. McHenry was considered the best vote counter the Republicans had on their side. Surely he wouldn't be standing there if McCarthy didn't have the votes.

McHenry, however, had known by 6 P.M. that they weren't done. For close to two hours that evening, he huddled with Gaetz, who had been unable to convince his cohort of remaining holdouts to vote "present."

Garret Graves, a Louisiana lawmaker who had become a key McCarthy ally during the Speaker's race, also knew it wasn't over yet. When he entered the celebratory suite, he functioned as a human record scratch: "Put the cork back in the bottle," Graves, who hadn't slept in days, said to the group. "Cut that shit out." Someone tried to give him a hug, and he shrugged it off.

Republicans began panicking when they realized McCarthy was going to fail again. On the floor of the House, North Carolina Rep. Richard Hudson, the chairman of the National Republican Congressional Committee, told a moderate Democrat that the NRCC would promise not to spend money running against vulnerable Democrats in exchange for members' voting "present" to give McCarthy the win.

"Can you guarantee that other outside groups won't spend money, either?" the Democrat asked him.

Hudson could not. There was no deal to be had at the eleventh hour on the fourteenth vote. It took yet another vote, accompanied by threats of violence, to get over the finish line close to 2 A.M. on Saturday.

Rep. Mike Rogers, an Alabama Republican and incoming chairman of the House Committee on Armed Services, stepped up to Gaetz on the House floor after the fourteenth vote looking ready to fight. He had to be physically restrained by another congressman, who grabbed Rogers by the chin to yank him back.

Heavy drinking had been a longtime problem during late-night votes, especially when members had had nothing to do all day. A large contingent could be reliably inebriated by 7 P.M. (One little band of heavy drinkers became known among their Republican colleagues as "the Drunk Caucus.") That night, one Republican member, Rep. Beth Van Duyne from Texas, approached Boebert on the floor to try to reason with her. McHenry thought Van Duyne was intoxicated, in no position to be inserting herself into delicate negotiations at this late hour. He told people she was drunk, though video of Van Duyne captured by C-SPAN that night shows no visible signs of intoxication. He pulled her into the cloakroom for a less-than-friendly chat.

"Obviously, your plan is not working," Van Duyne told him. "I'm friends with Lauren, I'm a donor to Lauren, why aren't you asking her friends to talk to her?"

McHenry was livid. "We've got this," he said, pointing his finger in Van Duyne's face. "Don't fuck this up for me. I've worked too hard for this."

The Rogers lunge may have been captured on C-SPAN, but tensions were running high throughout the chamber, much of the fury aimed at McHenry. Tennessee Rep. Tim Burchett, a member of the Twenty, thought that McHenry had bumped into him. "If you touch me again," he said to the diminutive congressman, "I will drop your ass."

McHenry looked him in the eye and laughed. "You must think I'm somebody fucking else," he said, "because I don't give a shit."

On the floor, Rep. Derrick Van Orden, a hulking newly elected Wisconsin congressman and former Navy SEAL, placed his hand on Gaetz's shoulder, leaned in, and quietly told him to go fuck himself. Even Gaetz seemed rattled.

Trump phoned Gaetz personally after the fourteenth round of votes, trying to intervene on McCarthy's behalf.

Gaetz had already won seats for his allies on key committees, a pledge to bring down spending, a new investigative subcommittee, and a rules change that made it easy to kick out McCarthy if he violated their deal. But he and Boebert found one more thing to torture McCarthy with: an assurance that centrist Republicans like Rep. Tony Gonzales of Texas wouldn't tank the package of rules changes when it came to a vote. This last demand infuriated McCarthy. He confronted Boebert on the floor after the fourteenth vote. "Change your vote," he insisted. "Say my name."

She refused. But with fights nearly breaking out on the floor, the rebels eventually tired of the drama and felt they had proved their point. By the final ballot, all the holdouts, including Gaetz, Boebert, and Crane, voted "present," allowing McCarthy to claim the gavel.

Kevin McCarthy was finally elected Speaker of the House on January 7, 2023, fulfilling his years-long quest after a historic fight that served as a preview of what governing in Washington would look like under a leader who was willing to let the tail wag the dog.

That night, McCarthy, who does not drink, had a glass of champagne, the first and last time any of his longtime aides ever saw him imbibe.

McCarthy encouraged members to forgive, forget, and come together, first citing the Lord's Prayer to "forgive us our trespasses as we forgive those who trespass against us." He ended on a lighter note, quoting Ted Lasso, the fictional soccer coach whose life advice is to be like a goldfish, the happiest animal in the world because it has a ten-second memory.

After the vote, Graves and McHenry, wired and tired, retreated to the congressional prayer room to process what had happened. They sat in silence for a long time, until Graves broke the stillness. "So, June?" he said, his prediction of how long the fragile coalition would hold.

McHenry laughed. "Let's hope it's a little longer than that. Maybe the end of the year."

It was like Subway before Subway.

—KEVIN McCARTHY

KEVIN McCARTHY LIVED IN A RENTED BEDROOM IN A $4.3 MILLION condo made up of four penthouses that had been combined into a twelve-bedroom, twelve-bathroom political fun house about two miles from the Capitol. The spread belonged to Frank Luntz, the longtime Republican pollster and consultant, and the place felt more like a political museum than a home, a cross between Mar-a-Lago kitsch and Saul Goodman's office in *Breaking Bad,* with its faux Roman columns and U.S. Constitution wallpaper. Luntz's fantasyland contained a carefully curated fanboy's collection of marble busts, political tchotchkes, and campaign buttons. "Nixon for President" and "Humphrey for President" pillows decorated couches; historic campaign posters ("Lindbergh for Governor"; "Keep Coolidge President") took up every inch of space on the walls; and there was a room dedicated to vintage *Time* and *Life* magazines—the entire space was filled with bookcases displaying old issues. A secret bookshelf door led to a hidden room with walls painted to look like the views from the Oval Office.

In 2021, McCarthy's rented room in Luntz's palace caused a minor stir when Fox News host Tucker Carlson broke the story and tried to claim there was a conflict of interest in McCarthy's renting from a longtime friend who consulted for corporations. "Kevin McCarthy promises Republicans he shares their values," Carlson said—that is, fighting against the Washington Swamp class. "At the end of the day, Kevin McCarthy goes home to Frank Luntz's apartment in Penn Quarter and laughs about it."

McCarthy said at the time that the arrangement lasted only a few months and he had since returned to sleeping in his office, a strange but common practice among members of Congress looking to save money on housing. Many members slept on their couches and then showered and changed in the morning in the members-only gym. The practice was more common among Republicans and men. (When she served in Congress, Kristi Noem of South Dakota was one of the few female office-sleepers.) Some invested in Murphy beds with Tempur-Pedic mattresses. Others just put mattresses on the floor next to their desks and stored blankets and pillows, along with their wardrobes, in their closets. It was awkward and not common anymore, especially after the MeToo movement, but the price was right.

McCarthy had temporarily become an office-sleeper. But eventually, he quietly moved back into the Luntz condo. After a stressful day on the Hill, this was the alternative universe McCarthy returned to each night, a political swag palace that fetishized his own obsession: the campaign. After all these years, this was what counted as his home away from Bakersfield, California—as much as anything counted as home for a man who lived mostly out of hotels on the road. McCarthy chose the arrangement in part because he felt like he was being a loyal friend: Luntz was in bad health and he was happy to be around to keep an eye on him. McCarthy also hated being alone.

For all his flaws, Kevin McCarthy was a powerhouse campaigner, a prodigious fundraiser with a recipe for picking successful candidates that matched their districts across the country. He would not officially back any candidate until he had visited their district, and before arriving, he would ask the candidate to put on an event for him to attend. The test wasn't in the delivery of the stump speech or the advance work that made the event look nice. McCarthy was grading the *audience*. "If people didn't come who knew you in childhood—from Little League, or someone who babysat you, or you babysat them—I didn't think you had a chance of winning," he said.

McCarthy understood that the business of politics, which people said was not personal, was nothing but. Failing his test as a candidate meant you lacked the roots that grounded you to a place and to a community. As a longtime member of Republican leadership, McCarthy felt his fellow members were his constituents, and he prided himself on knowing everything about their families and their districts and on being there for them in times of personal crisis. When Andy Harris, a Maryland Republican, lost his wife unexpectedly in 2014, McCarthy used his personal airline miles to fly Harris's kids, who lived in California, back and forth for the funeral. (This act of personal kindness still left Harris a McCarthy holdout until the thirteenth vote of the January Speaker debacle. It wasn't personal.)

His own origin story was a by-his-own-bootstraps tale of the American dream. The son of a firefighter, McCarthy opened his own deli, Kevin O's, at age twenty-one with a five-thousand-dollar windfall from a lucky lottery ticket. "It was like Subway before Subway," McCarthy often said of the deli he started in his father's garage in Bakersfield, a tale that had become part of his political lore. With the money he made selling sandwiches and then flipping used cars, he was able to pay his way through college. He went to work for Rep. Bill Thomas's office as an unpaid junior aide to the congressman whose seat he would eventually win for himself.

McCarthy never lost that entrepreneurial streak. He was always reading self-help/leadership books, like *Good to Great: Why Some Companies Make the Leap . . . and Others Don't* and *Start with Why: How Great Leaders Inspire Everyone to Take Action.*

But he had never been viewed as one of those great leaders himself. McCarthy had always been considered a policy lightweight who gave off the vibe of a laid-back parent who took the car keys and let the kids drink at his house. Even worse, for years, he had been generally regarded as a non-intellectual who had trouble putting together cogent sentences, garbling his words and peppering his sentences with misnomers. (He once said of Pelosi, "She will go at no elms to break the rules." Hard to argue with that.) In a 2015 address, he said that he had visited "Hungria" and that Russia was "keeping the place of the band on America." Throughout countless gaggles and television hits during the debt ceiling negotiations in 2023, McCarthy talked constantly of the need to "curve inflation." But more important, he had groveled before Trump, once sorting his Starburst candies for him and bringing him a bag of only his favored flavors, pink and red, behavior that helped earn him the demeaning Trumpbestowed nickname of "My Kevin." With his visit to Mar-a-Lago after the January 6, 2021, attack on the Capitol, one that helped resuscitate Trump, McCarthy cemented himself as a national symbol of Republican leaders in the Trump era—politicians willing to put aside any allegiance to higher principles or the substance of what the party had ever stood for in order to kowtow.

At his core, McCarthy was a political schmoozer and survivor, not a guy who anyone thought was cut out for the heavy lifting of high-stakes negotiations. A highlight of the spring 2023 Republican retreat in Orlando for him was a selfie with Mike Tyson, who was doing some late-stage celebrity autograph signing in the same resort hotel where Republicans had gathered. McCarthy's closest friends in Congress described him as someone who could not stand to be alone and had a preternatural need to be liked. His need to be surrounded by people at all times helped McCarthy build a base of power over the years. He often asked his colleagues to come with him to meetings with big donors or world leaders, preferring to roll deep. "McCarthy would just bring you in, plus-one it," Patrick McHenry recalled. "He shared the benefits. And even if people firmly did not like him, he thought it was his mission to flip that."

It's a style that mostly served him well in Congress, where the trust level is so low that unless you're actively trying to woo someone, they automatically assume you're trying to screw them over. But McCarthy's desire to be loved meant he cut so many deals over so many years with so many different people that a lot of people felt there was no way to trust him.

Just after McCarthy secured the speakership, one of his former top aides agreed to meet the authors of this book for breakfast near the Capitol. The former aide, now a successful lobbyist on K Street, was thrilled with McCarthy's rise, something the two had spent many late nights in the Capitol together fantasizing about over the years. How would McCarthy define success a year down the line? The aide stabbed at his scrambled eggs with his fork as he thought about the question.

"Still being Speaker" was the short and honest answer.

THIS WAS NOT A political moment in which anyone could enjoy much of a honeymoon. From the minute he won the gavel, McCarthy's first major test was looming, and it was the most important job he would perhaps ever encounter in politics—preventing an impending economic default by raising the nation's debt ceiling against the will of the hard-right members who had a yoke around his neck. No one was certain that the weakened Speaker was up to the task. Many were sure he wasn't.

McCarthy tried to make the most of the months he had before that test, banking some goodwill he knew he would need. He filled out the various high-profile committees with lawmakers who hated him and brought to the floor a series of partisan messaging bills that pleased them.

Eli Crane did not end up in the broom closet, as he had anticipated, but on the committees on Homeland Security, Veterans' Affairs, and Small Business. Matt Gaetz finally got a seat on the committee of his choice after personally pleading with McCarthy to give it to him. "Hope you saw me say long live the speaker," he texted McCarthy after the race, in one of many private exchanges between them. "Saying publicly what I said privately, working to build trust." (Filed under: Things you shouldn't have to say out loud.) "Who made the decision to leave me off weaponization?" Gaetz added in another text. "I'll do the work of ten members on that sub," he wrote, using congressional slang for "subcommittee." In February, McCarthy quietly pulled Chip Roy, the shouty Texas Republican, off the committee and gave the seat to Gaetz.

McCarthy also got to work on a campaign of political retribution against some of Trump's biggest targets. He removed Reps. Eric Swalwell and Adam Schiff—two California Democrats who had helped lead impeachment proceedings against the former president—from the House Intelligence Committee. And he elevated Marjorie Taylor Greene, whom Democrats had removed from committees altogether, by placing her on the Oversight and Homeland Security committees.

Greene, once a CrossFit fanatic who owned a construction business in the suburbs of Atlanta, was living a normal private life before she discovered Donald Trump and QAnon and became political by making wild, conspiratorial, and bigoted statements online. When she was first elected to Congress in 2020, she was treated like a liability by members of her own party. Steve Scalise had put his weight behind her opponent in the primary. Members of leadership said they were disturbed by some of her behavior and comments and were frightened of any association with her.

But McCarthy, who had decided that the key to holding power in his party was embracing the hard right, forged an unlikely bond with Greene. They were both aware of what they could offer each other, and then, on top of it, they grew genuinely fond of each other. Thanks in large part to McCarthy, Greene, a former QAnon follower who still often made conspiratorial and bigoted statements, was no longer treated like a liability. Now she was welcomed inside the tent and treated like an asset: someone who spoke MAGA fluently and could say "I told you so" to Republicans who had, for a brief moment after January 6, 2021, assumed they might finally be able to move on from Donald Trump. Greene had *never* wavered on Trump.

And when McCarthy began embracing her as a respectable lawmaker, she never wavered on him, either. "I will never leave that woman," he told colleagues after Greene stood by him through fifteen rounds of Speaker votes. "I will always take care of her." He treated her like a top adviser, a friend, and a serious member of Congress—which led other members to take her more seriously.

If appeasing the far right was his goal with his new friend, McCarthy's strategy made some sense. But the problem was that he'd picked someone who could not move any votes other than her own. Greene acted like a party of one, deeply unpopular even with her colleagues on the right. McCarthy succeeded in winning over Greene, but if anything, that counted against him with the rest of his hard-right flank.

One of McCarthy's first bills in the Republican-led House delivered on a campaign promise: It cut funding for the Internal Revenue Service, a longtime hobbyhorse of the right. Like most of what the House did, the bill had no chance of passage in a moment of divided government when Democrats controlled the Senate and the White House, but it served its purpose as a messaging vehicle that helped rally the base and build goodwill with members.

Entranced with his own celebrity, the Speaker also got to enjoy some perks of the job. He re-decorated the office he had coveted for so long, painting the walls to make it brighter and taking up the carpet to show the historic tile underneath. He had a mural created in one of the House office buildings, a photographic collage with his own waist-up image stacked atop those of the other members of Congress, his gaze skyward—looking presidential, even—with the Capitol Dome behind him.

Elon Musk visited him at the Capitol on the Speaker's birthday, a fact McCarthy gleefully shared with the reporters permanently camped out in the hallway across from his office. Donald Trump, Jr., trekked to Capitol Hill to record an episode of his podcast with McCarthy in his office. This was a welcome change for the politician who was more famous for traveling to Mar-a-Lago to bend the knee than for having anyone with cachet on the right go out of their way for him.

At the Conrad hotel in downtown Washington, there was a lavish party in McCarthy's honor. South Carolina Republican senator Tim Scott gave a toast and offered words of advice to the new Speaker as he stared ahead at the high-stakes debt ceiling negotiations to come: In a game of chicken, Scott said, you have to toss the steering wheel out the window and crash the car. McCarthy threw his head back and laughed.

He was living his dream. Still, deep down, he knew it couldn't be forever. The class photo of the entire House of Representatives is usually taken at the end of the two-year session. McCarthy scheduled the shoot for the 118th Congress in May, to be on the safe side.

4

Now I'm fucked. I look like a flip-flopper.

—NANCY MACE

NANCY MACE, A SECOND-TERM REPUBLICAN FROM SOUTH CAROLINA, was blossoming. Mace entered the 118th Congress as something of a unicorn: a seemingly center-leaning Republican who had walloped a Trump-backed candidate in her primary (thanks in large part to McCarthy's financial help). A onetime Trump campaign staffer, Mace claimed that all of the former president's accomplishments had been "wiped out" by his behavior during the mob attack on the Capitol Building on January 6. In response, Trump called her a "grandstanding loser."

Mace constantly criticized her party for its hard-line stance on abortion and contraception, claiming that if they wanted to keep winning elections, Republicans would need to support policies that were nicer to women.

Her big, toothy smile and dark Disney-princess hair made her a highly telegenic presence—and she loved going on television almost as much as the bookers for cable news shows loved a Republican guest who sounded somewhat reasonable and was willing to be critical of Donald Trump. Mace also had that thing a politician can't fake: a real narrative.

She was a high school dropout, a rape survivor, and a Waffle House waitress who had pulled herself out of a deep depression and downward trajectory to become the first female graduate of the Citadel, a military college in Charleston, South Carolina. Her Waffle House era was a difficult time in Mace's life, but these days it was political gold. ("Former Waffle House waitress" was in her Twitter bio, and she often met reporters at a Waffle House, where she would order her hash browns in front of them with confidence: scattered, diced, capped, and peppered.) A divorced mom of two kids, she had sold commercial real estate before entering politics and becoming the first Republican woman elected to Congress from South Carolina, a critical state in the presidential race.

At the beginning of 2023, Mace had the potential to carve out a unique lane for herself in a tribal party that was totally devoted to Trump. She wasn't looking to become some sort of political martyr like Liz Cheney, who had sacrificed her own career in Republican politics because of her criticisms of Trump. But Mace seemed to be searching for her own path. McCarthy had helped get her elected, and while she often made noise about breaking with the party, he didn't see her as one of his more serious problem children. Sure, she required more tending than your average member. And her quick-trigger tendency to frame herself as the victim of sexism or mistreatment raised red flags for him, so he told people that he would never meet with her without a female attorney in the room. But she mostly fell in line on votes when he needed her to.

At the Washington Press Club's annual black-tie dinner that February, just weeks after the Speaker's race, Mace served as the emcee and brought down the house with a roast of her colleagues. "Did you watch McCarthy during the Speaker vote?" she said, dressed in a revealing nude dress decorated with strategically placed black flower cutouts. "I haven't seen someone assume that many positions to appease crazy Republicans since Stormy Daniels."

As for Gaetz, Mace said, "I do have a message from Matt—he really wanted to be here tonight, but he couldn't find a babysitter." (Gaetz had been under investigation by the Justice Department, which ultimately declined to bring charges, for possible sex trafficking of a seventeen-year-old.)

The crowd ate it up. Mace was well on her way to becoming a bona fide Republican star in Washington. By April, she had gotten used to the high profile she enjoyed in D.C. and was accustomed to being at the center of attention on Capitol Hill—a position that could really belong to any Republican who wanted it. The slim majority meant that any single member could make noise about being the critical vote that needed to be won over or make demands that needed to be met to earn their vote. And

Mace often put herself in the middle of the action by threatening to buck the party, milking the moment for attention, before ultimately backing down.

On a cool day in late April, when McCarthy's time to make difficult legislative decisions had finally rolled around, Mace sat in a leather armchair in the corner of her office, dressed in a tight royal blue sheath dress and nude high heels, a staple of every Republican woman's closet, pecking at her phone. Three male aides sat arranged around her, weighing in as she composed a text message to the number three House Republican, Tom Emmer.

Nervous energy permeated the room, the antsy mood exemplified by Mace's dog, a Havanese named Liberty (aka "Libby"), scuttling around the office, jumping in and out of the congresswoman's lap. It was a critical day on Capitol Hill for House Republicans, but even more, it was a critical day for McCarthy, whose brief honeymoon in the job was officially over.

April 26 was the date of McCarthy's first real test, the first hard thing he had to do—pass a bill to raise the debt ceiling while cutting spending and taking apart President Biden's domestic agenda. The test would prove whether he had, in fact, learned how to govern, as he had so confidently stated after the debacle of the Speaker's race.

The House needed to pass *something* to jump-start negotiations with the White House and put the ball in Biden's court. McCarthy had proposed a hard-line bill called Limit, Save, Grow, that would cut nearly five trillion dollars from federal spending in exchange for raising the debt limit. He reasoned that only an ultraconservative bill could unite his rightward-lurching conference. But even cuts so deep they could impact veterans' medical care, meals for seniors, and cancer research weren't enough for some right-wing members who were refusing to back any increase to the debt limit under any circumstances.

McCarthy could afford to lose just 4 votes, and it was not at all clear he had the votes for passage shored up. Most Democrats, in fact, were convinced that the hard right actually wanted to steer the country into economic default and that McCarthy had no way to stop them. "I think I have the support of America," McCarthy told CNBC's Sara Eisen, speaking from the New York Stock Exchange on his one hundredth day as Speaker, when asked if House Republicans supported his proposal, and notably avoiding a direct answer to the question. "I'll get the party behind it."

Which is why Mace was running her text by a roomful of wired aides. A fiscal conservative, she didn't want to vote for the bill, which she said went against her principles. But the Speaker was desperate for her support. The precarious situation placed Mace right where she liked to be: at the center of the action, hoovering up airtime on television, a deciding vote with leverage.

Or so she thought.

Her chief of staff, Dan Hanlon, a longtime Republican Hill operative and former Trump administration official with a gravelly voice and long hair—making him both look and sound a little like Michael Douglas in his Gordon Gekko era—laid out what was really at stake. "This is a vote of confidence in McCarthy," Hanlon said. "This is not about the debt ceiling. This is inside-the-Beltway stuff."

"I love Kevin," Mace said, briefly looking up from her phone. "He's been very helpful to me. My position is principled." She turned back to the screen in her hands. "I want to lead a balanced budget amendment," she said, reading her text out loud as she pecked. "I want the cannabis bill that Dave Joyce is trying to fuck me on—and fuck him—and a floor vote on an active-shooter alert."

Mace really wanted the Active Shooter Alert Bill, which would incentivize an Amber Alert–style text messaging system for communities where a mass shooting was occurring. Two weeks earlier, her two kids had been a mile away from a mass shooting near Charleston. She was concerned as a mother, and showing that she was pushing for some pragmatic response would also go a long way toward helping her win re-election in a purple district. Her aides snickered at her f-bombs. "Is that going in the text?" Will Hampson, her communications director, asked. It was. The aides cackled.

"Does that make sense?" she asked them, and they nodded their unanimous approval. "Should I send it?"

"Send it," the chorus responded.

"Done. I sent it." Her anxiety set in immediately. "But now I'm fucked," she said. "I look like a flip-flopper." Mace had declared herself a hard "NO" in an op-ed published that very morning on the website *The*

Hill. And yet here she was, privately and profanely negotiating her way to yes.

Her concerns about how this behavior would be interpreted were well founded. In her two-plus years in Congress, Mace, whose purple district in South Carolina included Charleston and the Lowcountry along the coast—it was later re-districted to become solidly red—was quickly gaining the reputation of the congresswoman who cried wolf. She often criticized her party on issues like abortion and guns, racking up the television hits and social media clicks that came with being a somewhat independent voice in a tribal Republican House majority. But she had also built the voting record of a mostly reliable GOP foot soldier.

Her most egregious flip-flops had to do with Trump. As a rape survivor, she said that Trump triggered her. Watching an accused rapist climb back to power put her back in the mindset of her fourteen-year-old self, who had been assaulted in a pool by a friend of her swim coach. For years, she'd blamed herself for the episode because she had been wearing a two-piece swimsuit that day. She was also still blaming herself for being raped at sixteen.

Not to mention January 6, 2021. "I hold [Trump] accountable for the events that transpired, for the attack on our Capitol," Mace said during her first floor speech as a member of Congress, a week after the attack. A little over two years later, in the spring of 2023, sipping a skinny margarita in Charleston after a meet-and-greet with constituents at a local coffee shop, Mace vowed that if Trump became her party's nominee again, she would take herself off the airwaves rather than do anything to support him publicly.

But she was also ambitious, and her unique political profile, coupled with her good looks, made her future look bright. Mace wanted the Senate, or maybe the governor's mansion, or, hell, she thought maybe she could become the first female president one day. But if she wanted any of that, she had to figure out how to talk about Trump.

Mace was also a habitual oversharer, which could be a disarming tool. Within minutes of our meeting her, she confided that she had been up since five that morning. Work? Television hit? Hair and makeup? No, perimenopause, she volunteered.

On a bipartisan congressional delegation to London, she held hands with her fiancé in a theater and turned to a Democrat seated next to her. "This, by the way, is appropriate behavior in a theater," she said, poking fun at her colleague Lauren Boebert, who had jeopardized her own political career after she was caught on surveillance tape vaping and groping her date during a Denver performance of the family-friendly musical *Beetlejuice*. (More on that later.)

But bucking the party and carving out her own lane was hard work, and Mace, it turned out, wasn't cut out for navigating a tough road despite her Citadel credentials. She was an erratic boss who trusted nobody, but she was also petrified of making decisions for herself, according to former staff. She leaned on her consultants at every move but then dismissed their advice as sexist when she found herself in a corner. She devoured her own press, sometimes falling all the way down the rabbit hole and reading comments on Reddit to see the nasty things people were anonymously saying about her. Moving the needle of her extreme party and showing that there was a viable lane for a "reasonable" and re-electable Republican who was not backed by Trump seemed more and more difficult—maybe actually impossible. Falling in line was easy.

That spring, months before Mace ultimately succumbed to the path of least resistance and made a full-bore turn to Trumpism, her negotiating tactics were quickly making her D.C.-famous but had done little else. She knew what was being said about her, but she had a clear theory when it came to media, one that was authentically Trumpy. "People will say I'm overexposed," she said. "People may disagree with me, they may not even like me. But if people see you on TV, they think you're important, they're going to vote for you." She knew she couldn't pull this kind of shtick forever. But the day of the vote on McCarthy's debt ceiling bill was not the day to start breaking the trend.

Hanlon assured her that she was fine, despite her hard-line op-ed. "You forced a floor vote on your issue," he said. "Seventy percent of the country would say you're a great negotiator." (Those floor votes would never come.)

But fine. In the moment, she was somewhat convinced.

In any case, there wasn't much more time to ruminate that morning. Mace was now late for a Republican conference meeting in the basement of the Capitol Visitor Center, and she was also worried about getting "ambushed" by the reporters stationed outside. But there was also a sense of adrenaline in the room as Mace and the team prepared to be mobbed by microphones and television cameras on their way into the meeting. They claimed to be concerned about it, but it was clear they didn't hate it.

In 2023, after all, were you even *really* a member of Congress if CNN's ever-present congressional correspondent Manu Raju wasn't chasing you down the hall with a cameraman in tow?

"So, what do I say?" Mace said.

Hanlon offered some language as they moved briskly through the halls. "I'm open to a deal, I'm coming to the table, leadership knows what I want. Put the ball in their court. Do they want to win a national election? Keep hitting them on everything."

"Okay," she said. "Let me hit the head real quick."

Mace could act like one of the boys. Her bro-ish staff often climbed out the window of their office in the Longworth House Office Building and drank beers on the roof, overlooking the Capitol.

At lunchtime, Mace's team received word that she was being asked to attend an afternoon meeting with McCarthy to discuss her crude morning text. "Summoned to the principal's office again," as Mace liked to say.

It was time for another strategy session with her staff, this time at a taqueria on Pennsylvania Avenue, walking distance from the Capitol. The team drove. Mace insisted that all she wanted was that the bills dealing with guns, access to contraception, and marijuana be brought to the floor.

"You're a sophomore," Hanlon said. "You want to be like, 'I had this brought up in the House. My colleagues didn't vote for it.' That's an easy ask." McCarthy's weakness, he argued, was an opportunity for Mace to build a name for herself. "He's promised so many things to so many people, why would he not do it," Hanlon said. "He understands he doesn't control the conference."

"I want people to understand that if I'm going to modify my position there's a substantive reason for it," said Mace, eating the filling out of her tacos and leaving behind the shells.

At around 1:30 P.M., she trotted into McCarthy's office with Hanlon. About thirty minutes later, she emerged and told reporters that she was voting for the bill because she had felt "heard" by the Speaker.

That evening, McCarthy passed the bill that many in his conference hated, with 4 "no" votes, the exact number he could afford to lose. Gaetz couldn't be won over. Neither could Tim Burchett, a folksy hard-liner from Tennessee, nor two House Freedom Caucus members, Andy Biggs of Arizona and Ken Buck of Colorado. Those four would stick together and later plot to oust McCarthy.

But McCarthy now had a "House product" that would put him in the Oval Office, face-to-face with the president, who had insisted he would not negotiate over the debt limit. Mace's decision to back the bill in exchange for concessions on her pet issues meant that McCarthy had passed his first big test, which gave him leverage and altered the dynamics of the debt ceiling negotiations as the country crept closer to default.

It wasn't immediately clear exactly what Mace had extracted in return—assurances of vague things that would happen in the future—but she claimed she was satisfied. "I was the last one," she said. "I got a balanced budget amendment, I got movement on women and also the gun violence–related bill. These are all good things."

Except she never got them. And then she got tired of trying. By Christmas of that year, almost all her staff had resigned or been fired, replaced with at least two staff members whose résumés included having previously worked for the national punch line that was former Rep. George Santos, the serial fabulist who had conned his way into office and would be booted out before the end of his term. Hanlon would be gone—and on such bad terms that he even filed paperwork to run against his old boss for her seat.

5

It's going to require them to continue on a week in, week out basis to obstruct.

—RUSSELL VOUGHT

RUSSELL VOUGHT WORKED OUT OF A BARE-BONES OFFICE JUST A FEW blocks from the Capitol, tucked away around the corner from a Starbucks, up two rickety flights of stairs. His Nordstrom Rack ties hung on the bathroom door. The only art on the walls was newspaper clippings with headlines commemorating an undeniable highlight of Vought's career: McCarthy's flailing fight for Speaker. Framed on his wall was a *New York Post* front page, known as the wood, with the headline "Grow Up!" and featuring a photo of Gaetz and Boebert sabotaging McCarthy.

Some sort of animal had burrowed into his walls—rats or pigeons—and sometimes clawed so loudly from behind his desk that it was hard to carry on a conversation without picturing what it was after in there. (It helped to assure oneself that they were pigeons, not rats.) It was out of this infested office that Vought, who had served as budget director in the Trump administration, ran the Center for Renewing America, a pro-Trump think tank that served as a critical outside adviser to the hard-right faction of House Republicans. Vought was also helping to craft the agenda for a second Trump term, and his name was often floated as a potential White House chief of staff. (He would end up in his old job, serving a second tour as head of the Office of Management and Budget.)

Skinny, serious, and bespectacled, Vought had cultivated a reputation as a budgetary savant with extreme views. He wanted two trillion dollars in cuts to Medicaid, more than six hundred billion dollars in cuts to the Affordable Care Act, and more than four hundred billion dollars in cuts to

SNAP, or food stamps. He wanted to cut the State Department and the Labor Department in half. He was staunchly opposed to funding the war in Ukraine and adamant that the so-called "X date," when the treasury secretary said the United States would default on its debt, was a made-up deadline that should be ignored.

Vought had a particularly close relationship with Rep. Chip Roy of Texas, the policy chairman of the House Freedom Caucus and a self-styled spending expert of the hard right. Roy was an aggressive communicator. He loved grandstanding on the House floor and yelling into the chamber as much as he loved burying himself in the charts and mind-numbing minutiae that gave his grandstanding some intellectual heft. If you watched C-SPAN on mute and saw his floor speeches, you could somehow still hear how loud he was. If you turned on the volume mid-speech, you'd inevitably hear him railing about "slush funds" and "back-room deals" and posing rhetorical questions like "When are Republicans going to put up or shut up?"

Roy was an interesting member of the hard right in that he had voted to certify the presidential election in 2021. After the January 6 attack on the Capitol, he said that Trump "deserves universal condemnation for what was clearly in my mind impeachable conduct" and that it was "foreseeable and reckless" of Trump to whip his supporters into a frenzy over the lie that the election had been stolen. (Roy did not vote to impeach Trump, however, because he said the Democrats had drafted articles that were "flawed and unsupportable.") Unlike other Republicans who had made similar statements in the immediate aftermath of the attack on the Capitol, Roy never tried to eat, spin, or disappear his words. In 2023, he made an early, bad bet on the doomed presidential campaign of Florida governor Ron DeSantis.

Roy may have hated Trump, but he often checked in with Vought—one of the few former cabinet secretaries who remained fiercely loyal to the former president—for an "all clear" on his position on spending. As McCarthy's team began negotiating with the hard right on their debt ceiling plan, they would often read Roy into their machinations in the hope of winning him over. It would often seem like Roy was amenable to their negotiations with Biden, which involved raising the debt ceiling in exchange for work requirements, permitting reform, and other conservative priorities.

But that would curdle after Roy returned from a meeting with Vought. McCarthy allies always rolled their eyes at the mere mention of Vought and his influence. From McCarthy on down, they would all ask the same question: "When has Russ ever been elected to anything?"

Vought was not in Congress and never had been, but there are plenty of other ways to wield influence in Washington, and his shabby office counted as an unlikely power center. It was from there that he helped organize the opposition to McCarthy's speakership, with members checking in with him regularly for strategic advice. It was from there that he cranked out memos and briefing papers for Republican lawmakers, explaining to them how to confront Biden over the debt ceiling and where to impose drastic cuts on federal agencies.

Whether McCarthy liked it or not, Vought hovered over the negotiations from start to finish—sometimes literally. At one point, McCarthy's hand-picked negotiators, Reps. Garret Graves of Louisiana and Patrick McHenry of North Carolina, were meeting with Biden officials in a conference room in the Eisenhower Executive Office Building, a room decorated with framed portraits of former budget chiefs. Graves snapped a photo of Vought's portrait and texted it to him.

"Don't worry," he joked, "you're overseeing the negotiations."

Vought had a clear view of how Republicans should be governing with their House majority. "You figure what the maximalist conservative position you can accomplish is and get 218 votes for it," he said. "That's what success looks like." That's not what he saw McCarthy doing, and in his mind, it left the hard right with only one option to get the Speaker in line. "It's going to require them to continue on a week in, week out basis to obstruct," he said.

Obstructing was all the House Freedom Caucus had ever really been successful at or trained to do. And even now, despite all the concessions hard-right members had won during the Speaker's race, it was still in the group's muscle memory.

In Vought's mind, the roadblock to the transformational change he had been hoping to see was Rep. Thomas Massie of Kentucky. Massie was a far-right, raw-milk-guzzling libertarian-minded member, perhaps best known in the national consciousness as the congressman who posed for a Christmas photo with his wife and five children, each holding a semiautomatic rifle and grinning in front of a heavily ornamented tree. "Santa, please bring ammo," Massie captioned the family photograph, which he posted online in 2021 just days after a mass shooting at a Michigan high school in which four students were killed.

McCarthy respected Massie, unlike some of the other thorns in his side. An inventor and MIT-trained engineer who held twenty-nine patents, Massie didn't play manipulative games, and he wasn't driven by petty personal disputes. He just followed his own libertarian leanings.

Massie was one of three congressmen aligned with the House Freedom Caucus who, after the January Speaker fight, were given a seat on the Committee on Rules, known in the past as the Speaker's Committee because it was stacked with loyalists and served as the Speaker's mechanism for controlling the House floor. Before a bill can come to the floor, it has to get past the Rules Committee. One of the concessions McCarthy had made with the holdouts was to give them 3 seats on this powerful internal tool of a committee. People like Vought assumed this meant that his wing of the party would control the House floor: The trio could exert their power to tank legislation they didn't favor, like a bad debt ceiling deal, even before it could come up for a vote.

But assuming Massie would do what was expected of him was a misread of his character. On the Rules Committee, he took a principled approach to his position: He didn't think it was his job to achieve a specific legislative outcome, especially if it was the opposite of what a majority of the conference wanted. Massie didn't intend to use the assignment to hold legislation hostage.

For Vought, this constituted a huge problem. The entire *point* of having Massie on the Rules Committee was to hold legislation hostage. If Massie had held his ground, Vought thought, the right could have been transformational, stopping any less-than-conservative debt limit deal from coming to the floor, halting any efforts to fund the government, and blocking a Ukraine-aid bill from ever getting a vote.

In truth, there are ways to pass bills that don't go through the Rules Committee. Many of the bills Vought wanted to halt relied primarily on Democratic votes for passage, and the Speaker could have circumvented the Rules Committee altogether and brought those bills to the floor under what's known as "suspension of the rules," which requires a two-thirds majority to pass. Or, members could have used a discharge petition, a rarely used maneuver that amounts to a demand, with signatures from a majority of the House, that forces consideration of the bills on the floor. Some of these maneuvers would be used regularly over the next two years to circumvent the hard right.

Still, Vought sighed at all that could have been.

The Speaker's race had put twenty hard-right members into positions where they had real power and influence. Vought was struggling to find someone to blame for the fact that they would not have a single policy win to show for it. "It could have been earth-shattering if Massie was different. He has a very old view, a leadership view, of who gets to decide what's on the floor," he said. "I think his view is problematic."

McCarthy tended to agree. "I knew when I had him on the Rules Committee, he was my secret weapon," he said.

Serious people put shit on paper.

—SHALANDA YOUNG

IN NEGOTIATIONS, THE CONSEQUENCES OF FAILURE TYPICALLY MEAN A lost opportunity for progress. If talks fall apart before the finish line, as they often do, it means something that could have been done is lost, whether that be instituting gun safety laws or border security measures.

Rarely do the consequences of a failed negotiation lead to an immediate, catastrophic economic result. Once a crisis like America's defaulting on its debt has been averted, it's easy to forget the stakes, like moving on with your day after stepping into traffic and almost being hit by a bus. *Not* being hit by a bus doesn't become a formative experience. Avoiding a terrible outcome is not much of a message on which to run a campaign. Still, Biden officials consider the debt ceiling negotiations of 2023 to be one of their greatest successes, because the alternative would have been so unthinkable—a potential global recession, the loss of millions of jobs, a sharp drop in stocks that would have hit retirement funds. "We knew we had to close here," said one top White House official. "Even if Republicans owned it more, it would have been Biden's economy, and we were beginning to feel like we were making some progress on the economy."

In June 2023, the White House had no margin for error. Democrats lived in a constant state of anxiety over Biden's age and electoral strength, and economic competence was going to have to carry the day for Biden if he wanted to beat Trump.

Democrats mostly stayed quiet on the topic of his age, but privately, they admitted that it was a subject of great concern long before the June 2024 presidential debate that ultimately forced Biden out of the race altogether. "I think he's one fall away from not being the nominee, or one TIA, or something like that," Rep. Don Beyer, a longtime Virginia Democrat, said in July 2023, weeks after Biden tripped on a sandbag and fell after speaking at the U.S. Air Force Academy graduation. "I worry about his being eighty-six at the end of his term, and I do worry about Kamala, who I like, but her positioning in the public consciousness chases independents to the right."

Despite all of Biden's accomplishments, Beyer said, "there's no affection from voters. And he seems fragile."

Rep. Marie Gluesenkamp Perez, a vulnerable Democrat representing a rural district in Washington state, was asked by a donor at a private fundraiser that winter if Democrats had any mechanism by which to ditch Biden. She didn't have much that was positive to tell the group gathered at the wine-and-cheese-and-folding-chairs gathering back home in Washougal, Washington. "The reality is, the ship has sailed, Biden is going to be the nominee," Perez told the gray-haired crowd. "I'm not here to apologize for his performance or his messaging."

Rep. Josh Gottheimer, a centrist Democrat from New Jersey who would go on to run for governor, fretted in September 2023, as a potential shutdown loomed, that Biden was simply not dynamic enough to do what was needed to help his party out of a mess he thought they would all be blamed for. "I'm extremely worried that he's not up to it," Gottheimer said. "I don't think he's senile. I just think he can't control the room. He can't go work the phone." But at the time, most kept their concerns private, for fear of damaging Biden even more if they vented them in public.

Biden was on shaky ground even before the earthquake of the debate that forced him out of the race, and he couldn't afford a massive hit to his economy. That there was even going to be a negotiation over raising the debt ceiling was a fairly remarkable occurrence—a showdown between a Democratic White House and a Republican House on this issue hadn't happened since 2011, when everyone involved had vowed it should never happen again. And this was a far more perilous situation, because a solid group of House members might tank the economy for the sheer spectacle of it.

Biden had played a key role in the 2011 negotiations, but he took the more historical perspective that it was morally and politically imperative for Congress to lift the debt ceiling on its own without the White House's involvement. Biden's longtime chief counselor, Steve Ricchetti, spoke on the phone regularly with McCarthy, and it became clear to Ricchetti that the Speaker did not want to risk defaulting. But there was a solid group of House members over whom McCarthy had no control, who were far too dangerous to play chicken with.

That spring, Garret Graves, the square-jawed Republican from Baton Rouge who bore a passing resemblance to actor Luke Wilson, would emerge as a key player. At fifty-one, Graves was a longtime Hill staffer who was first elected to Congress in 2015. He was something of a throwback, a low-key policy wonk who loved the details of permitting reform and bemoaned the loss of trusted voices in news. (Despite being too young to have grown up watching Walter Cronkite, he claimed to long for the days of Walter Cronkite.) Graves disliked the incentive structure created by social media and cable news, which served only to amplify the loudest MAGA voices in the party.

A former wilderness instructor and river guide, he enjoyed long morning bike rides with McCarthy in Washington and fishing trips with the Speaker back home in Louisiana, and on sleepless, stressful nights, he would stay up kneading cinnamon rolls from scratch. When he was in Washington, he slept in his office, and he would bake his rolls in the oven of the Lincoln Room, a historic space off Statuary Hall in the Capitol, and present them to his surprised colleagues at high-stakes morning meetings.

Graves was a rarity among Republicans in Congress in the year 2023—he wasn't looking for fame as much as, he claimed, seeking a way to make his party less embarrassing and more focused on governing. To be clear, he was still a modern-day member of the Republican Party who wanted to be successful. That meant he had voted against both of Trump's impeachments and had voted to overturn the 2020 election results. He had opposed Biden's $1 trillion infrastructure bill. He voted for the political impeachment of Secretary of Homeland Security Alejandro Mayorkas and supported the hamstrung Republican efforts to impeach President Biden. He voted against sending aid to Ukraine, arguing that he couldn't justify spending billions more on a foreign war unless the White House gave out "some metrics of success or milestones, so this isn't an endless war." (Some of Graves's Republican colleagues had the same criticisms of the White House, but they still voted to approve the aid, arguing that not doing so would cost the United States dearly later.)

Despite his own votes on Trump, Ukraine, and the 2020 election, Graves could grow cynical about how his party had changed since he first arrived in Congress, and he viewed himself as operating outside that change. And on those sleepless nights when he was kneading dough, he fantasized about leaving it all behind and leading a simpler life working in a bakery. (It's a common fantasy for anyone in a stressful job, but an especially popular one among top decision makers in Washington, who often suffer from decision fatigue. Rahm Emanuel, who served as chief of staff to President Barack Obama, said the two of them often sat in the White House and fantasized about opening a T-shirt stand in Hawaii that sold only white shirts in a size medium, leaving them with absolutely no decisions to make.)

Graves thought the "reward mechanism" in politics was broken, which encouraged the provocative tweets and personal feuds and disbursement of misinformation. There was no reward mechanism, as he saw it, for the people like him, the quiet types who were actually trying to solve problems. "It's twenty-four months of political crap and beating the hell out of the other party and weaponizing everything you can," he said. "That whole thing really needs to be reset."

Graves often referred to the far right of the party as "exotics." The term, which never caught on, was meant to tag hard-right extremists as the exception to the rule rather than the norm. The "exotics" may have been the minority, but they represented the id of the party, and their ranks were growing.

Graves wasn't the chairman of a powerful committee and hadn't been elected to any leadership post. But during the Speaker's race, he distinguished himself in McCarthy's eyes by helping to corral the various factions to end the embarrassment and deliver him the gavel. "It was complete ridiculousness, in my opinion," Graves said. "I'm looking at it on TV and think we look like a bunch of freaking idiots. The American people gave us the majority; we're unable to pick up the reins and start actually governing."

"What do you want?" McCarthy asked Graves after winning the gavel, working under the fair assumption that everyone wanted something from him.

"I want you to be a good Speaker," Graves said.

In a world where McCarthy was widely viewed as a politician of low principles, someone who would do and say whatever it took to survive the day, Graves, somehow, was a devout McCarthy-head. He didn't ask for anything, but he got a few goodies. McCarthy created a faux leadership position for him and gave him a coveted hideaway in the Capitol. So Graves became McCarthy's man on the Hill, filling a gap in a toxic leadership team built on suspicions. "It got to where I was spending three-quarters of my day in the Speaker's office," Graves said. McCarthy's actual staff started thinking of Graves as a sort of super-staffer, a helper with a member pin.

McCarthy didn't trust Steve Scalise, the elected majority leader and his number two on paper, and told people he found him ineffective. He cut Scalise out of all decision-making, and it didn't help soothe giant bruised egos that he essentially replaced him with Graves, a more junior congressman from Scalise's home state.

Rep. Elise Stefanik of New York, the number four House Republican, was seen as someone consumed with ambition to rise in a potential Trump administration, either as his vice presidential pick—she always knew it was a long shot but not a no shot—or a cabinet secretary. She was less interested in the politics of the Hill.

Instead of empowering the people who had the top jobs on paper, like Scalise and Stefanik, and had been elected by the members to hold leadership positions, McCarthy built his own small team of loyalists to lean on. So when it came time to negotiate a debt ceiling deal with the White House, it made sense that McCarthy turned to Graves first. But when he informed the White House that Graves would be his chief negotiator, the unconventional arrangement raised eyebrows.

Shalanda Young, the budget director who would be helping to lead the talks, was a staffer's staffer at heart. The first Black woman to serve as White House budget director, she'd left her heart behind in the House, where she had made her bones as the Appropriation Committee's majority staff director. Young knew the ins and outs of negotiations and could work out the complicated, technical bills that funded the government. She was also the rare "normal" person among those in top jobs in Washington, and the rare person beloved by both Democrats and Republicans. She had lived and worked in D.C. government since the George W. Bush administration, but she still ordered crawfish from back home in Louisiana and picked it up herself from the loading dock at National Airport.

Trained in the Pelosi school of politics, Young held a deep belief in the value of following protocols. She trusted institutions and the structure of congressional committees. "They are there for a reason," she said, sitting in her ornate office in the Eisenhower Executive Office Building, across the street from the White House. "Even if you don't trust the chair, there's a lot of staff knowledge that's built in."

All this made her very anxious when she was informed that Graves, someone who was not in leadership and had never chaired any committee, would be her negotiating partner on a high-stakes deal to avoid catastrophic economic collapse. He seemed nice enough, but Young couldn't help but wonder, *What is Garret even doing here?*

Graves understood the starting point for many House Republicans: They simply did not support debt ceiling increases. Period. Most of them, from all wings of the broken party, agreed that Washington had a fundamental budgeting problem that needed to be addressed. And Graves firmly believed that the House would have no credible negotiating position if it didn't have a "House product," i.e., a bill it passed on its own to address the debt ceiling, one that he said would "guarantee us a place in the room, if not actually a place leading discussions."

To think House Republicans would be "leading" the discussions was a gross overestimation of the leverage they had with a White House that believed raising the debt limit was the exclusive and autonomous responsibility of Congress and that the administration should never have been dragged into this mess in the first place. But Graves was right that they needed to show they could pass something on their own to even earn a seat at the table.

McCarthy's little band of trusted voices on the issue were old-school Republicans who didn't get airtime in the modern-day moment dominated by Marjorie Taylor Greene and Matt Gaetz. They would also all be gone by the end of the 118th Congress, their names lost to history, while

Greene and Gaetz would carry on and become celebrities with national profiles.

Along with Graves, the group included Patrick McHenry, the elfish forty-seven-year-old Republican from North Carolina who had been in Congress since 2005, a lifetime during which he had transformed himself from a young bomb thrower into what passed for a statesman two decades later. He wore bow ties, hated Donald Trump, and had chosen to chair the Financial Services Committee rather than take a leadership position where he would be expected to weigh in on what he considered news-of-the-day nonsense, like Trump's "truths" and George Santos's lies.

That McHenry didn't want anything was his superpower in Congress. "When people think they have leverage over you, this place changes for you," he said. "The way I operated the whole year is because I don't actually want to be Speaker."

As long as McCarthy was in charge, however, McHenry had a chance of getting roped back in, and he would quickly be asked to help find a path out of the debt ceiling debacle. Even if he wasn't a social media star, McHenry knew how to work the traditional media, and he understood the contours of the assignment he was given—to figure out how to say that Republicans were reducing federal spending, even if Democrats were going to try to stave off any significant cuts from domestic programs.

McHenry took pride in being able to speak in perfect quotes, and while Graves might have been McCarthy's latest friend crush, McHenry was McCarthy's oldest friend on the Hill, the longtime Robin to his Batman. Plus—and there's no nice way to put this—he was just smarter than the majority of his Republican colleagues.

Still, the White House was set on not negotiating with anyone McCarthy sent to sit with them.

With the help of Graves and McHenry, however, McCarthy, for a moment, looked like he might be able to make it all work on his terms and make Biden bend to his will. He muscled through the Limit, Save, Grow Act, his bill, the "House product" that raised the debt ceiling while cutting spending and whose sole purpose was to get him to the negotiating table. (Thank you, Nancy Mace!) McCarthy sold the bill to his members, who hated it, seeing it as nothing but a messaging bill—he promised them it was the floor, not the ceiling, of cuts he would fight for in the negotiations. None of it could have ever passed the Democrat-controlled Senate, and Biden immediately threatened to veto a bill that rolled back parts of the Inflation Reduction Act and imposed expansive work requirements on social programs like SNAP.

The last member to cast his vote on the tied bill was not Mace but Santos, the law enforcement target who had been calling himself a solid "no" vote just a week earlier. But on this vote, like Mace, Santos had seen an opportunity to show his worth and to demonstrate to leadership they needed him as much as he needed them. In a meeting with his staff, he had pitched them the idea of his waiting until the very end to cast his vote. They were uniformly opposed to such a stunt, arguing that what he needed was *less* attention, not more. But later, as they watched the floor vote, they noticed Santos refusing to vote as every other member cast theirs.

"Oh my God," one staffer said out loud. "He's actually doing it."

Santos positioned himself as the man who gave McCarthy his big win. Maybe it helped him hang on for a few months longer. Probably it was just another news cycle he butted into for no real purpose.

Republicans had passed the bill, and passing it at all, even by a slim 217–215 margin, served its purpose. The meetings in the Oval Office would now begin.

Leaning into the role of the perpetually underestimated man, McCarthy took a victory lap for what amounted to a half measure. His precarious position required constant maintenance of what some lawmakers referred to as McCarthy's "red meat tank," which he had to empty and refill on a regular basis after spending down his capital with the hard right. Negotiating a debt ceiling deal with Biden would leave the tank empty, and he would try to refill it by launching an impeachment investigation into the president. But that would be later.

In May 2023, there he was, playing against all those unflattering (if accurate) caricatures of who he was, set to negotiate one-on-one with the most powerful person in the world—and he was holding that person hostage, refusing to raise the nation's $31.4 trillion borrowing limit without spending cuts.

On May 9, McCarthy was the Speaker of the House, and not in name only. He attended his first Oval Office meeting with the president as part of the Big Four—the group of top House and Senate leaders from both parties that included Sens. Chuck Schumer and Mitch McConnell and Rep. Hakeem Jeffries—and the bargaining was being conducted on his terms. This was an elevating moment for the former owner of Kevin O's, sitting across from the president of the United States, the two of them speaking as almost-equals.

The group arranged themselves on the cream-colored couches by po-litical party: McCarthy and McConnell sharing a couch across from Schumer and Jeffries, who wore sneakers. Biden sat apart, in a chair at the center.

It wasn't McCarthy's first time in the Oval Office—he had been there plenty during the Trump years. But stylistically, things had changed. The cream-colored carpet had been swapped out for a dark blue one bearing the presidential seal. The portrait of Andrew Jackson that had once hung near the Resolute desk had been replaced by a portrait of Benjamin Frank-lin. There was a bust of Rosa Parks next to the bust of Martin Luther King, Jr. That was definitely new.

In the meeting, the Democrats asked McCarthy, "Will you take de-fault off the table?"

He refused. Instead, he pressed back. "We have now just two weeks to go," he said, looking at Biden. "Does he not believe there is any place we could find savings?"

As McCarthy and the Big Four left the White House after their first debt ceiling meeting, the press-loving Senate majority leader, Chuck Schumer, gleefully headed for the "sticks," the stakeout on the White House driveway where lawmakers could speak to reporters after a meet-ing and spin their version of events.

McCarthy put a hand on Schumer's shoulder and pulled him back. "The Speaker goes first," he said as he strode out to meet the cameras, where he purposefully took his time and made the others wait. He later confided to one of his aides, "I don't know if that's a rule. I just made it up."

There were two types of people on McCarthy's negotiating team. In one camp were the true believers who wanted to shrink government. That group included a young man named Brittan Specht, McCarthy's top policy adviser, who would leave a lasting impression among White House officials as a staff member who once challenged Biden in an Oval Office meeting, at a moment when the chaotic, MAGA-fueled Hill clashed with the guarded Biden White House. In the meeting, Biden had started reciting his well-known talking points. "No one else could have achieved the economic success we have achieved," he said. "Nobody could have brought the unemployment rate down. Nobody would have imagined we had done this."

Specht, a smart, young, confident ideologue who regularly made it through the day by drinking eighteen cups of coffee, did not have much of a poker face, and he smirked as Biden spoke.

The president noticed. "You tell me you would have believed we could have done that," he said, wagging his finger at Specht.

"With all due respect, Mr. President, I don't think that's right," Specht replied. He had more to say about why he thought the economy would have come back after the pandemic in many scenarios, but he didn't have time to finish his thought.

"You're a lying, dog-faced pony soldier," the president shot back angrily at the young policy staffer who had dared to speak up. (A senior Biden staffer denies that this exchange occurred.)

While Biden's senior staff cringed, the Republicans in the room, meanwhile, felt like the most cartoonish caricature of Biden had emerged in a real-life setting, as Specht backed down and everyone tried to move on from the awkward moment as quickly as they could.

In the by-the-book world of Biden's West Wing, what Specht did counted as a stunning breach of protocol. In an Oval Office meeting with the president, a staff member simply does not speak unless called upon to answer a specific question. Staff were in the room simply to support their bosses and to provide information if called upon to do so. Even Shalanda Young, the budget director and lead negotiator, had asked permission to speak up during the meeting. "Mr. President," she asked, "is it okay if I explain where we are?" Speaking out of turn was not how serious people conducted business in the corridors of power. But that's what Specht had chosen to do.

"Total amateur hour," Young told people in shock after the meeting.

Back at the Capitol, the entire episode got a good laugh. "Guys, you're not going to believe what happened," McCarthy said, eager to recount the incident to the rest of the team. The Republicans who had sat through the meeting also came away shocked at how business was conducted in Biden world. Top staffers seemed to walk on eggshells around the president. McHenry described the vibe there to people as a "WASPy, passive-aggressive Thanksgiving." So what if Specht had spoken out of turn? Everyone needed to lighten up.

At other times, Specht, the right-wing ballast in the discussions, told the team he understood the limitations of their negotiation—he understood that those at the table represented a small majority who controlled one chamber of Congress, and whose only power was to block legislation. It wasn't the Tea Party wave—Republicans hadn't just won an election they'd run on the issue of federal spending. Still, they had to reflect that many of their members did want to overhaul the federal government.

When it came to reining in spending, "our members want gastrointestinal surgery, they want someone's stomach stapled," Specht told the Biden negotiators in one meeting. "We're more in the mode of 'Put down the donuts and get a dog.'"

Still, there were conversations where the Biden economic team thought Specht overstepped. "We're really just trying to help you with the labor shortage," Specht told his White House counterparts at one meeting in the Capitol, trying to convince the White House to include more work requirements for SNAP and other safety net programs. "You passed all these big bills to build manufacturing plants; there's no workers. Nobody wants to work anymore, and we're trying to help you with that." To the White House negotiators, he spoke as if all the evidence that work requirements don't produce more workers didn't exist and he was going to convince the other side of his point of view.

Negotiations at this stage were not about convincing the other side. They were about getting to the other side of a crisis House Republicans had created, finding some landing zone that enough Democrats and Republicans in the House could vote for.

The other part of McCarthy's negotiating team was made up of brasstacks people like McHenry, who understood that they simply needed to emerge from the deal with some kind of agreement that would avoid default and include enough concessions from the White House to earn at least 150 Republican votes. McHenry understood that there would be no grand rethinking of the way government was funded, no overhauling of the annual budget process, no winning ideological battles with lifelong Democrats over work requirements. There would be small wins on the margins: some federal spending caps, reclaiming unspent funds that had been designated for the Covid-19 emergency, imposing stiffer work requirements for safety net programs, and some permitting reforms for energy projects.

Behind the scenes, McCarthy was working multiple angles. He spoke regularly with Steve Ricchetti, Biden's trusted adviser, who had been tapped to lead the debt ceiling negotiations on the president's behalf.

Ricchetti was as inner circle as it got in Biden's incredibly insular world. When Biden was vice president, the two shared an office, with Ricchetti working out of Biden's closet. Biden liked the cramped arrangement—when Ricchetti tried to lobby for a bigger space in the Eisenhower Executive Office Building, arguing that it was impossible for him to hold any meetings under the current arrangement, Biden said he would simply leave and let Ricchetti use the main desk for meetings but that he needed to stay close.

"I've been told you're the person I need to talk to," McCarthy said to Ricchetti on their first call after he was elected Speaker. The two developed a fruitful back channel and spoke more openly and regularly than anyone knew at the time, with McCarthy giving Ricchetti many quiet heads-ups about his next moves.

For the most part, the negotiations with the White House were cordial. The White House didn't think much of Graves—"useless, absolutely useless," was how one person deeply involved in the negotiations described him, noting that he seemed to lose all interest in anything other than his pet issue of permitting reform—but they thought highly of McHenry, who was viewed as bright, creative, and clear-eyed about the goal: finding a face-saving solution for everyone.

Sometimes McHenry would appear to be performing for the true believers on his side of the table. At other moments, he back-channeled with Young. Republicans wanted a win on a border security measure, and McHenry would call Young to say, "I need some help. Give me some ideas I can pitch to you guys that you'll accept. Give me something you'll say yes to on the border." The White House would give them nothing on the border.

In public, McHenry bemoaned the leaking and the scooplets that threatened to derail a careful dance House Republicans were coordinating with the White House. "Everyone wants a detail of this, everyone wants a tweet," he said one night as he walked into McCarthy's office while news outlets were reporting that a deal was taking shape.

Young tried to be as transparent as possible throughout the negotiations. For example, Republicans wanted to secure a budgeting mechanism known informally as Paygo—a pay-as-you-go plan for government agencies that says any actions that cost money have to be offset by savings elsewhere. Young insisted that as budget director she would have the ability to issue waivers from that requirement. And she told them she intended to give herself great latitude to do so. "If you want to do this," she told them, "the waiver authority has to be big enough that I can waive it because it's a Tuesday." Republicans complained, but Young explained to them that their victory would be mostly symbolic. She wasn't pretending otherwise, and ultimately they relented.

And so the negotiations went, mostly cordial.

Until May 19.

After meeting with McHenry and Graves in the Capitol, Young had reached her limit of speaking in generalities. They had been talking for weeks about a deal over a certain construct on federal spending caps, and she was starting to feel like she was doing their job for them. She would come up with something that fit their construct only to have them shoot it down. On May 19, a beautiful Washington Friday, when they had been cooped up inside all day, she had had enough. "Serious people put shit on paper," Young told them bluntly. "We have talked around your needs long enough. We're at the paper phase, or we won't get finished." With Republicans refusing to offer anything in writing, there seemed to be no point to continuing the talks.

Long nights and no sleep were also adding up. Ricchetti and Young were accusing Graves and Specht and their party of being responsible for the entirety of the deficit increase.

"It's all related to the 2017 tax cuts," Young told them.

"That's bullshit!" Specht yelled at her across the table. If every negotiation has a good blow-up meeting, this one counted as the breaking point.

Graves told Young he was going to tell reporters after he left the room that they were hitting pause on the negotiations.

"Maybe you should use different terminology," Young warned him, noting that the markets were parsing every word and that *pause* was a dangerous and loaded term to use with just two weeks left before the date that the treasury secretary had said the nation would go into default.

"I'm going to say 'pause,'" Graves responded.

Graves came out of the meeting and said the talks were on "pause" because the White House was making "unreasonable" requests.

There were consequences to the gamesmanship. In August, Fitch Ratings would downgrade U.S.-backed debt and remove the United States from the group of fiscally top-rated countries like Germany and Denmark, citing an "erosion of governance."

Personally, Young was happy for a brief break. She hadn't seen her toddler daughter in weeks, relying on her parents' coming in from out of town, along with her best friend, for around-the-clock babysitting. For some thirty-six hours, the teams that had been talking three times a day didn't speak.

Young's principal remaining hang-up was work requirements. Republicans insisted on imposing new or expanded work requirements for safety net programs like SNAP, other federal programs for low-income families with children, and Medicaid for adults without dependents. Democrats were deeply concerned about making such a concession. Biden, however, was clear with Young that the ramifications of a first-ever default would fall squarely on him. It was his economy that was on the line, and anything to disrupt it would become a central story as the election neared. He was willing to make those compromises to get the win.

Biden had his own red lines: He refused to cut discretionary spending below the previous year's spending levels, but he very much needed a deal to come through. It was, however, a tough pill for many Democrats to swallow that the deal meant that people in their fifties were going to lose access to the food stamps they depended on.

"There's not a damn thing in here for Democrats," Ricchetti often complained during the negotiations.

It helped sell the cuts to Democrats when the independent Congressional Budget Office said that under the terms of the deal, enrollment in the programs would actually increase and spending on the programs would grow by $2.1 billion over the next decade. Veterans were added, as were people experiencing homelessness and young adults who were in foster care at the time they turned eighteen. But this didn't change the fact that some people would be kicked off.

"The president wanted to finish and not default," Young said. "I was worried about work requirements, but at the end of the day, it was balanced."

One of McCarthy's great victories of the debt ceiling negotiations was making sure Trump stayed quiet. Florida governor Ron DeSantis had come out strongly against the deal in an attempt to outflank the front-runner in the Republican presidential primary from the right. Vivek Ramaswamy, the entrepreneur and political upstart who was also running for president, had also criticized the deal. But McCarthy told Trump he was expecting to have some 150 Republicans voting for it. His argument to Trump was that if 150 of DeSantis's former House colleagues didn't listen to him, it would show he didn't have any juice and Trump would look stronger.

Trump waited until after the deal was signed to criticize it. "Well, it is what it is," he told a Des Moines radio host. "It has passed," he said, adding: "We'll get it properly fixed in two years."

The White House's strategy was to let McCarthy claim the negotiations as a victory to win over his conference. They thought they had won in the fine print, but they would sit back while McCarthy did his victory lap, if that's what it took to avoid default.

The problem was his members didn't fall for it. "A disappointment across the board," the Freedom Caucus said in a statement issued after the deal was settled. Rep. Dan Bishop, a hard-right Republican from North Carolina, raised the prospect of ousting McCarthy because of it.

Democrats, meanwhile, went into briefing overdrive. The White House had cut House Democrats out of all negotiations on the bill, which they found frustrating, given that they were the ones who had to vote to pass it. Now Biden's team didn't want any lawmaker to be able to say they had not been briefed into oblivion about the deal before the vote.

Young was scheduled to deliver a commencement speech in New Orleans, at Xavier University, as the rollout was proceeding. "This is the most fun I've had in two weeks," she said in her speech. "If you haven't read, we're having a few budget problems in Washington, and the president gave me a two-hour break to come be here with you, and I'm not kidding about that."

She really wasn't. On the way to the commencement, Young circled the airport in her car so she could brief Vice President Kamala Harris on the deal, with her parents distracting her daughter in the back seat with Cocomelon videos. On the way back to the airport, Young's father pulled over at a gas station as she was briefing the cabinet, and she finished doing so on the side of the road. Her daughter was being too loud in the car.

When she landed, she went straight into a briefing on Zoom for Senate Democrats (which, because it was the weekend, featured a number of significant others milling around in the background or sitting in recliners and watching television) and then to four separate in-person briefings for House Democrats. Some Democrats were distraught over the concessions the White House had made on work requirements, but they had faith in Young, whom they still viewed as one of their own.

The White House ended up with an outcome they felt they could defend. Republicans extracted some modest cuts but enough to be able to feel—at least temporarily—like the effort to drag the White House through it was worth it. Everyone could claim some kind of win.

The deal was unquestionably a monumental victory for both parties involved, and for the country at large. It also set the stage for a semifunctional relationship between some top White House officials and some House Republicans, who would have to meet again to negotiate a deal to send billions of dollars to Ukraine.

Thanks to McHenry, Graves, and Young, the world economy would no longer be threatened. McCarthy's negotiators had pulled off a deal that could likely get enough votes to pass into law, even as a sense of nihilism and fiscal madness had overtaken large swaths of the right.

The problem remained for McCarthy that enough far-right members weren't buying what he was trying to sell.

7

We're going to force him into a monogamous relationship.

—MATT GAETZ

IN ORDER TO PASS THE DEBT CEILING BILL, REPUBLICANS FIRST NEEDED to pass a rule, a bit of congressional arcana that few who work outside Capitol Hill would have had any need to pay attention to until now.

Ahead of any major legislation, the House needs first to approve a "rule" for debate, laying out details like what amendments on a given bill can be offered. The passage of the rule was always treated as a foregone conclusion—even if lawmakers planned to break with their party on a bill, they would stay in line on the rule.

For decades, it had been assumed that you voted your conscience on the bill and your party on the rule. But things had changed. The hard-right Republicans didn't care about how things had been done in the past, and for them, the rule was a useful tool for controlling the floor.

By 2023, more than two decades had passed since the majority had lost a vote on their own rule. By the end of the 118th Congress, it had happened seven times.

"Who cares?" Eli Crane told *The New York Times*'s Carl Hulse about violating a longtime House norm and voting down a rule. "I could care less and neither could my voters." (About a month later, Crane would make headlines for referring to Black Americans as "colored people" on the floor of the House, words that Democrats immediately requested be stricken from the record. A few months after that, Crane wrote on X, formerly Twitter, that an upcoming visit to the Capitol by the Ukrainian president, Volodymyr Zelenskyy, was a reason in and of itself to support a government shutdown. But those were all one-offs: He would eventually find his animating issue in promoting conspiracy theories that shadowy "deep state" forces had tried to assassinate Trump.)

"It's the only tool they have in the toolbox. It's legal; it's in the rules," said Tim Burchett, the folksy hard-right member from Tennessee who had started to regularly vote down rules.

Members of leadership didn't know how to handle the shift. "This is a whole new mindset," House Majority Whip Tom Emmer said. "I'm telling you, the new representatives, they're going to be the voice of the people who sent them here."

McCarthy needed 218 votes to pass the rule that would allow him to bring the debt limit legislation to the floor. But so many Republicans were so livid about the agreement that they planned to vote against the rule simply to register their objections. This left just one unpleasant way forward for McCarthy: He had to ask Democrats to provide him the votes he needed to pass the rule and cover the gap.

McCarthy never called Hakeem Jeffries directly to ask for his help. Instead, Steve Scalise was tasked with speaking to Rep. Katherine Clark of Massachusetts, the number two House Democrat, about how many Democratic votes they would ultimately need to get the rule passed, given the mutiny on their side. They had concluded they would need a sizable chunk: around 30.

About an hour before the vote, Jeffries called Josh Gottheimer, the New Jersey centrist who co-chaired the bipartisan Problem Solvers Caucus and had good relationships with Republicans. "I need thirty people in the well for the vote," he told him.

Jeffries held a stark view of his role in that Congress. In his view, lawmakers had basically one job: to avoid a catastrophic default on the country's debt. The rest, however awful and dysfunctional it got, was just details by comparison. If there was one thing House Democrats were going to do, it was ensure passage of the debt ceiling bill negotiated by Biden and McCarthy.

McCarthy's need for Democratic votes to pass the rule marked a major milestone in the crumbling of his fragile coalition: Once beholden to the far right, he was now forced to run to the opposing party for help. It's hard to put it better than Matt Gaetz put it himself.

"We're going to force him into a monogamous relationship with one or the other," Gaetz said on *War Room,* the podcast hosted by Steve Bannon—who, like Russell Vought, worked relentlessly to push the House to the right and was agitating for default. "What we're not going to do," Gaetz added, "is hang out with him for five months and then watch him go jump in the back seat with Hakeem Jeffries."

Some House Democrats carried a small chip on their shoulder about how they were being treated. They had been excluded from negotiations between Biden and McCarthy, but now they were expected to come save the country from economic crisis. On the House floor, Democrats held back their votes to see how many Republicans would vote against the rule. For thirty-one excruciating minutes, Democrats simply waited for it to become clear that, by a large margin, the rule would fail and, without their help, there wouldn't even *be* a vote on the debt ceiling bill negotiated by the Republican Speaker. In what passed for a dramatic moment for the always-collected Jeffries, the minority leader finally gave the go-ahead, holding up a green voting card in his right hand that unleashed the Democrats. Gottheimer cast the first Democratic vote for the rule, walking up confidently to the front of the House and cementing himself as a centrist power broker; then 51 more Democratic votes poured in, far more than needed for the rule to pass. In the end, 29 Republicans, including Gaetz, voted against the rule.

Some Democrats had wanted to allow the rule to pass but give Republicans the votes they needed and nothing more, like giving a prisoner a sip of water and a hunk of bread to stay alive but not enough to feel satiated. Instead, Democrats, many of whom were enthusiastic about the deal, flooded the rule with "yes" votes.

The number of Democratic votes ultimately didn't matter. But it mattered a lot to one important person, who still despised McCarthy and prided herself on her ability to count votes. Pelosi, the Speaker emerita who generally took the position of offering advice only when asked—she often said her goal was to act as the dream mother-in-law to the new leadership team—in this case couldn't help but give them her unsolicited two cents. She sidled up to Reps. Pete Aguilar, Clark, and Jeffries on the House floor and told them pointedly, "Not how I would have done it. But I understand you can't control every member."

Jeffries heard the comment but chose not to engage with the criticism. In his book, it was a clean win. "At the end of the day," Jeffries said, "what McCarthy was asked about and criticized for was handing over the floor to House Democrats. We made this happen as House Democrats, not them, even though they were in the majority."

On May 31, just days before the date when treasury secretary Janet Yellen predicted the federal government would not be able to pay its bills, the House passed the Fiscal Responsibility Act, avoiding catastrophic default. McCarthy managed to pull the country back from the brink of crisis, but he did it by passing a bill that had more Democrats voting for it than Republicans. This left him in a complicated position.

There was little time for celebration. As McCarthy's top aides took off immediately for delayed family vacations, they got word that Rep. Ken Buck of Colorado, one of the founding members of the House Freedom Caucus, a guy who kept a (nonfunctioning) AR-15 mounted on his office wall and had no love for an establishment-minded Speaker, was mulling a motion to oust McCarthy.

Brittan Specht, of "that's bullshit!" fame, joked to one of Jeffries's top advisers, Gideon Bragin, that the Republicans could co-opt Jeffries's oft-repeated line about Democrats: "Our diversity is our strength."

"You know what the second half of that line is?" Bragin responded. "Our unity is our power."

Most people believe McCarthy could have survived the debt limit deal, maneuvering through it and "piling on some bullshit elsewhere," as one person put it, to make amends with the angry far right. And most people believe he made the deal because he had been in leadership long enough to have internalized the need to be somewhat responsible.

But one difficult decision had just led him to the next. Now he would have to pass a short-term spending patch that would only further enrage those members who already wanted his head on a pike.

GAETZ HAD PRIVATELY TOLD McCarthy he thought the deal was solid. "The debt limit is a kidney stone: You gotta pass it and move on," he said. "I'm going to vote against it, but I think it's a pretty good deal."

Garret Graves had been in the room for that conversation and so many more like it, and now he was enraged about the public reactions from Gaetz and the House Freedom Caucus. The reactions he had gotten from many of them internally ranged from positive to simply too uninformed to have any strong opinion about what the bill did or didn't do. In one hours-long meeting before the bill came to the floor, Gaetz had told Graves, "If you can just get work requirements strengthened alone, that's all we need for a victory."

When the measure finally passed—a deal that included pushing 750,000 people off food stamps—Gaetz dismissed all the "purported policy 'wins'" as "largely cosmetic budget gimmicks or waivable at Biden's whims" and patted himself on the back for opposing both the rule and the bill itself. (Gaetz wasn't exactly wrong: The White House had wrangled other changes to expand other portions of the food stamp program, SNAP, and had allowed only Republican wins that were either illusory or so small they could live with them.)

Still, Graves came to his own conclusion that, of the Republicans who were railing against the bill, "none of them knew what it was that was in there. It was not merit-based reasons. It just goes back to theatrics and egos and all that stuff."

Nancy Mace, for her part, had staked out a firm "no" position on the debt ceiling bill, and this time she didn't budge. "Republicans got outsmarted by a president who can't find his pants," she tweeted after voting against the Fiscal Responsibility Act, a mean comment about Biden's mental acuity that Democrats pounced on as a delicious self-own by a member of the opposing party, admitting that they had somehow gotten outsmarted by a guy they regularly accused of having dementia.

But hours before the evening vote on the rule, Mace was in her office feeling more upset and jaded about Washington than she had since she got there. She was smarting over a rebuke by Rep. Bryan Steil, a young Republican from Wisconsin who had gone on Fox News and criticized her opposition to the bill. "There's some of my friends who would like to be on TV and raise money off this bill, rather than read the details of it," he said. Adding insult to injury, Mace said leadership had informed her that if she voted "no" on the rule, they would renege on the promises they had made to her. Mace sat in her office looking stunned. "I don't do business that way," she said. "I started my business with a handshake. I don't operate that way."

As she sat there debating what to do—potentially tweeting about leadership's threat, potentially taking a walk during the vote on the rule or simply voting "present"—Graves arrived at her office in the Long-worth Building. Mace told an aide to tell him she was tied up speaking with a *New York Times* reporter. As she hid from Graves in her office, her aides explained to him that Mace was upset with Steil. They played him the offending clip. And when Graves sauntered off, Mace asked them for a blow-by-blow.

"He seemed like he did not think that was helpful," an aide told her. "He thought from your text that you wanted to talk. It seemed like he could maybe come back?" The aide added: "The Steil thing made him pensive." Graves did not return.

In the end, a lot of trust was broken. As punishment for their own leader, a dozen hard-right lawmakers staged a protest a week later on the House floor to block a piece of their own party's strange culture war agenda: a bill to protect gas stoves. (There was no actual plan by the Biden administration to ban gas stoves.) They voted against the rule, and this time, no Democrats came to save the day. The floor was frozen and would stay that way for an entire week, with no votes being taken as McCarthy huddled in his office with various lawmakers traipsing in and out as they tried to find a way out of the impasse.

"We're not going to live in the era of the imperial Speaker anymore," Gaetz said. He himself may have had no problem with the debt ceiling deal. But what he saw in front of him was a useful band of angry members whose rage he could deploy to unseat McCarthy.

"This is the difficult thing," McCarthy said after meeting with those demanding ransom from him. "Some of these members, they don't know what to ask for."

8

I can't move forward and move up and be anti-Trump.

—NANCY MACE

A S THE CRIMINAL INVESTIGATIONS AGAINST DONALD TRUMP BEGAN piling up, House Republicans contorted themselves into ever-more-awkward positions to defend him. After prosecutors released photos of Trump storing classified documents next to a toilet at Mar-a-Lago, McCarthy argued that such a practice was actually secure.

"A bathroom door locks," he explained, with a straight face.

And as it became clear that Trump would be his party's inevitable presidential nominee, Nancy Mace, trying to keep up, would conveniently find herself less triggered by the former president and actively looking to make peace. On television, she began berating the Justice Department for indicting him, and privately she started machinating about what it would look like to position herself as a potential vice presidential pick on the Trump ticket. "I'm willing to bury the hatchet to save the country, and I know President Trump is, too," she told *Politico* that summer.

It all induced a collective eye roll from her colleagues and the reporters who covered her, especially because it was clear she had an approximately zero percent chance of joining Trump on the ticket—not after having criticized him for the January 6 assault on the Capitol and after her vote to certify the 2020 election. So, what was the point of throwing away her personal credibility?

"I have to make a decision on where I'm going to be in all of this," she said. "I can't move forward and move up and be anti-Trump. That's just not where the country is. If I want to have a career going forward, then I have some decisions I have to make. I'm in the most complicated place I've ever been."

In June 2023, Mace and Trump had started texting, since she had taken to defending him on television. He sent her one of his Sharpied letters, thanking her, though they hadn't actually spoken yet. But someone had planted her name in a story about potential vice presidential picks, she said, and now Mace's mind was off to the races.

"I would take a conversation," she said. "He's going to be the nominee; if we want Republicans to win, you need a woman on the ticket. It's something I would consider. Biden is corrupt. What are your choices? You have a chance to serve your country at that level. Do you turn it down? I don't know that you do."

It was a stance that was enraging Nikki Haley, the former South Carolina governor who at the time was still running against Trump. Two years earlier, Haley had endorsed Mace and campaigned with her when Mace was being viciously attacked by Trump. Haley expected the favor to be returned.

Mace fully acknowledged that she would not have won her race without Haley's backing. But she was in the process of making a series of justifications that so many "adults in the room" had made before her when they decided to attach themselves to Trump—one that Haley herself had made at one time and would make again. Just like the people with burned careers and reputations who preceded her, Mace thought her own story might turn out differently. "I think I understand what works and what doesn't work. It's four years, it's a placeholder for doing other things," she said. "Stranger things have happened."

Mace was not alone on Capitol Hill in her tendency to look in the mirror and see a future president staring back. Many lawmakers grew accustomed to being treated like visiting heads of state abroad, appearing on influential Sunday news shows whenever they want to and attending lavish fundraisers as the guests of honor.

The jobs also came with just the right amount of celebrity: Many lawmakers were recognized and thanked for their service enough to feel important and fulfilled, but remained anonymous enough to lead mostly regular lives, where they could order coffee at Starbucks and have their names misspelled on the sides of paper cups like any constituent. Beneath the Capitol Dome, they were greeted with a world of convenience available to anyone with a member pin, including a barber, a pharmacy, members-only restaurants and dry cleaning services, and a private gym for lawmakers. At the D.C. airports, members of Congress enjoyed another major perk: reserved parking spots.

The successful lawmakers generated a deep sense of loyalty among those who worked for them, to the point where being a staffer to so-and-so became the core of one's identity. And they became accustomed to being attended by staff members whose lives were dedicated to making the unpleasant hassles of their own fade away. The less successful left behind a trail of disaffected aides who wanted to share all the unflattering truths about their bosses' private behavior.

Mace was in the latter camp, and as she shed staff, stories of her erratic behavior began permeating Capitol Hill. She had an "eight-minute rule"—everyone who worked for her had eight minutes to return phone calls and texts or risk losing their job. *The Washington Post* reported that during the January 6 riot at the Capitol, as she hid with staff in the Cannon House Office Building, Mace floated the idea of confronting the rioters and purposely getting punched in the face so she could become the face of anti-Trump Republicans.

She so enraged her former chief of staff, Dan Hanlon, that at the Republican National Convention, where he was working as a volunteer, Hanlon made sure he got the assignment of escorting her to the main stage ahead of her speech so he could rattle her before her national star turn. And some of the lore about her erratic behavior didn't come from disgruntled former staffers gossiping anonymously over drinks—it was on display for everyone to see. At a prayer breakfast in Washington hosted by Sen. Tim Scott of South Carolina, Mace stunned the crowd when she told them she had turned down morning sex with her fiancé to make it to the event on time. "I was like 'No, baby, we don't got time for that this morning. I've gotta get to the prayer breakfast,'" she told the religious crowd. "He can wait. I'll see him later tonight."

In truth, Mace's relationship with the prayerful was sometimes theoretical. She liked to tell people that she regularly attended church in Charleston with Sen. Scott, and on Sundays, "church" was always on her calendar. But "church" could conveniently move around depending on what Sunday shows she had been invited to appear on, according to former staff. Sometimes "church" would move on the calendar from 10 A.M. to 7:15 A.M. Sometimes it got pushed to 11 A.M. or noon. "Church" was flexible, sometimes taking second place to where Mace often worshipped on Sunday mornings: greenrooms.

By the winter, Mace had broken up with her fiancé, a wealthy entrepreneur, and was embroiled in a series of lawsuits related to their shared real estate in Washington, D.C., and Isle of Palms, South Carolina, outside of Charleston. And she was no longer in a complicated or unique political space for a Republican: She was all in with Trump, not just endorsing him but campaigning with him and unapologetically counting herself as one of his biggest cheerleaders. So much for taking herself off the airwaves.

It was a tale as old as 2016—Mace was just behind the curve.

Shame! Shame! Shame!

—DEMOCRATS

Back in 2021, Democrats took the extreme measure of removing Marjorie Taylor Greene from the two committees on which she'd served: Education and Budget. It was a step that was usually reserved for lawmakers facing indictments or criminal investigations and had never before been used by a party in power to punish a member in the minority.

In this case, Greene hadn't broken any laws. At issue were some of her social media posts from before she was elected, in which she endorsed executing top Democrats and repeatedly promoted anti-Semitic and Islamophobic conspiracy theories. She "liked" a post that stated a "bullet to the head would be quicker" than removing then-Speaker Nancy Pelosi through a peaceful transition of power.

That same year, Democrats also censured Rep. Paul Gosar, a dentist turned Republican congressman from Arizona, for posting an animated video depicting him killing Rep. Alexandria Ocasio-Cortez and assaulting President Biden. Democrats also voted to strip Gosar of his committee assignments. Both measures were taken as near-party-line votes, with almost all Democrats supporting the measures and almost all Republicans opposing them: Reps. Liz Cheney of Wyoming and Adam Kinzinger of Illinois were the only two who voted with Democrats in support of the measures. One Republican, Rep. David Joyce of Ohio, voted "present." Most pledged payback down the line.

At the time, McCarthy, who was then the minority leader, promised that if Republicans took back control of the House, Gosar and Greene would be rewarded with "better" committee assignments and Republicans would remove Democrats they didn't like as retribution.

Promises made, promises kept: After becoming Speaker, McCarthy promptly elevated Greene and Gosar and removed Rep. Ilhan Omar of Minnesota, one of the few Muslim members of Congress and a member of the progressive "Squad," from the Foreign Affairs Committee. The reason given was that she had made past statements about Israel that had been criticized as anti-Semitic. McCarthy also blocked Adam Schiff and Eric Swalwell, both lead players in the impeachments of Donald Trump, from their posts on the House Intelligence Committee.

Pelosi, by then relishing her role as Speaker emerita—she joked to colleagues that *emerita* meant "happy"—placed a rare call to McCarthy, personally requesting that he not remove Schiff, one of her favorites, from the Intelligence Committee. "Don't equate it with what I did," she told the new Speaker. (Pelosi denies ever placing the call.)

At the time Democrats removed Republicans from committees, many of them made the vote seem unambiguous. "I hope we are setting a clear standard for what we will not tolerate," said Rep. Jim McGovern, the Massachusetts Democrat who delivered some of the most animated floor speeches lambasting Republicans. "Anyone who suggests putting a bullet in the head of a member shouldn't serve on any committee, period."

But even in real time, the votes to remove Greene and Gosar from committees made some moderate Democrats queasy. With Republicans back in control and seeking retribution for how their members had been treated, some Democrats blamed themselves for the politics of payback that Republicans were now practicing.

Don Beyer of Virginia said the votes didn't sit well with him at the time but that he felt immense pressure to fall in line. "I just thought, bad precedent," Beyer said of removing Greene from the committees. Gosar, he thought, had posted violent and offensive content online, but at the end of the day, it was a cartoon. He wasn't so sure it merited a formal censure. But Beyer feared the social media backlash that would ensue if it looked like he was breaking party ranks to stick up for two Republican extremists. He knew there was little room for nuance to explain his vote on what was being presented by people like McGovern as a good-versus-evil issue. "The penalty for having voted against it would not have been worth it," he said. "It wasn't what I wanted, but supporting it was the safer move."

Rep. Chrissy Houlahan, a Democrat from Pennsylvania and a former U.S. Air Force officer, also said she came to regret those votes she took as a freshman. "In some ways, we started it," she said of the personal politics of retribution Republicans have taken to an extreme. "I don't think you can pin it on the Republicans for Adam Schiff. There was precedent there. I had to take those votes. I was really disturbed by that pressure and voted, in my opinion, the wrong way. It was the wrong thing to do." Houlahan said she's tried to make up for it. She voted "present," rather than "yea," to formally censure George Santos, whom even Republicans wanted evicted from Congress.

It may be that the past actions of Democrats had little effect on how Republicans behaved and they would have done what they wanted to do, no matter what. To assume that Republicans would give them credit where it was due or operate in good faith was naïve in the current political climate.

Democrats typically played by a different set of rules than Republicans—so much so that at times it could feel like members of the two political parties in Congress had the same job title but were playing two different sports. Democrats generally wanted to come to Washington to make government work, while many Republicans thought government was too big, ultimately ineffectual, and needed to be dismantled. Democrats wanted to build things; Republicans often wanted to break them. And the basic laws of physics deemed that building was the harder job. Whether or not Democrats were to blame, they now operated in a world where censures and committee removals were part of the business of the Capitol.

"We should not be censuring speech of members, and to do that begins down a road of eroding all sorts of things about our democracy," Katherine Clark, the number two House Democrat, said in November 2023.

Greene, for her part, didn't buy that any Democrat had remorse for kicking her off committees. "I don't think they regret it, because they are using this demonized persona of me that they've created and they're raising more money off of that than anything, other than Donald Trump," she said. "I don't think they regret it. It's been too profitable. And no one has ever apologized."

The censure of Rep. Rashida Tlaib, a Democrat from Michigan and the sole Palestinian American in Congress, proved to be more complicated and tested Democrats in their commitment to standing for free speech. In November 2023, as the war between Israel and Hamas exposed a sharp divide within the Democratic Party, Marjorie Taylor Greene tried to censure the far-left progressive for "anti-Semitic activity." Greene accused Tlaib of participating in an "insurrection" at the Capitol, citing her role in a House office building protest of Israel.

Insurrection was a loaded word to use around the Capitol Complex, given the events of January 6, 2021, and one that made even a solid group of Republicans balk. There had been no violence at the pro-Gaza protest, and Tlaib had addressed the group only outside the Capitol. Greene's censure seemed to be tailored to attacking who Tlaib was—a Palestinian American with family living in the West Bank—and less about what she was saying or doing.

Still, Tlaib was a complicated figure to defend. "We're going to impeach the motherfucker," she said about Trump shortly after she was sworn into Congress in 2019, giving Republicans ammunition in their case that Democrats were simply trying to take Trump down without any specific proof of high crimes and misdemeanors. Tlaib at another time claimed that it was impossible to be a true progressive and back "Israel's apartheid government."

Tlaib had been criticized by her colleagues in the past for her anti-Israel rhetoric, but Democrats held together to strike down Greene's censure, and 23 Republicans joined them in voting to table the motion—i.e., to stop it from ever coming to a vote. "Really for the first time in this Congress, I thought, 'There they are, there are some moderates, or people who were voting on a principle,'" Clark said, noting that it was a low bar to celebrate 23 Republicans using their votes to agree the censure was racist nonsense. "I thought, 'There's some pulse over there! We still believe in a democracy and the free-speech and debate clause.' Okay! I'll take it where I can find it."

But things grew more complicated when Tlaib posted a video on social media that accused Biden of promoting the "genocide of the Palestinian people" and used footage of demonstrators chanting the loaded phrase "from the river to the sea," a pro-Palestinian rallying cry that has been deemed anti-Semitic by the Anti-Defamation League because many view it as a call for the eradication of Israel.

So, just one week after Greene's censure of Tlaib failed, 22 Democrats joined with most Republicans to pass a new censure of Tlaib, introduced by a lesser-known Republican lawmaker, Rich McCormick of Georgia. A married man with seven children who commuted around the Capitol Complex on a skateboard, McCormick was openly dating Rep. Beth Van Duyne of Texas, the divorcée who had tried to insert herself into negotiations during the final hours of McCarthy's Speaker battle. The two made no effort to hide their relationship: They left late-night votes together and held hands under the table at dinners they attended. At the Washington Press Club Foundation's annual congressional dinner in 2023, McCormick left early, remarking loudly in a room full of reporters, "I've got to take Beth home." There was nothing remarkable about lawmakers cheating on their spouses in Washington, but what made McCormick and Van Duyne stand out was that they appeared to be in a full-blown relationship right out in the open, even though one of them was married.

It came as little shock when McCormick eventually announced he was getting divorced, after the *Daily Mail* began sniffing around one of the worst-kept secrets on Capitol Hill. He said he had long been separated from his wife, Debra Miller, who didn't make it sound that way when the *Mail* knocked on her door in Georgia and asked if she was splitting with her husband because of an alleged affair. "You should ask Rich and his colleague," Miller said.

McCormick's censure resolution stripped out any diverting language about an "insurrection" and simply accused Tlaib of "promoting false narratives" and "calling for the destruction of the state of Israel." Some Republicans said they still opposed the use of censures and kicking people off committees as retribution, but they weren't going to burn any political capital defending Tlaib.

Greene voted for McCormick's resolution, even though the whole escapade had been her idea. But tension lingered. After the vote, McCormick approached Greene in the hallway off the floor, grabbed her hard by the shoulders, and started shaking her, according to Greene. "He was squeezing my shoulders really hard," she said. "I had to knock his arms off of me. He was out-of-control angry. I've never had that happen to me." It was so disconcerting that she reported the assault.

As with most interpersonal issues with her colleagues, Greene chalked it up to jealousy, even though in this case it was her censure that had failed. "He was angry at me over the Rashida Tlaib censure thing," she said. "He felt we were competing." (McCormick called Greene's allegation "ridiculous" and "fictitious" and said her claims had been investigated and dismissed.)

Clark dutifully whipped a "no" vote on McCormick's censure resolution, but it was a rare moment that year when leadership failed to keep House Democrats united. "I think that comment so resonated," Clark said about Tlaib's use of "from the river to the sea." "We had members in tears, who never, ever are in tears, saying, 'Wow, only twenty-two Democrats care enough to vote to say that's not right?' There is such raw emotion on all sides of this. Once it got to that, it was very hard to contain."

After the vote, Tlaib stood on the House floor, where she was embraced by progressive Democrats like Rep. Ayanna Pressley of Massachusetts, a Black member of the Squad, who said the censure was "blatantly Islamophobic, anti-democratic, and an utter waste of time."

Tlaib was the second Democrat censured that year (Adam Schiff of California was the first, a few months prior), but she wouldn't be the last. In the waning days of 2023, Republicans also voted to censure Rep. Jamaal Bowman, a Black progressive New York Democrat (which we'll get to later). The following year, they drafted a resolution to formally rebuke Ilhan Omar for suggesting that some Jewish students at Columbia University were "pro-genocide."

What had once been a rare form of congressional punishment—used against just two members of the House in almost four decades and just twenty-four times in history—now counted as a regular part of what a do-nothing Congress busied itself with. Part of it had to do with the fact that leadership had no control over its members.

The decision to censure Schiff over comments he had made in the past about Trump's 2016 campaign and its connections to Russia was the brainchild of Rep. Anna Paulina Luna, a former *Maxim* model and cocktail waitress from Florida who insisted on bringing it to the floor despite McCarthy and others pleading with her not to. They argued that what she was doing would ultimately help Schiff position himself as a Democratic martyr and the top target for Republicans as he ran for Senate. (They were right. Almost a year later, Schiff was still blasting out fundraising emails with the subject line "the thing about my censure.") But Luna bypassed leadership by bringing it up as a privileged resolution. Her resolution failed on her first try, but Luna came at it again, stripping the measure of a $16 million fine she originally said Schiff should have to pay if the House Ethics Committee determined he had lied.

Outmaneuvered by Luna, McCarthy had to pretend he supported the censure and embrace it as his own. Luna's insistence on forging ahead produced one of the more contentious moments of the Congress. As McCarthy called the vote, Democrats stood in the well of the House and began chanting, "Shame! Shame! Shame!" over his actions.

"Censure all of us!" one Democrat yelled out.

Rep. Gregory Landsman, a freshman Democrat from Ohio who had developed a good relationship with McCarthy during a bipartisan trip to Israel, looked up at him on the dais.

"What are you doing?" he said to the Speaker with disgust.

In Landsman's telling, McCarthy looked sheepish, knowing he had screwed up. He later dispatched an aide to meet with Landsman and smooth things over.

There would be no olive branch extended to Swalwell, McCarthy's sworn enemy, who called the Speaker "weak" on the House floor that day. The next day, with Indian prime minister Narendra Modi in town, McCarthy and Swalwell ran into each other again.

"If you ever talk to me that way again, I'll kick your ass," McCarthy said to Swalwell. "I'm just telling you right now. You don't speak that way. Call me a pussy again, and I'll kick your ass." McCarthy turned and began walking away.

"You. Are. A. Pussy," Swalwell responded.

10

I'm like a prodigy compared to my hometown.

—JAMES COMER

A HOUSE AS EVENLY DIVIDED AS THE ONE McCARTHY PRESIDED OVER has two options: The parties can enter into a coalition government, working across the aisle to advance broadly popular bipartisan legislation. Or House leaders can put legislating on the back burner and throw everything they have into investigating the other party.

There was never much doubt which path House Republicans would choose—investigating and impeaching Democrats was what they had repeatedly sold voters during the 2022 midterms. And partisan payback was what their representatives intended to deliver.

What they didn't necessarily anticipate was that Democrats had outgrown Michelle Obama's proclamation at the 2016 Democratic National Convention, "When they go low, we go high." Many of the new faces on Capitol Hill subscribed to a different code: The only way to deal with a bully is to punch them straight in the nose. Those Democrats planned to match their Republican counterparts by undermining, in showy and embarrassing ways, what they viewed as baseless political investigations.

McCarthy, at his core, was still a Chamber of Commerce Republican, and he often needed to be dragged to the right by movement conservatives. He hadn't been convinced before the midterms, for instance, that House Republicans needed to create a brand-new, robustly funded congressional investigation to take on the "deep state."

★   ★   ★

ON AUGUST 8, 2022, the FBI had executed a search warrant at Trump's Mar-a-Lago estate. Within twenty minutes of news of the raid breaking, Russell Vought, from his infested office, began calling for a "Church-style" committee to investigate the "weaponization" of government. (The phrase invoked the famed Church Committee of the 1970s, which exposed abuses of power and is widely regarded as the paragon of a productive congressional inquiry.)

Vought began talking with his allies on the Hill. "If they can do this to Trump," he told them, "they can do this to any of us."

Vought actually believed what he was selling—he half-expected agents to knock on his door, demanding to rummage through his files. He wanted the so-called Weaponization Committee to have a large budget and the power to cross traditional jurisdictional lines at the Capitol. It would have to be able to look at classified materials to get to the bottom of anti-conservative bias in the federal agencies. But McCarthy fought the idea. Even as he railed against the Justice Department for the Trump raid and raised questions about whether justice was being applied equally, he'd put the Weaponization Committee on ice.

We'll see about that, Vought thought.

Vought's opportunity came after the midterm elections, when the red wave didn't crest, forcing McCarthy to court the extremist allies he had thought he would have the power to sideline. As he negotiated for the speakership with Matt Gaetz and Chip Roy, who were both being instigated by Vought, McCarthy suddenly discovered he was more open to the idea. A weaponization subcommittee would be one of the concessions he gave to the rebels to win the gavel. Vought won.

The "weaponization" investigation would fall under Jim Jordan of Ohio, the Judiciary Committee chairman. If you met Jordan and had no clear idea who he was—and this would happen only if you had never seen Fox News, where he has appeared more often than any other sitting member of Congress—you could easily think he was just another polite Midwesterner.

With his light brown comb-over and the slightly hunched posture of a former wrestler, Jordan does not come across in person as anything like the combative attack dog he is. Short and lean, his body curled from his years training to become a three-time All-American and two-time NCAA wrestling champion, he often scurries through the halls of Congress with his head down, looking like someone who could pass for a high school math teacher, not, as former House Speaker John Boehner famously described him, "a legislative terrorist."

"I'm just a little country boy from western Ohio," Jordan often says.

An evangelical Christian, Jordan married Polly, his high school girlfriend, whom he met when he was thirteen and she was fourteen. By all accounts, Jordan is a decent family man, the father of four home-schooled kids who does his own mowing and yard work, exercises aggressively, and is not stalked by any rumors of infidelity or bad behavior when he's left to his own devices in Washington.

(The only major scandal that has embroiled Jordan during his time in office is one in which he was accused of turning a blind eye. In his twenties and thirties, Jordan was an assistant wrestling coach at Ohio State University. A doctor at the university was accused of sexually harassing and fondling athletes. Some former wrestlers accused Jordan of being aware of the doctor's behavior and doing nothing to stop it. In Trumpian fashion, Jordan aggressively defended himself, and his supporters rallied to his side, casting him as a victim of the same "deep state" conspirators who wanted to take down the former president.)

No, Jordan's demeanor would give you a completely wrong impression of the role he has played in his party, doing more than any single member of Congress to drag it to the right. He is a deeply competitive hard-right brawler—a limited-government, burn-it-all-down conservative who helped found the House Freedom Caucus in 2015. He doesn't like to lose, and he often tells colleagues, "My brand is 'fighter.'" In high school, his wrestling record was 150–1, and that lone loss still eats at him today.

Jordan had been a mainstay in Congress for years, but his fortunes really took off with Trump. In 2016, after the release of the infamous *Access Hollywood* tape, when Republicans were distancing themselves from Trump, the Jordans doubled down. Polly Jordan flew to North Carolina to join a Women for Trump bus tour. On the Hill, Jordan positioned himself as Trump's number one attack dog, and whether the issue was leading the charge in Congress to question and undermine faith in the 2020 election results or using the power of the House to go after Trump's prosecutors, Jordan was Trump's man. It was during the Trump years that Jordan became a conservative media superstar, with a political operation that reaped the benefits. In 2016, his campaign brought in about $732,000; during the 2022 election cycle, it took in $14 million.

During his entire career in Congress, Jordan has never passed a bill into law as its sponsor, but he's opposed plenty. He tried to block funding for the Affordable Care Act; he voted against funding for Ukraine; he served as a key force behind government shutdowns; and perhaps most consequential to his legacy, he was intimately involved with the plan to overturn the 2020 election by delaying certification of the electoral college vote. One prominent think tank in 2023 ranked Jordan the 436th least bipartisan House member, which was especially impressive because there are only 435 members of the House. Trump awarded him the Presidential Medal of Freedom.

In Congress, Jordan represented a more mature version of Trump sycophancy. He didn't need to show up at criminal court appearances for Trump to prove he was a loyal fighter. He didn't need to stage press conferences at Mar-a-Lago to demonstrate his fealty. Because by 2023, Jordan was a made man in Trumpworld.

And he was such a true believer that he would have been willing to do anything Trump asked of him. If Trump had asked him to serve as undersecretary for research, education, and economics, Jordan would have said, "Yes, sir. When do I start?"

Sitting in the basement of the Mansfield Noon Optimist Club for lunch in Ohio in early 2023, Jordan recounted his plans for the "weaponization" subcommittee. He wanted to take on the FBI and the U.S. Intelligence Community, which he believed had waged an unfair war against Trump during his administration.

On the Judiciary Committee, Jordan targeted former intelligence officials he believed were anti-Trump. If a prosecutor investigated the former president, Jordan and his staff planned to investigate them back. If a witness turned against Trump, Jordan worked to discredit them. In August 2024, he even subpoenaed a company connected to the daughter of the judge in Trump's hush money case, New York State Supreme Court judge Juan Merchan, arguing that his daughter's political work for Democrats influenced his ruling in the case against Trump.

Hearing of McCarthy and Jordan's plans for the weaponization panel, Hakeem Jeffries adopted his own approach: He began referring to the panel as "the Select Committee on Insurrection Protection."

And for it, Jeffries would have to select the perfect counterweight to Jordan, someone with the legal acumen to challenge Jordan on the facts, but also someone who relished a fight.

In his office in downtown Brooklyn, Jeffries described his thinking on who might be perfect to name to such a committee. "Stacey Plaskett!" he said, referring to a little-known congresswoman who serves as the non-voting delegate from the U.S. Virgin Islands. "Jim Jordan doesn't know what to do with Stacey Plaskett. She's a former federal prosecutor, she was an impeachment manager, she's tough, she's a woman, she's Black. It's his worst nightmare. That's exactly what we wanted."

But what Trump wanted even more than an inquiry into the Justice Department was an investigation into the overseas business activities of Joe Biden's son Hunter and brother James. Trump and his top aides had been trying for years to dig up dirt on the Bidens, but now Republicans had subpoena power through their control of the House. This was their best chance to prove Joe Biden was corrupt ahead of the looming presidential rematch with Trump.

Committee jurisdictional practices meant the Biden family inquiry would fall to the Oversight Committee and its new chairman, Rep. James Comer of Kentucky, a man who up until then was best known in Congress for striking a bipartisan deal on a postal service reform bill.

Comer was no one's idea of the kind of fire-breather needed to lead the premier investigation Republicans had promised their base and their leader. He was not yet a MAGA figure—he had voted to certify Biden's 2020 election and had been well liked by Democrats in the Kentucky state legislature. Comer was also known as an aw-shucks good old boy, not someone who could master the encyclopedic details of a complex investigation. He was more comfortable discussing the finer points of his whiskey collection, whose bottles lined the walls of his office. "For it to be a Kentucky bourbon, a licensed bourbon, it has to be aged a minimum of two years in a charred white oak barrel that can never be used again," he said. "That's the key. It can never be used again."

But due to timing and circumstance, Comer found himself the top

Republican on the Oversight Committee, historically the panel where leadership has stashed the party's bomb throwers, conspiracy theorists, and other broken toys.

As a lead Republican investigator, Comer was expected to be omnipresent on conservative television, an aspect of the job that worried him at first. "I'm not the best interviewer on TV. It's hard to do those interviews," he said. But he was also a multimillionaire farmer and a large landholder, which raised questions about whether his whole "dumb old country boy" persona was an act. He insisted it wasn't. "That's pretty much what I am," he said. "I'm like a prodigy compared to my hometown."

In 2015, Comer ran for governor of Kentucky and lost the Republican primary by just 83 votes, a near miss that sent him into a spiral. Now he saw the job leading the Biden investigation as a second chance to prove himself. "This has worked out," he said with a sense of self-satisfaction. "I think I'm in a much-higher-profile position today than I would have been if I had been finishing up my second term as governor of Kentucky."

As the requests for TV interviews flooded in, Comer discovered he actually enjoyed the public-facing portion of his job quite a bit. Some weeks, he did more than a dozen TV hits. Comer went into the job planning to cast himself as the voice of reason leading the Republican inquiries. But he quickly discovered the obvious: Calm, measured, and reasonable weren't what viewers tuned in to see. They wanted revenge for Trump and the destruction of Biden, so Comer began catering to their desires. With donations and attention pouring in, he would try to deliver the facts to them—and if he couldn't deliver facts, then, well, he would have to deliver rhetoric.

He promised fantastical connections between Hunter Biden accepting a Chinese diamond and his father's mishandling of classified documents; he made wild assertions that a Chinese spy balloon could have contained "bioweapons"; and he lamented that Beau Biden, the president's other son, who died of cancer in 2015, was never investigated.

All this would prove to be wasted energy after 1:46 P.M. on July 21, 2024, when President Biden stunned the world by announcing that he would not run for re-election and, minutes later, endorsing Vice President Kamala Harris. Biden's decision roiled the Trump campaign, which had been designed as a specific machine to take on the weak sitting president. But Biden's abdication also made so much of the work of Congress more useless than it had already been. Republicans had devoted hours of hearings and indictments and airtime to Hunter Biden, whose misdeeds would now have very little to do with the course of the election.

Gaetz's efforts targeting Hunter Biden dated to 2022, when, sitting at the dais of the Judiciary Committee, he held up a black thumb drive and attempted to introduce the "laptop from hell" into the official *Congressional Record,* the transcript of all the proceedings of Congress. For more than two years, Republicans had obsessed over a laptop that Hunter Biden had abandoned at a Delaware repair shop. It was full of salacious material: evidence of hiring sex workers, of crack use, and of foreign business deals of a dubious nature, as well as texts and emails revealing a dysfunctional First Family riven by tragedy, jealousy, bitterness, and drugs. Republicans saw it as their golden ticket to end Joe Biden's presidency and pave the way for a second Trump victory.

No one had ever attempted to enter an entire hard drive of scandalous material into the *Congressional Record* before. Lawmakers had no idea how to even do that. After much discussion, they finally settled on a strategy: They would have congressional aides print out individual files and photos from the laptop. But the work proved extremely time-consuming and extremely NSFW. Staffers spent weeks printing out pages before redacting personal information, bank accounts, and pornographic photos. The work was considered inappropriate for younger congressional staffers, so senior aides had to step in. In the end, the job was never completed, and the laptop's contents were never formally entered into the *Congressional Record.*

Democrats, former intelligence officials, and social media companies, meanwhile, sought to discredit the stories about the laptop, pushing their own censorship and misinformation campaign. Social media companies in 2020 blocked links to the first *New York Post* story breaking the news of the laptop, and a group of fifty-one former intelligence officers wrote a letter, coordinated with the Biden campaign, that alleged the laptop was part of "Russian information operations."

Mark Zuckerberg, the co-founder of Facebook, later admitted in a letter to Jordan that the FBI had influenced him to suppress the laptop story by suggesting that negative information about Hunter Biden and Burisma, the Ukrainian energy company, could be part of a foreign plot. "The FBI warned us about a potential Russian disinformation operation about the Biden family and Burisma in the lead up [*sic*] to the 2020 election. That fall when we saw a *New York Post* story reporting on corruption allegations involving then–Democratic presidential nominee Joe Biden's family, we sent that story to fact-checkers for review and temporarily demoted it while waiting for a reply," Zuckerberg said. "It's since been made clear that the reporting was not Russian disinformation, and in retrospect, we shouldn't have demoted the story."

The laptop was real, and now the hard drive was in Comer's hands, if not the *Congressional Record*.

Using documents from the laptop, Comer promised to deliver the kind of damning revelations against the Bidens that Fox News and Newsmax viewers wanted to hear: There was always some judgment day about to come for the Bidens, if he could just get one more interview, one more document, one more bank record.

Comer knew he was on the B-list of Republican investigators. He was envious of Jordan's stature on the right. Comer was also aware of how lower-ranking members of his committee were better known than he was. He compared himself to a low-profile NBA coach in charge of star players he couldn't control. The LeBron James of his committee? That was Marjorie Taylor Greene. "We've got some very high-profile members of the committee, and they're often the lead messengers for our conference, for better or worse," he said.

Comer courted right-wing media, but he also craved the legitimacy that legacy outlets could bestow upon a member of Congress. To them, he portrayed himself as one of the more responsible Republicans, one who would neither tout allegations without facts nor traffic in innuendo.

But what would happen, for instance, if Greene wanted to display nude photos of Hunter Biden from the laptop during a hearing?

That, he vowed, was a line Republicans would not cross. He insisted that his inquiry would remain serious, focused on influence peddling, not drugs and sex. He wouldn't allow his room to become a venue for airing revenge porn.

"That's not gonna be part of what we do," he insisted. That pledge wouldn't last even half a year.

COMER HAD HIS HANDS FULL with his band of firebrands on Oversight. In addition to Greene, there were Boebert, Mace, and Gosar, the former dentist, who had ties to white nationalists.

In January 2023, staffing Oversight also became an unusually high priority for Democrats. Leaders stayed on Zoom calls until after 10 P.M., making lists of whom they could place on the undesirable committee to counter the Republicans. Part of the focus on Oversight had to do with the fact that Anita Dunn, a top Biden adviser who was overseeing the White House response against multiple investigations, was closely monitoring exactly how they planned to push back on investigations against the president.

One problem for Democrats: So many Republicans had sought spots on Oversight that McCarthy had expanded the number of members on the committee. This left Jeffries and other top Democrats to recruit people to the panel, and most Democrats wanted to be on a more respected committee, like Appropriations or Judiciary, a perch from which you could shape government spending and, perhaps most important, raise money.

Democrats decided to keep "older institutional folks" off the Oversight panel in favor of younger combatants. They wanted members who intuitively understood how media is driven online, and most of all, they wanted people who knew how to embarrass Comer. Alexandria Ocasio-Cortez, the political phenom from New York, was named the number two Democrat on the committee under Rep. Jamie Raskin of Maryland, a former professor of constitutional law who had developed a beloved following in the Democratic Party for his work on the January 6 Committee.

Ocasio-Cortez told people her goal on the committee was to so thoroughly embarrass Comer every time he overstepped and smeared the president that he would eventually question whether he would be employable after leaving office. "What we recognize is the damage of the mere insinuation," Ocasio-Cortez said. "What we have to do is show there is a political consequence to doing this. If you just try to say, 'Oh, let's be the bigger people, let's not lower ourselves to having to address something so outrageous,' then there is no political or professional consequence to launching investigations without merit. And one of the best forms of doing that is shame and embarrassment.

"If these members don't want to stay here, they are eventually going to have to work somewhere," she said. "And if your time in Congress is spent beclowning yourself with completely baseless and low-quality work, there has to be a consequence for that."

It was an approach fully endorsed by Raskin. "If you guys continue to blindly follow Trump," Raskin would tell those Republicans on his committee, "you're going to be fit to sell incense at Dulles Airport." It had no effect.

Democratic Rep. Dan Goldman, a former federal prosecutor from New York, was placed on the committee and made it his mission to beat Republicans to the microphones outside closed-door interviews to frame testimony before they had the chance.

And then there was Rep. Jasmine Crockett, a former Dallas attorney and first-term congresswoman. "Every single one of us wanted Judiciary," Crockett said of the band of rowdy freshman Democrats who became central to the action on the Oversight Committee. "There just wasn't space, so they threw us onto Oversight." It didn't take long for Crockett, a feisty forty-two-year-old Black woman, to see the upside.

Crockett was a product of the Texas statehouse, where, at one point, Republicans issued a warrant for her arrest over a dispute about Texas voting laws. The framed warrant now hangs in her Dallas office. She knew how to handle a bully, and from her seat on the Oversight Committee, she became a viral star. "These are our national secrets," she said at one hearing, waving over her head pictures of classified documents Trump had stored in a bathroom at Mar-a-Lago, "looks like in the shitter to me."

"Every single hearing, y'all spin, spin, spin," she'd jab at the Republicans in the committee room. "I don't know how y'all are still standing right now because you should be quite dizzy from all the spinning you're constantly doing."

Crockett's first major assignment on the Oversight Committee was unexpected. Marjorie Taylor Greene was organizing a sympathy tour for the January 6 prisoners at the jail in Southeast Washington where they were being held. Her plan was to go there and present them as victims of a politicized justice system.

Senior Democrats were so used to taking the high road that they were not sure how to respond, or if they should respond at all. For Crockett, it was a no-brainer. When they went low, she trailed after them.

It was raining off and on the day of the tour. Crockett dressed in black for the occasion, wearing her newly acquired congressional raincoat, ready to do, as she called it, some "truth squadding." She accompanied Greene, Boebert, and other House Republicans inside the D.C. jail where about two dozen of the January 6 rioters were being held.

The tour was designed to show how badly the men were being treated, but Crockett couldn't get over how good they had it. There were yoga classes and air-conditioning in this jail. Each inmate had access to an iPad for twenty-two hours a day. And, truly shocking, they even had the freedom to record a jailhouse song, singing "The Star-Spangled Banner" over a prison phone line, which Trump later played at rallies. The song went to number one on iTunes, briefly beating out hits by Taylor Swift and Miley Cyrus.

These were not the jail conditions the young brown and Black men Crockett represented as a public defender in Texas had ever experienced. She also noticed that the Republicans and the rioters seemed "starstruck" with one another, high-fiving each other. She found it sickening.

After the tour, Crockett watched as Greene made her way to the television cameras. She was relishing the spotlight and the chaotic press scene outside the jail, even as a protester loudly blew a whistle in her ear. Greene even held multiple reporters' mics for them. "They told us stories of being denied medical treatment," she said. "They told us stories of assault. They told us stories of being threatened with rape."

Once Greene had finished, Crockett stepped up to the mics. "My frame of reference comes out of Arkansas jails, Texas jails," she said. "Listen, this is so much different and so much better. I don't think the January Sixers would want to go the other way."

It was a small but important early sign of how Democrats were finished with being bullied onto the high road; the Democrats on the Oversight Committee changed the way Democrats responded to Republican attacks, and Crockett's jailhouse tour signaled their new approach. Greene saw what was going on. But game did not recognize game, in this case. "She's trying," she said of Crockett later, "but I don't think she's there."

11

You always want to keep a record and keep proof of your bribes.

—MARJORIE TAYLOR GREENE

THE TRUMP CAMPAIGN HAD BEEN CUSTOM-BUILT TO TAKE ON BIDEN AND so had the House of Representatives. For two years, the Republican-led investigative committees had been scrutinizing everything Biden—from his administration to his campaign to his family.

Everything Congress does is political to some degree, and House Republicans, who saw themselves as Trump's foot soldiers, were eager to do their part ahead of the 2024 election. But they spent a tremendous amount of time and money on the wrong opponent. It would be Vice President Kamala Harris who would face off against Trump in the November election, and she was left largely untouched for the first twenty months of the administration.

Republicans were caught flat-footed, not anticipating a candidate swap in part because they couldn't fathom a party abandoning its leader after a bad debate. They had stood by Trump through so much worse: two impeachments, four indictments, and thirty-four felony convictions. They fully expected a Biden-Trump rematch, and they'd aimed their artillery at the biggest target in the Biden family: the president's troubled son Hunter.

COMER LAUNCHED HIS INVESTIGATION into the Biden family by hiring James Mandolfo to oversee the inquiry. A former federal prosecutor with salt-and-pepper hair who looked like he had been born to closely exam-

ine other people's taxes, Mandolfo set out to prove the Bidens were corrupt.

Comer, Mandolfo, and their staff began issuing subpoenas for the
bank records of Hunter Biden's business partners, obtaining thousands of
pages containing financial transactions and hauling in witnesses to testify
behind closed doors.

It all looked very bad. The bank records showed that Hunter Biden
and his uncle James Biden received tens of millions of dollars from overseas companies. There was nothing in any of the documents Mandolfo
obtained tying Hunter's and James's financial dealings to the president,
but that was a minor detail. Comer could just refer to the "Biden family"
getting the money, implying they were all part of the same corrupt family
business and their funds were comingled, even if that wasn't true.

Comer rushed to bring his findings to Fox and Newsmax, and he de-
lighted in how the innuendo resulted in polls showing that more Americans believed President Biden was corrupt. "We have made astonishing
progress," he boasted at one press conference, touting his investigation.

But because of the missing link between Hunter and Joe Biden's fi-
nances, Comer's findings weren't taken all that seriously in the mainstream
press. Comer often grew short-tempered dealing with any reporter in the
hallways of the Capitol who didn't work for *Breitbart, The Epoch Times,*
or other conservative outlets. Why don't they report my allegations? he
complained.

Then, out of nowhere it seemed, help arrived.

It was May 2023 when Republican Chuck Grassley strode to the Senate floor as quickly as his eighty-nine-year-old legs could carry him. (At a
moment when the gerontocracy reigned, age was an obsession in Washington, but no one ever seemed to complain that Grassley was too old for
the Senate. The Iowan boasted that he still went for morning runs. After
undergoing hip surgery, he carried his catheter bag around the Senate,
and most people just averted their eyes.)

In his many years in Congress, Grassley had earned the reputation as a
king of oversight and became known on the right as the "Patron Saint of
Whistleblowers," cultivating leaks from inside federal agencies. Rising on
the Senate floor to speak, Grassley announced that he had heard from one
of his whistleblowers about a shocking development. He had learned, he

said, of a document in the FBI's possession that could reveal "a criminal scheme involving then–Vice President Biden."

He suggested to any American listening that there was a single document, an FBI Form FD-1023, that could confirm the most sensational corruption allegations against Biden—and that the Federal Bureau of Investigation was engaging in a cover-up.

The document contained an unsubstantiated allegation that Biden himself had taken a five-million-dollar bribe from a Burisma executive. "Did they sweep it under the rug to protect the candidate Biden?" Grassley asked conspiratorially.

This was the breakthrough Comer and the House Republicans had been waiting for.

Over the next few months, the obscure document took on a life of its own. It became a fixation and then a foundation of the Republican push to impeach the president. Republicans demanded the FBI turn over the document, and when the agency resisted, they threatened to hold the bureau's director in contempt.

The FBI warned Grassley and House Republicans not to run wild with the allegations. They were unverified and shouldn't be released until they could be corroborated or shot down. But Republicans were in no mood to wait or carefully evaluate the claims. They wanted them out, and eventually the agency relented.

In a secure facility in the House basement known as a SCIF, where lawmakers can review sensitive or classified documents, Republicans took turns reviewing the allegations. At a bank of microphones set up outside, each member tried to outdo the last in their descriptions of how damning the claims against Biden were.

"This specifically indicates Joe Biden's involvement in these corrupt schemes, and this is not a Republican source," Lauren Boebert said after emerging from the SCIF. "This is not a Democrat source. This is the FBI's source."

"This is serious. This is legitimate. This is credible," Nancy Mace told reporters. "It looks like classic racketeering. Classic RICO. It looks like money laundering. It looks like bribery."

Marjorie Taylor Greene emerged from the SCIF carrying handwritten notes. She said the form showed that a trusted FBI informant knew of ten million dollars in bribes directly to Joe Biden and his son. "This owner of Burisma kept a record, especially of the bribes," she said. "And if you're in an industry where you have to pay bribes to get your business deals done, then you always want to keep a record and keep proof of your bribes, because that's how you make sure you get people to follow through." She added: "What I read today is, again, shocking." The Republican case against the Biden family seemed to be picking up steam, even if the claims in the document were still unverified.

A drumbeat would begin to build toward impeachment.

Trump made his view on the matter crystal clear. On his social media site, Truth Social, he gave a direct command to House Republicans: "Either IMPEACH the BUM, or fade into OBLIVION."

Around the same time, Republicans got another boost: Two veteran IRS agents came forward to allege political bias within the agency with regard to the Justice Department's investigation of Hunter Biden. Their emergence was another example of how outside organizations can play an important role in Hill investigations. The Republican investigations were fueled by a constellation of conservative groups.

The IRS agents were shepherded through Congress by a group called Empower Oversight, the brainchild of a former Grassley staffer, Jason Foster, who had left the Hill after he was exposed for making anti-Muslim and anti-gay online posts under a pseudonym. Foster soon realized he could be even more effective working off the Hill.

Foster and other former Grassley staffers learned the IRS agents had sensitive information on Hunter Biden and his taxes, but if they revealed the documents publicly, they could be charged with felonies. Foster knew how to maneuver through Byzantine congressional rules and the laws protecting government whistleblowers better than anyone, given that Grassley had helped write them. He knew there was a way to get Hunter Biden's private tax information out legally, and he set out to make that happen.

Within weeks, the two IRS investigators had turned over Hunter Biden's text messages and personal tax information to the House Ways and Means Committee and testified behind closed doors about them, detailing their claims that a corrupt Justice Department provided preferential treatment to the president's son.

Empower Oversight was funded by a nonprofit linked to allies of

Trump called Informing America. Empower Oversight received at least $1.3 million from the nonprofit, which counts Mark Meadows, Trump's final chief of staff, among its leadership.

Informing America also was providing funds for conservative outlets that promoted Empower Oversight's work, including a website called *Just the News,* which was run by Trump ally John Solomon (who had a dual role as a Trump representative to the National Archives). Solomon credited himself with initially finding the IRS whistleblowers and promoting their claims.

While Foster and Solomon worked to fuel the GOP inquiries, powerful behind-the-scenes forces on the left were aligning to tank them. No one was more involved with the liberal effort to counter Republicans than Anita Dunn and her former consulting firm SKDK. Dunn, one of Biden's top advisers in the White House, worked with a group called the Congressional Integrity Project to undercut the Republicans at every step. Its leaders created graphics of Comer in a cowboy hat with the phrase "All hat and no cattle" to mock his endless predictions of anti-Biden revelations that never materialized. They filed ethics complaints against the lawmakers, drove mobile billboards around town, and even flew a plane over the Kentucky Derby carrying a sign that read, "Investigate Comer."

This last stunt succeeded in getting under Comer's skin. "Nothing spells 'INTIMIDATION' more than Biden's dark money PAC paying a plane to fly over #KentuckyDerby to attack me for simply investigating public corruption," he fumed in a Twitter rant about the stunt.

THE OVERSIGHT HEARING ROOM buzzed with excitement in July 2023 on the day the two IRS agents were set to testify publicly. One of Empower Oversight's lawyers, another former Grassley staffer, sat directly behind the men.

The agents, Gary Shapley and Joe Ziegler, had produced seemingly damning WhatsApp messages implicating Hunter Biden in a political shakedown. "I'm sitting here with my father, and we would like to understand why the commitment made has not been fulfilled," Hunter Biden warned a Chinese businessman in one message. "I will make certain that between the man sitting next to me and every person he knows and my ability to forever hold a grudge that you will regret not following my direction."

Hunter Biden claimed he was drunk or high when he sent the message and denied that his dad was beside him. "I was out of my mind," he would later testify. "I can also tell you this: My father was not sitting next to me." There were unposed questions on this topic to ask: If Hunter Biden was so high he couldn't remember sending the message, how could he be so sure his father wasn't with him?

But instead of holding a serious hearing recounting the revelations against Hunter Biden and whether they could plausibly be linked to his father, House Republicans tacked in a different direction. Greene approached Comer with a plan. She wanted to display sexually explicit material from Hunter Biden's laptop in the committee chamber to show that he had broken prostitution laws and that the FBI had failed to investigate him for political reasons.

She encountered no pushback from the chairman, who felt he had no control over the true star of the Republican House.

"These were Hunter Biden's own pictures that came from his laptop. He took those pictures himself. He took the videos himself," Greene said later, defending her stunt and arguing that her efforts were part of legitimate oversight of the Bidens. "Hunter Biden's not ashamed of it. He filmed the pornography and uploaded it to—what is that site called? Pornhub. He's got five or six Pornhub channels. He's not afraid for people to see it."

In a spectacle seldom seen in a Capitol Hill hearing room, Greene followed through with her plan. "Parental discretion is advised," she warned before displaying blown-up nude photos of Hunter Biden engaging in sex acts as she alleged that his solicitation of prostitutes amounted to human trafficking by the Biden family.

There was stiff competition, but a lawmaker displaying pornography on the floor of a committee hearing may have marked a new low in the annals of congressional oversight. "Should we be displaying this in the committee?" objected Raskin, the top Democrat on the panel.

Jasmine Crockett was sitting in the hearing room at the time. She prided herself on always being ready for a good "clapback" against Greene. But even she had no idea what to say. "It was one of those 'we're frozen' moments. Like, what do we do?" she recalled. "We were all looking at each other, like, 'Did that just happen?' We were all in shock and awe. Clearly there's nothing else that this crazy woman can do. Every time you think there's nothing crazier she can do, she finds a way."

The IRS agents, Shapley and Ziegler, testified that day and made allegations about a two-tiered system of justice in which Hunter Biden had received preferential treatment. They recounted how a prosecutor had told them they were not to ask questions about the president, even when his son's communications clearly referenced him. They argued that Hunter Biden should have been charged with felony counts, and eventually he was—the Justice Department would bring multiple indictments, alleging he committed tax crimes and lied on a gun application, against the president's son later that year.

But Shapley and Ziegler's testimony had lost top billing at the hearing. Greene and the nudes had stolen the show.

Afterward, Comer backed up Greene and defended her actions in interviews with reporters. He joked that he wished photographers covering the hearing hadn't angled their shots in ways that featured his face so close to Hunter's nude body, but he added, "The Democrats keep saying, 'You don't have any evidence.' Marjorie showed them evidence. She showed them evidence of the president's son committing a crime."

In her office months later, Greene also defended her behavior and compared displaying the photos of Hunter Biden engaging in sex acts to Alexandria Ocasio-Cortez's defense of abortion rights. "Why is it sensitive?" Greene said. "AOC wants to talk about abortion. Well, that's killing babies. That would be sensitive."

12

It'll be the prayer, the pledge, and the motion to vacate.

—MATT GAETZ

THE DAY AFTER BIDEN WAS SWORN INTO OFFICE IN 2021, MARJORIE
Taylor Greene had introduced articles of impeachment, accusing him of
"abuse of power by enabling bribery and other high crimes and misdemeanors." To cover all her bases, she followed up with more impeachment articles in May 2023, accusing Biden of mishandling the border. At
the time, Greene had asked Lauren Boebert to co-sponsor the impeachment articles and Boebert refused.

But on June 22, Boebert decided to take matters into her own hands
and one-up her chief rival, demanding to move ahead with charges that
Biden's "open-borders agenda" was failing the nation and somehow met
the constitutional standard for impeachment. To do so, she took advantage of a House procedure that allowed her to circumvent leadership and
call for a floor vote on articles of impeachment.

McCarthy, loath to resort to an impeachment for political purposes,
fought back. In late June, he and other top Republicans convened to discuss how to deal with Boebert's play.

Byron Donalds, a Black MAGA-aligned Florida congressman who
was often mentioned low on a list of potential vice presidential picks for
Trump, started things off rather bluntly. "Hey, we all know what this is:
a political weapon," Donalds told the group. "So, when can we vote?"

"What the hell's wrong with you guys?" McCarthy said.

His ire was directed at Steve Scalise as much as Donalds, who, as he
was later being considered for Trump's running mate, made the comment

that "during Jim Crow, the Black family was together." McCarthy blamed Scalise for never managing the party's more reckless members, leaving him to clean up the mess.

"So you want to pick something political instead of doing what constitutionally is right or wrong?" McCarthy said. In a Republican conference meeting later in the basement of the Capitol, McCarthy told members, "I'm voting to table. If I'm the last person to vote for table, I'm going to be the last person, because it's wrong."

Boebert's move also didn't sit well with Greene, who accused her of stealing her impeachment articles. As the House was voting down Boebert's attempt to impeach the president, Greene approached her on the House floor. "I've donated to you, I've defended you," she yelled at Boebert, in an exchange that was first reported by *The Daily Beast*. "But you've been nothing but a little bitch to me. And you copied my articles of impeachment after I asked you to co-sponsor them."

The two women, forever linked in the public consciousness by the image of them jumping out of their seats during the State of the Union to heckle Biden, had always despised each other. Greene made fun of Boebert's tight dresses and often-on-display cleavage. At one point, she tried to turn Trump against her nemesis by falsely telling him that Boebert was going to endorse Ron DeSantis for president.

Boebert mocked Greene for suggesting that space lasers controlled by Jews had caused a wildfire in California and for constantly seeking attention. Each viewed the other as a total embarrassment to her own brand. "Any time there was a bad story written about her, I was immediately lumped in as if we were besties," Boebert said of their relationship when they first arrived in Washington. "I did want to create separation with that."

Greene and Boebert, both elected to Congress in 2020, seemed like natural allies. They were hard-right, Trump-adoring women who loved guns, hated pandemic restrictions, and had, at times, bought into QAnon conspiracy theories. There were Republican lawmakers who had changed because their party had changed. Greene and Boebert were Republican lawmakers who only existed in Congress because of that change.

Greene arrived in Washington assuming she and Boebert would find common ground. "I called her and congratulated her, I tried to be her friend," she said. "Our staff tried to work with her staff. I genuinely tried to be an ally." Instead, what she encountered, she said, was "non-stop rejection." Boebert wanted nothing to do with the "Jewish space lasers" lady. "If there was an event where we were both invited to speak, she would decline; she didn't want to be on the same stage as me," Greene said. "If a vendor was working for me, she would not hire them."

Greene chalked it up to jealousy. "She thought she was going to be *it*," she said, "and that there would not be any competition." Boebert denied rejecting vendors because of an association with Greene, but she admitted she didn't want to be saddled with Greene's baggage as she was trying to make her own way in Congress. "I just didn't want her negative headlines to be attached to me," she said. "I can create bad headlines on my own, I don't need assistance in that." She proved to be as good as her word in 2023.

That September, Boebert, thirty-six and embroiled in an ugly divorce from the father of her four teen and tween sons, was in Denver during a congressional recess week. It had been a difficult year, personally and professionally. In May, she had missed the most important vote in Congress—the vote on the debt ceiling, which she had railed against—and then lied about it. First, she said obliquely that she had been "unavoidably detained." Then she told people that she had missed the vote on purpose in order to stage a "no-show protest" vote. But that excuse was immediately undermined by video showing her sprinting up the steps of the Capitol trying to make the vote and getting turned away when she was told she had missed it.

One night during the recess, Boebert called her aide Drew Sexton and told him she was going to lie low at home for the weekend and see a play on Sunday night before returning to Washington. Sexton was thrilled with this plan for his impulsive boss, who kept him on his toes. He hadn't pegged Boebert for a theatergoer, but this sure sounded like good, clean fun.

The trouble began Monday morning when Sexton received a call from a local Denver reporter, Ernest Luning, who was running down a strange tip. Boebert, Luning said, had been removed from the theater for disruptive behavior. The political reporter had received the tip from a colleague who had attended the *Beetlejuice* cast party, where Boebert's rowdy behavior at the performance and subsequent ejection were all anyone wanted to talk about. Sexton said he would do some digging and call Luning back.

"How was your weekend?" he asked Boebert on the phone.

"Good," she said. "How was yours?"

"Fine. Anything you want to tell me?"

"About what?" she said.

"Did anything happen at the play?"

Oh, that.

Boebert responded flippantly that, yes, she and her date had been asked to leave, but she brushed it off as no big deal. She had taken pictures and, not being a regular theatergoer, hadn't realized that was prohibited.

Sexton was relieved. There was no police report detailing the incident, and when he called Luning back, he convinced the reporter to skip what he assured him was a non-story. When a second reporter called about the play, this time from *The Denver Post,* Sexton confidently waved the paper off, again noting that there was no police report and therefore no story. But the *Post* followed up by tracking down a fairly detailed "incident report" from the Buell Theatre, one that described "vaping, singing [and] causing a disturbance." It was becoming clear that Sexton's day of damage control was far from over. There was also now a surveillance video that was going viral of Boebert and her date getting escorted out of the packed theater.

Still, Boebert was adamant with Sexton that she had not been vaping. Taking her word for it, Boebert's office released a statement denying the vaping and insisting that any haze in the room had been caused by fog machines from the stage—which weren't even operating in the second act of the play. "I plead guilty to laughing and singing too loud!" Boebert said.

But, just as when she lied about her debt ceiling vote, there was video to prove her wrong.

Another surveillance tape showed that Boebert was, in fact, vaping, and she and her date could be seen aggressively groping each other in their seats. This time, Boebert knew she'd been caught and couldn't deny her way out of it.

"There's another video," she told Sexton on another phone call. "It's bad."

"How bad?" he asked her.

"You'll see," she said.

The story immediately became late-night-comedy chum. In his first show back after a five-month-long writers strike, Jimmy Fallon opened his show by saying "I'm more excited than a guy seeing *Beetlejuice* with Lauren Boebert."

Stephen Colbert, the host of *The Late Show,* said that "causing a disturbance" was apparently "code for 'yanking her date's crank at a family-friendly show.' According to witnesses, she was apparently trying to start him like a lawnmower."

The story got stranger still when it was discovered that Boebert's date that night was a Democrat and the co-owner of an Aspen cocktail bar that hosted drag shows during Aspen's Gay Ski Week. One of Boebert's hobby-horses was the indecency of drag shows.

Boebert had long been known as an impetuous boss who carried a chip on her shoulder as big as she was. This was a woman who had grown up never knowing her father and had moved around the country with her young mother, staying with her mother's various boyfriends and an abusive stepfather until Lauren left home altogether. When she got pregnant at sixteen, she dropped out of high school. By thirty-six, she was a grandmother. And against all odds, she was now a member of Congress, with the same job title as historical giants like John Lewis and Abraham Lincoln. Boebert had gotten there by herself and by being herself, and she was wary and dismissive of anyone who offered her political advice.

"I have never changed a damn thing," she said. If some people ever saw a softer side, "it's because you're paying attention more."

Boebert's staff treaded delicately around her, never outright telling her what to do. But there were so many unforced errors. For one, she didn't seem to understand that she couldn't simply lie her way through Congress. To this day, she still denies that she was "consciously vaping" in the theater that night.

"It was an unconscious thing, that I was vaping," she said. "I look at this video, I totally blew out my vape like nothing. If I was truly trying to vape in there consciously, I would have held that in and sneaked it out. It was totally unconscious."

She added: "It wasn't weed."

The level of crisis that *Beetlejuice* created for Boebert may have been clear to the people around her, but it took a while for her to realize that this scandal wasn't going to be shrugged off. Part of the problem for her was that there was no partisan flag to rally around.

Texting with a Fox News producer in the heat of the crisis, Boebert agreed to make an appearance on Jesse Watters's show, but on the condition that he would devote just one minute to the *Beetlejuice* episode and focus on "policy" instead. Watters didn't pretend to have an agenda beyond probing for more gossip.

"So, what happened that night?" he asked.

Boebert blinked uncomfortably into the camera. "Well, Jesse, what happened is I messed up," she said. She described the entire episode as "taxing" for her family and said, "The best apology is changed behavior." Boebert said she was going to proceed with more humility as she reassured voters she knew she had fallen short.

"Just a little too much to drink?" Watters pressed.

Boebert, visibly uncomfortable, claimed it was just the excitement of the theater that had gotten the best of her. Her neural inhibitors had apparently gone on the fritz, overrun by pure, unadulterated *Beetlejuice* enthusiasm.

"You seem contrite, and I respect that," Watters said. "I don't want to pry or anything like that. Who's the guy? You guys still friends?" So much for any policy discussion. Watters ended the interview by telling Boebert to "have a great weekend and behave yourself."

"Thanks, Jesse." Boebert smiled. The whole thing was uncomfortable to watch. Steve Bannon later came to her rescue, giving Boebert a slot on his show, where she spoke about the southern border for a good fifteen minutes.

On her contrition tour, Boebert soon realized what a political hole she was in. There was something in her scandal for everyone to hate. Some voters told her they had to pray after seeing a mother of four getting so handsy with someone in public. Others said they were offended that her date was a Democrat, and some just didn't like the ugly image of a congresswoman being so rude to the theater staff. Even people who think smoking looks cool hated the way the vaping looked.

But her entire political brand had been built on her abrasive persona, and contrition was not a comfortable pose for her. Boebert was a hardcore election denier who bragged about carrying a loaded Glock pistol around Congress and how she was the tip of the spear in the efforts to impeach President Biden.

"If there's anything that has hurt me about the entire theater scenario, it's that I have been denied the ability—by Republicans, by Christians, by my supporters—to be authentically myself in my response," she said, reflecting on the episode a year later.

What she found most difficult about it, she said, was that "it's not accepted to make light of the situation. In my personal life, it's brought up almost daily. We have fun with it."

When the *Beetlejuice* incident proved difficult for Boebert to shake, she embraced it. She hung up a *Beetlejuice* poster with her face on it. She took her boys to see the film's sequel in the theater. "My son paid for it and said, 'I'm a much better date than your other date,' " she recalled.

And at the end of the day, Boebert said she wasn't embarrassed. "I get groped more in a GOP click line than I ever was in a theater," she said, referring to lines of selfies with supporters at rallies and public events. "I literally have to tell people, 'Don't *Beetlejuice* me.' I know it's not going anywhere."

When she toured the campus of George Washington University in the spring of 2024 with a group of House Republicans looking to score political points by criticizing pro-Palestinian protesters, Boebert was singled out for heckling. "What about you in that theater?" a woman called out. There was a deeply sexist tinge to it all—you almost wanted to have sympathy for a young woman in the throes of a painful divorce who had messed up and was being shamed for it. But the political persona she had cultivated, which included calling House progressives "the Jihad Squad," made it hard for many to give her much grace. She wasn't really one who wanted sympathy, anyway. She just wanted to make some crude jokes and move on.

"We thought I'd never get away from QAnon, don't worry, I got rid of that one," she said. "It may trail me, but it is what it is. I just wish Michael Keaton had invited me to the premiere."

The *Beetlejuice* episode became a defining moment of her career to date. And with Boebert publicly humiliated, Greene seemed to have, at least temporarily, won their competition for relevance in MAGA world.

"I lost total respect for her when she was caught vaping in the movie theater," Greene said. "She was vaping in a movie theater, and a pregnant woman asked her to stop. She is a mother of four children! And a pregnant woman is asking her to stop, and she tells her no, and she's nasty about it."

Greene, forty-nine at the time, has three children—two daughters and a son—but they are all grown, she notes, and both her daughters are married. She has never had to juggle taking care of her kids and her job in politics. Her office is decorated with framed family photos and pictures of her with Trump. She went through a semi-public divorce herself and was dating Brian Glenn, a right-wing media personality on Real America's Voice who was always at her side at Trump events and on Capitol Hill and often promoted her on air.

But her own experience didn't leave her any more sympathetic to Boebert. "Then she gets caught doing whatever they're doing in the movie theater, and then she walks out. She looked drunk or high, she had this skanky-looking dress," she said. "The behavior was so unbecoming of anybody that respects themselves or wants other people to respect them."

When Boebert went to support Trump outside the courthouse at his hush money trial in Manhattan in 2024, Greene noted that five days earlier, she had failed to show up for her son Tyler Boebert, who had been arrested in Rifle, Colorado, and was facing felony charges of criminal possession of identification documents. "She had not gone to her own son's court appearance," Greene said with disgust. "He's eighteen years old, with some very serious charges. I always go home. I want to see my mother, I want to see my children. I call them all the time. This woman never went home. She went all over the country, and then her son is screwing up really bad. He goes to court, and he appeared there with no attorney and no parent. And she's all, 'I must go and defend President Trump.'" Greene shook her head. "I don't respect her enough to fight her or say anything to her," she said. "That's how I feel. Not even worth it."

Boebert dismissed Greene's derision as "liberal talking points."

"It's really unfortunate that Marjorie would side with some of the nastiest people on the left who attack my family," she said, noting that she is in constant contact with her son and has attended court hearings with him. In the case Greene brought up, she said, "He went there to say, 'I'm working on getting an attorney.' I don't think that's something I need to leave Washington and be present for."

She added: "It's interesting to hear that she's saying it's not worth it to say anything about me, yet she seems to always have something to say about me."

The "little bitch" remark became an emblematic moment of the Congress: two MAGA mean girls fighting loudly on the floor of the House over who had the right to call a baseless, attention-seeking impeachment of Biden her own.

On that front, the House ultimately voted with McCarthy and sent Boebert's impeachment to a committee for further study, like when a dog is sent to "a nice farm upstate." But the move still troubled McCarthy and his allies. "I'm in a box now," the Speaker vented. "They're going to do this shit all the time."

He had watched Anna Paulina Luna use the same tactic to censure Trump's impeachment enemy Adam Schiff. Even after she failed on her first attempt, she forged ahead despite his requests that she not. "I'll be filing to censure you next week," Luna said to Schiff, scooting by him in the hallway on a contraption she was using to wheel herself around after a leg injury.

"Better luck next week!" Boebert shouted as she followed. "We're gonna get you!"

McCarthy couldn't control these members and decided he would have to call for an impeachment inquiry into Biden himself, knowing it would ultimately lead nowhere. "We were finding more information than people thought," he said, recounting his logic at the time. "But did it rise to the level of impeachment? No."

McCarthy spoke with lawyer Jonathan Turley, a legal scholar, civil libertarian, and skeptic of executive power who was a favorite witness for Republicans on impeachment and other matters. He told McCarthy it was appropriate to move forward with an inquiry.

"I thought what the Democrats did was wrong," McCarthy said. "And I didn't want to do the same thing. I wanted to break the cycle."

Matt Gaetz was also breathing down his neck, now threatening to kick him out of office over spending deals Gaetz argued weren't conservative enough.

On the evening of September 11, 2023, the day the House returned to Washington after its annual six-week summer break, Gaetz put out a press release announcing his plan to make a floor speech detailing all McCarthy's failures. It landed in the inboxes of members of McCarthy's team, raising resting heart rates. Was the moment everyone had been anticipating since January finally upon them? Was it *vacate* time?

Speaking on the floor of the House on a ninety-degree Tuesday afternoon, Gaetz didn't pull that trigger—he made it clear he was going to take his time and draw out the torture. (And why not? This way, the cameras would stay on him for longer; the fundraising appeals would write themselves.)

"I rise today to serve notice, Mr. Speaker, you are out of compliance with the agreement that allowed you to assume this role," Gaetz said. The floor was empty, as it always is during the open-mic portion of the day, when members can come and talk about whatever they want— congratulating a local high school girls' basketball team on a recent victory or, say, threatening to vacate the Speaker. Gaetz had the chamber almost to himself that day, except, randomly, for George Santos, who was seated in the front row waiting his turn at the mic. Other members trickled in and out to give their one-minute speeches, but Santos stayed awhile. (When it was his turn, Santos urged his colleagues to "put partisan rhetoric aside" to avoid a government shutdown, blasted the "din of the media's attempts to influence what comes out of these chambers," and ended with a moment of silence for "all who have fallen due to the unspeakable acts of September 11, 2001.")

Gaetz was the newsmaker that day. "The path forward for the House of Representatives is to either bring you into immediate, total compliance or remove you," Gaetz barked into the mostly empty chamber. He said there had been "insufficient accountability for the Biden crime family and instead of cutting spending to raise the debt limit, you relied on budgetary gimmicks and rescissions so that you ultimately ended up serving as the valet to underwrite Biden's debt and advance his spending agenda."

In a follow-up conference call with reporters, Gaetz said that if

McCarthy didn't drop his plans for a short-term funding bill to avoid a government shutdown and make other concessions to the far right, he would make snap votes to oust McCarthy a regular part of the legislative day. "It'll be the prayer, the pledge, and the motion to vacate," he threatened.

McCarthy needed to get ahead of Gaetz. And in his mind, a Biden impeachment inquiry could accomplish two goals: give him more control over impeachment proceedings and buy him some more time in his job.

An hour before Gaetz's speech, McCarthy decided the time was right to make some news of his own. Just before 11 A.M., his staff rolled a lectern out into the narrow hallway in front of his office, a pathway typically filled with tourists taking guided tours of the Capitol. At the top of the hour, McCarthy emerged to announce he was opening an impeachment inquiry into President Biden.

McCarthy aides had tried to convince the White House that their path meant slow-walking an impeachment inquiry that they assumed was going to happen one way or another, either officially through the Speaker's office or by Gaetz or some other hard-liner freelancing and bringing it up on their own. This way, they argued, at least they could manage it. But what it looked like to most people was a last-ditch attempt to refill his tank of red meat by giving the hard right something its members had been clamoring for.

"House Republicans have uncovered serious and credible allegations into President Biden's conduct," McCarthy said, which was such an exaggeration of the sparse facts they had turned up as to make it a lie. "Taken together, these allegations paint a picture of a culture of corruption."

He didn't take any questions; after reading his brief statement, McCarthy retreated into his office.

But afterward, he continued to play his double game, assuring his old pal Maryland Rep. Steny Hoyer, one of the longest-serving and most respected Democrats in the chamber, that this was not what it seemed. The impeachment effort was a way *not* to impeach Joe Biden, McCarthy emphasized. It was the same thing he told Steve Ricchetti back at the White House.

Whatever he claimed his intentions were, the whole thing appeared to be a slap-dash attempt to get ahead of Gaetz's floor speech.

When Nancy Pelosi had announced that she was opening an impeachment inquiry into Trump in 2019, she chose as a backdrop the stately Speaker's Balcony hallway, a space she used only for photo ops with visiting foreign leaders and high-profile national addresses. Immediately after her carefully prepared speech, she went to address her caucus and get everyone on the same page about what they were doing and why. It was all carefully choreographed.

McCarthy, in contrast, looked wholly reactive to Gaetz.

Gaetz seemed to know exactly what McCarthy was up to and immediately dismissed his impeachment inquiry as too little, too late. He denounced it as "failure theater," a move designed to look like effort but never intended to succeed. "I think that Kevin McCarthy just wants the specter of impeachment so that he's able to subjugate any threat to his power as an impeachment impediment," Gaetz told Bannon.

But he did seem to enjoy the fact that, once again, he was dictating McCarthy's moves. That evening, Gaetz arrived at Bannon's townhouse, just a few blocks from the Capitol, to record yet another episode of the *War Room* podcast. Bannon had spent his years since Trump left office promoting the lie that the 2020 presidential election had been stolen from Trump and discussing the out-of-control federal budget and the "criminal invasion of the southern border." His obsession of late was toppling McCarthy and taking out what he described as "uniparty" Republicans who had become indistinguishable from Democrats, which made Gaetz Bannon's star guest.

That night, Bannon was interviewing Gaetz remotely from the West Coast, and Gaetz, alone and relaxed, ambled into Bannon's lair a few minutes before the show was set to begin. He and Bannon had spent the entire weekend strategizing together, writing and editing Gaetz's floor speech and laying out a media rollout plan for increasing the pressure on McCarthy. Talking directly to the base on the podcast was a key plank of their plan.

"Do you think Steve qualifies as a hoarder?" Gaetz asked, scanning Bannon's mess of a recording studio as he stepped over wires and piles of books and other clutter looking for his chair. Books about China, Trump, and sensible weight-loss programs lived in messy piles on any flat surface that availed itself. Sharpied notes from Trump ("Steve! Your show is sooooo great—Proud of you! Donald") sat in piles with other miscellany.

"I watch *Hoarders,* and it makes me think of Steve," Gaetz said, taking in the mess. "Steve!" he yelled as a producer adjusted the volume on his earpiece and he was connected to Bannon. "I'm in the hoard!"

Gaetz had a few seconds to kill while he waited, and he mulled over the day's events out loud. "I said I was going to give this speech at noon," he said. "McCarthy rushes to announce that he's doing . . . whatever that was . . . at eleven." He paused, gleeful about the pitiful timing of McCarthy's impeachment announcement. "At eleven A.M.? Making major news at eleven A.M., as Speakers do. Didn't Pelosi do her big impeachment announcement in prime time?"

It was not surprising that Gaetz was mostly fixated on television's schedule. He was primarily a creature of the media. Despite being a sitting member of Congress, he had his own podcast, *Firebrand,* which he streamed on Rumble and other platforms, and he sometimes filled in as a guest host on Newsmax, the niche conservative news channel that was farther right than Fox News. During the Trump administration, Gaetz had distinguished himself as one of the president's biggest defenders on cable news, the stage that mattered most to Trump. Trump saw him as a useful and loyal ally on the Hill, someone who artfully defended him and looked the part while doing it. "Your message should be, 'This whole witch hunt must be stopped now,'" Trump told him in a 2019 phone call after Robert Mueller, the special counsel on Russian interference in the 2016 election, testified on the Hill. "You're handsome, so that's always good."

That was the year Gaetz came into his own. "I did one cable news hit during my first ten months in Congress," he told *The New York Times*'s Glenn Thrush in 2019. "And now it's only a couple of years later and *The New York Times* is sitting in my office asking me about my life. The only thing that's changed is a little bit of time and a whole hell of a lot of cable." That year, according to *Rolling Stone,* Gaetz appeared on 264 television hits, 174 of them on Fox News and Fox Business. He has described his first ten months in Congress, before he and cable news discovered each other, as "frankly some of the most unhappy times of my entire life."

He told *Vanity Fair,* "I view the Trump presidency not as a condition to be managed, but as an opportunity to be seized." And seize it he did. During those four years, Gaetz did everything he could to ingratiate himself with Trump and his family members. "Ivanka's favorite," Gaetz said one morning, picking out a pair of shoes he had once worn to the White House that had received a compliment from the First Daughter.

Gaetz had also undergone a notable physical transformation as he rose in prominence in a world where looking the part was at least half, if not the whole, ballgame. Once a pudgy young man with an uneven smile and a round baby face, he had shed a considerable amount of weight—so much that by 2023, his cheekbones looked chiseled and his tall frame lanky. He appeared to have had a new set of porcelain veneers put in that gave him a perfect white smile. He also appeared to have undergone a dramatic brow lift, Botoxed his eyebrows into a perpetual look of mild alarm, and started wearing his hair tall.

"I actually thought I saw Matt Gaetz here tonight," *Saturday Night Live* comedian Colin Jost said when he hosted the White House Correspondents' Association Dinner in 2024. "It was actually just my own reflection in a spoon."

His friends credited his new physique to the influence of his devoted young wife, Ginger Luckey Gaetz, whom he'd met at a Mar-a-Lago fundraiser and later proposed to at—where else?—Mar-a-Lago. (Ginger is the sister of Palmer Luckey, who founded Oculus VR, a virtual reality company, in 2012, when he was twenty. Two years later, he sold the company to Facebook for two billion dollars. With his windfall, he started Anduril, a defense tech company that makes AI weapons like drones.)

Before Ginger took over, Gaetz slept in his office in Washington and ordered Uber Eats most nights for dinner, which he would wolf down while watching cable news and placing sycophantic calls to Trump. Ginger was widely credited with "running a tight ship" and keeping him in line, physically and emotionally. She took pride in the role. In an interview with a Christian MAGA teenager who hosted a podcast, Ginger talked of marriage as the most important decision a young woman makes in her life, one that needs to be thought through carefully because she is choosing the person she plans to "co-brand with." On social media, she often shared before-and-after pictures of Gaetz, one pale and chubby, one tan and chiseled. "Spot the difference," she posted, with an unflattering picture of chubby Gaetz, alone, before he met her, and then one of them together, in which they looked like a golden couple. ("High protein, low carb!!!" she said. "Lots of FL white fish.")

The results of having a wife who kept him on a whitefish diet gave Gaetz a rakish appearance that made him a more chilling sort of villain, maximizing his look to match the character he was playing. And that character had a clear theory on how to work Washington. "The way that you're able to elevate your profile in Washington is to drive conflict, because conflict is interesting," Gaetz said in a 2020 HBO documentary, *The Swamp,* a quote that was eerily prescient of what was to come from him. "That's power that the leadership can never take away from you."

Gaetz's colleagues viewed him as immoral, but they conceded that he was clever and cunning. He could also be quite funny. "In America today, you can't even bribe Democrat senators with cash alone. You need to bring gold bars to get the job done just so that the bars hold value," he said in a hammy floor speech he wrote himself, referring to Sen. Bob Menendez of New Jersey, who was indicted by the Justice Department for accepting hundreds of thousands of dollars in bribes and was discovered to have bars of gold in his house when the FBI searched it. But perhaps more important than making Congress digestible in viral clips, Gaetz could count votes and had tended to a small band of hard-right members of whom he was now in control. Three obvious allies had presented themselves early in Congress when they had voted with Gaetz to oppose McCarthy's Limit, Save, Grow Act. Gaetz tended to them as he recruited more.

Sitting in Bannon's basement, waiting for his hit, Gaetz was skeptical about speaking to a *New York Times* reporter he didn't know well, and he kept his answers brief.

Why did he seem to hate McCarthy?

Gaetz demurred. "My heart is full of joy." He smiled. (A few days later, he tweeted, "Kevin McCarthy Is a Sad, Pathetic Man Who Lies To Hold Onto Power.")

Did he want to be the Speaker himself?

"I wanted to be Speaker once," he said with a rare flash of self-deprecation. "I ran for Speaker of the statehouse. I showed a tremendous capability to blow a lead."

What did Trump make of it all?

"I don't pretend to understand the contours of their relationship," he said, referring to Trump and McCarthy. (It was one of Gaetz's verbal tics when avoiding a question. "I don't pretend to understand the contours of their relationship," he also said about the unlikely partnership between McCarthy and Greene.) But on Trump and McCarthy, he couldn't help himself. "President Trump respects strength and has a keen eye for weakness," he added. "Those aren't the same thing. He has both. I can only imagine how that might create a lens for the events that are unfolding. This is a movement for winners."

As Gaetz finished his thirty-minute rant on *War Room*—example: "My plea to the posse: Contact your members of Congress and say you want a term limits vote, you want a balanced budget vote, you don't understand why there's not individual bills being voted on regarding our spending, and if Joe Biden hasn't committed impeachable offenses, then who has?"—he asked the new producer if Bannon had yelled at him yet. "He yells at me all the time," Gaetz said. He left Bannon's townhouse and ambled outside, where his car was waiting to drive him back to the Capitol. He had votes, and then he had a 10 P.M. hit on CNN. It had been another good day for Matt Gaetz.

Bannon, at this point, was deep into his role as big, bad MAGA daddy of the House. On the alt-tech social media platform Gettr, he called McCarthy a "total and complete sell-out" for the debt ceiling deal the Speaker had forged with Biden. In one six-minute-long rant days after the impeachment announcement, Bannon said that McCarthy needed to "stand up and be a man," and he asked, rhetorically, "Why have you not done anything in the first nine months?"

Bannon's aggrieved podcast persona was far more earnest than his real-world self, which was more aware of the ridiculousness of the world he operated in. But both versions of him were completely obsessed with the action in the House and the power he had to influence members from his townhouse.

"I stayed up till three A.M. watching the whole thing. It was riveting," he said one morning in September 2023 after a late-night floor debate on amendments to the annual defense spending bill. He still had C-SPAN on the next day as he sat in his basement keeping an eye on the House floor like a proud stage parent.

BANNON WAS ADDICTED TO the drama because he saw in it an opportunity to harness the power of the House floor for his far-right members. "They're coming in here. I say, 'Get an amendment, make it as outrageous as possible, just be on there,'" he said, gesturing at the House floor on C-SPAN. "'We'll cut it. Don't worry that you're not on Fox. We'll cut it, we'll play it, we're streaming this on Gettr right now,' I said to them, 'but you gotta jam it up and make it exciting.'"

None of the amendments being debated—like Greene's proposal to cut the salary of Lloyd Austin, the first Black defense secretary in history, to one dollar a year for "destroying our military"—had any chance of passage. But that was absolutely not the point. "You get five minutes!" Bannon squealed, referring to the time a member had on the floor to introduce an amendment. He saw before him a powerful backdrop for his lead actors, and with his help, they could harness it into a hit show. "Come on. You get five minutes!" he said. "You want to be Matt Gaetz, do what Matt Gaetz does."

To Bannon, Gaetz represented the whole package. "You gotta be detached from this," he said. "Not just to see the angles of attack, but know that you're going to be a pariah. The other things—it's like in sports, repetitions. He's been in that pit for a long time. It's a continuation of the fight."

The truth was that being Matt Gaetz took a ton of work, some natural performative talent, and a preternatural ability to tolerate the lifestyle of someone who could not eat out in Washington for fear of hecklers and was regularly cursed at, spat on, and mocked by half the country and most of his Republican colleagues in Congress, even as he was treated like MAGA royalty in safe spaces like Mar-a-Lago. Most people can't stand being despised. Gaetz had a high pain tolerance.

Bannon had been in a feud with Greene ever since she made her alliance with McCarthy. It irked her, even while she told people that Bannon's influence was overrated. She was frustrated that she had been banned from *War Room*. But even Bannon had to hand it to her—he liked the stunt of cutting Austin's salary to one dollar and said he planned to play her five minutes on the floor in full on his show later in the day.

Until he went to federal prison in July 2024 for contempt of Congress, Bannon broadcast his *War Room* podcast from his basement for four hours a day every weekday and two hours a day on Saturdays and Sundays. It was a desirable platform for members of Congress, and most members invited to speak to "the posse" came running over from the Capitol when given the opportunity.

Bannon offered them strategic advice and a way to raise money. But mostly what he had to offer them was his audience.

In past decades, right-wing rebels on Capitol Hill have encountered trouble getting real traction—shunned by lobbyists and big-money political action committees, excluded from leadership suites in the Capitol, and disregarded by Fox News. But with the help of Bannon, Gaetz and others didn't need to rely on any of that. They could speak straight to an angry right-wing base, and that was leverage.

Another thing Bannon did in his free time was terrorize Fox News hosts he thought were spewing McCarthy talking points. After one particularly testy exchange in September between Gaetz and Fox News anchor Maria Bartiromo over Gaetz's opposition to a funding agreement that could avoid a government shutdown, Bannon reached out to give her the business.

"You just humiliated yourself, you're better than that. You sounded like a moron carrying McCarthy's water," Bannon texted her.

"I try to be tough on both of them, Steve. I cannot win," Bartiromo wrote back. "I'm trying! This is so hard!" she added. "I agree with much of what Gaetz is saying but I have to push everyone on both sides."

"Maria, it's obvious to the world you're carrying the water for a failed speakership," Bannon said. "McCarthy wanted this to happen since late June, there were under fifteen days of work. They didn't want the individual appropriations bills because the lobbyists don't want massive cuts. This is all kabuki theater, we have finally broken the fever. Shutdown was a big winner in '14 and will be now."

After Gaetz publicly called her a "shill" for McCarthy and Bannon privately harangued her, Bartiromo complimented Gaetz on air the following morning and apologized to him on X. She also apologized personally to Bannon. "I think you're right," she texted him the following day. "My thinking has evolved. I made a mistake defending status quo. I see now that I was worried about the Biden investigation being shut down but I should not commingle the two, thank you."

Bannon immediately rewarded her. "We are starting the show with you today and saying what a star you are," he said.

"Oh stop," she responded. "You flayed me and I deserved it."

We've been in this fifteen-year burn.

—CHIP ROY

THE DYSFUNCTION OF THE HOUSE WAS DRIVEN BY THE FACT THAT THE MAGA hard right was at war not just with establishment Republicans, but also with itself.

Lauren Boebert and Marjorie Taylor Greene hated each other more than they hated Alexandria Ocasio-Cortez. Greene publicly referred to her forever nemesis as "vaping groping Lauren Boebert."

Greene was also often feuding with fellow hard-right conservative Chip Roy, whom she undermined by noting that he was a fake Texan and actually hailed from Bethesda, Maryland, a ritzy suburb of green juice purveyors and Botox med spas—in other words, he was no hat and no cattle.

When Republicans won back the majority, Jim Jordan used his power as chairman of the Judiciary Committee to pass over Ken Buck, whom he personally disliked, to lead an antitrust subcommittee. Buck had been the top Republican on the committee and had been carving out his own lane taking on big tech. But Jordan awarded that gavel to Thomas Massie instead. Buck's seniority should still have given him the chance to be among the first to speak at major Judiciary Committee hearings. But Jordan would sometimes not recognize him until the end of the hearings, hours after most of the press had left and attention had turned elsewhere.

These personal feuds helped create the dynamic that ground the House to what was basically a legislative halt: The Republican-led House passed just twenty-seven bills that became law in 2023, the lowest number since the Great Depression.

Despite ostensibly wielding more power than it ever had before, the House Freedom Caucus was in turmoil. Many of its members had been livid with Greene ever since she forged her alliance with McCarthy, and the "little bitch" incident with Boebert was a welcome excuse for them to say it was time to give her the boot. So on June 23, 2023, they convened an emergency secret meeting at which the group voted overwhelmingly to kick Greene out.

Jordan was one of the few who voted to keep her. "I just don't think you kick people out," he told his colleagues.

Greene was voting on the floor of the House that morning when she learned of her expulsion while scrolling through Twitter on her phone. She spotted another member of the group, Rep. Warren Davidson of Ohio (who would also later be booted), sitting a few rows in front of her on the floor.

"Is this true?" Greene asked, flashing him her screen.

"Yeah, they did it this morning," he told her. "They called a rush meeting at eight thirty A.M., and most members weren't even there."

Rep. Ben Cline, a Freedom Caucus member from Virginia, saw them talking and approached Greene to tell her that Scott Perry, the group's chairman, wanted to speak to her in person.

"I can't," Greene said in a huff. "I have a meeting with the Speaker's Office to discuss my bill to ban transgender surgeries for children, which the Freedom Caucus doesn't care about."

Greene and Perry never spoke, and Greene was never officially informed that she was out. But she embraced her new pariah status as a chance to pitch herself as someone who was more constructive than these far-right goons. "I'm not a member of the burn-it-all-down caucus anymore," Greene would tell anyone who listened. "I'm a greatly, very happily a free agent, and I want to do my job here."

Greene felt she was a brand on her own and was being punished for it. "Over half the Freedom Caucus also endorsed and supported McCarthy, but they singled me out. The men in the Freedom Caucus like the women they can control," she said, another implicit dig at Boebert. "They don't want them to be vocal and independent minded. There's a lot of patriarchy going on there."

The reality of the House Freedom Caucus in 2023 was that while some of the members of the group had never been so powerful, overall the group had never been so chaotic. When the Freedom Caucus was founded in 2015, its mission was clear: It was a small group of rebel conservatives who wanted to push the party to the right on fiscal and social issues. The movement grew out of the Tea Party, and the caucus sprang to life several months before Trump announced his candidacy. During the Trump presidency, the group of rebels rose to wield immense power in Washington. Two of its founding members, former Reps. Mick Mulvaney of South Carolina and Mark Meadows of North Carolina, went on to serve as White House chiefs of staff. Jordan, the group's founding chairman, eventually rose to become Judiciary chairman.

Over the years, Jordan identified and recruited conservative talent to Congress and the Freedom Caucus. Good Freedom Caucus members needed to be right-wingers with a libertarian streak. But most of all they needed to be troublemakers.

Perry, a former general in the National Guard who would go on to lead the group, at first wasn't allowed in, because Freedom Caucus members were skeptical of rule-following military types. He had to prove to them he was rebellious enough to qualify.

Others like Matt Gaetz and the libertarian-leaning Kentuckian Thomas Massie were too rebellious to *want* to join. Once, when Jordan was attempting to persuade Massie to join up, Massie told him, "I don't want to go to any more meetings. Just let me know when the prison riot starts. I'll be there with my shank sharpened."

But the Freedom Caucus had worked better as a small group of pirates plundering the ship than it did in captaining it—much like the Republican Party worked better at being in the minority than it did at being in the majority and having to govern. "They love the minority," Greene said of the group after she was booted. "They've created the identity where they only fight leadership, and it's just burn it all down."

As the hard right in Congress expanded, it also fractured. The group's bylaws included something known as the "80 percent rule," meaning that if 80 percent of the members wanted to support a bill or a position, the entire group would fall in line. But falling in line was anathema to these rabble-rousers, and they stopped adhering to their own rule.

There was no longer any binding principle. Some of the members were true fiscal hawks who believed in limited government and deep spending cuts. Others were Trump loyalists, fired up about social issues and election denialism, who didn't have strong views about the federal budget. And Perry, hand-selected by Trump, Jordan, and Meadows to lead the group, had proven he had zero ability to control his members.

In the fall of 2023, for instance, Perry tried whipping his members to vote for a conservative stopgap spending resolution. He told them it had border provisions in it that they should support. Despite his best efforts, 20 of his members voted against the bill, fracturing the group and undermining the power that came with being able to reliably vote as a bloc.

As the group expanded, so did complaints from members about the governing rules, and many of them dropped away. Jordan, for instance, stayed in the group despite an understanding that no committee chairman could stay in, and it meant his allegiances were split between leadership and the band of outsiders whose purpose was to make leadership's life a misery.

Some complained that when the group did manage to get it together to take an official position, they now did so on a messaging app, Telegram, and no longer took votes in person. Republicans aligned with the group privately grumbled that the quality of the members had diminished over time. And Greene, before she was expelled, was a constant source of tension.

Her expulsion wasn't the first time the group had tried to distance itself from Greene. There was a brief move to expel her in 2022 after she spoke at a conference organized by Nick Fuentes, a well-known white nationalist. Some members wanted to write a letter denouncing her for doing so. Others argued that it would simply draw more unwanted attention to the event. At the time, Greene falsely blamed Boebert for leading the charge, even though Boebert thought the letter was a mistake and wanted to ignore the whole incident.

"I didn't draft any letter, are you kidding me?" Boebert said.

"You're the communications director of the Freedom Caucus," Greene shot back, "so any letter that comes out of this organization is from you."

In meetings, Greene also had no time for the concerns of the fiscal hawks. She said that her concern was that the 2020 election had been stolen. Others in the group disagreed with her pet issue of putting into place a federal ban on transgender surgeries for children under the age of eighteen. People like Chip Roy argued with her, saying the issue should be left up to the states.

The group's next leader after Perry, Virginia's Bob Good, committed the cardinal sin of endorsing Ron DeSantis early in the Republican presidential primaries, a move that would ultimately cost him his seat in Congress. When DeSantis dropped out, Good may have set a world record for how quickly he professed his fealty to Trump, but it was too late. Trump endorsed Good's hard-right, election-denying challenger, John McGuire, telling Virginia voters that Good would "stab you in the back like he did me." The primary race split the MAGA coalition in two— Bannon was for Good, while Greene was for McGuire; Gaetz was for Good, and Trump was for McGuire. After a recount, McGuire squeaked out a victory by 370 votes, underscoring the divisions and weakness of a coalition based on personal feuds and raging egos. "Taking down the chairman of the Freedom Caucus was quite delightful for me," Greene said later.

As one of his last acts as chairman of the Freedom Caucus, Good made sure to kick out Warren Davidson, who had endorsed McGuire in that intraparty feud.

In 2023, the group still gathered on Monday nights at the Conservative Partnership Institute, Meadows's new home after leaving the Hill and the White House, but by then, it was more of a discussion group than anything else.

Their rising anger at McCarthy found its origins in events that preceded him. As Tom Emmer said, McCarthy was paying, in part, for the sins of others. "There's a struggle going on about changing this town, and it's been going back even really toward the end of the Bush administration," said Roy, who served as chief of staff for Sen. Ted Cruz of Texas before running for office himself. "We've been in this fifteen-year burn."

McCarthy had attempted to mollify the group in January when he gave hard-right members seats on the Rules Committee and invited its chairman to weekly meetings of the various Republican factions on the

Hill—what McCarthy would dub the "Five Families" meetings. Still, for some on the hard right, McCarthy had to go. "All of the animus toward the Swamp was being channeled and directed directly at Kevin," Roy said. And for some of them, this meant McCarthy's enabler Marjorie Taylor Greene also had to go.

To Democrats, the whole battle between the Freedom Caucus and Greene was simply proof that the Republican Party had lost its damn mind. "I go home and I just say, 'Sadly the Republican conference is being held hostage by the extreme of their party,'" said Rep. Andrea Salinas, a first-term Democrat from Oregon. "I say, 'They're so extreme that they kicked out Marjorie Taylor Greene.' The rooms just erupt. People are like, 'What?'"

Bring it on.

—KEVIN McCARTHY

Just did.

—MATT GAETZ

McCARTHY WAS GETTING INCREASINGLY AGGRAVATED BY THE CONstant threat of removal hanging over his head. "Move the fucking motion," he told Republicans at their weekly meeting in the Capitol basement days after Gaetz's speech. "I'm gonna lead the conference the best way I can. If you want to move the motion, move the fucking motion." In response, he received a standing ovation, a fact his allies promptly leaked to Twitter-happy reporters standing outside the door.

On the night of September 20, a perfect fall evening in Washington, when it would have been a joy to be somewhere other than that dank basement hallway, McCarthy gathered the entire conference for one of its semi-private meetings.

McCarthy had survived the debt ceiling battle. But now he had a government shutdown looming, and he had to muster his fractured conference to pass a short-term funding patch to keep the government open through Halloween. The hard right hated these short-term deals, known as "continuing resolutions."

"What I'm trying to do is break the fever dream that is the continuing resolution way of governing," Gaetz told CNBC. He said he was opposed to "one up or down vote to fund the entire government."

In the conference meeting that night, McCarthy said he would agree to deeper spending cuts as part of any bill to prevent a government shutdown, another attempt to appease the hard-liners threatening the shutdown. He hoped it would be a final breakthrough.

But Gaetz stood up at the meeting and declared, flatly, that he had a list of 7 members who would vote against a continuing resolution—no matter what. After the meeting, McCarthy approached Gaetz and quietly asked him for the list, which Gaetz happily handed over. "They're immovable," he said matter-of-factly. And the list was growing.

McCarthy's allies thought that the rebels just needed time to realize Republicans didn't have as many options as they thought they did. Patrick McHenry, for one, insisted that shutting down the government was a losing proposition for Republicans. "If you're the one executing it, you fail," he told less-experienced legislators. "It's been tried before, it's happened before, it's failed before."

Still, one week later, the hard right tried just that, blocking McCarthy's Friday night attempt at passing legislation to avoid a government shutdown. When he convened Republicans in the basement of the Capitol the following Saturday morning, a midnight shutdown appeared inevitable.

But McCarthy surprised everyone, Democrats, Republicans, and reporters alike, by announcing he was going to try again, a recognition that he was out of options to avoid a shutdown and was going to spare his party the political blowback, even if it meant relying on Democrats to pass it.

He would pass a short-term funding bill, pay the troops, keep the government running, and maybe lose his job.

"We're going to roll the dice," McCarthy said to John Leganski, his floor director. "How fast can we put this on the floor?"

"I can have it on the floor in twenty minutes," Leganski said.

The bill was stripped of policy proposals Republicans wanted, including deep spending cuts and hard-line immigration restrictions that would have made it impossible for Democrats to vote for it. Members were given about an hour to read and vote on the seventy-one-page bill they had never seen before, never mind the January promise McCarthy had made to allow lawmakers seventy-two hours to review any legislation before bringing it to the floor for a vote. Also, the bill would be considered under special rules that required a two-thirds majority for passage—that is, it would need substantial Democratic support.

McCarthy did not give Democrats any heads-up about what it was he was bringing to the floor, and he denied their request for ninety minutes to read the legislation before going to vote on it.

"This guy has lost it," Hakeem Jeffries vented to colleagues while sitting in his office that Saturday ahead of the vote. "He's done."

McCarthy's goal was to jam the Senate and make them vote on whatever the House passed, not the other way around. Democrats tried buying themselves some time to make sure they could vote for his bill. Jeffries used a "magic minute" (a privilege that allows top party leaders to speak on the floor for as long as they want) to give a fifty-minute off-the-cuff speech decrying—what else?—"extreme MAGA Republicans," his favorite phrase. And tensions were running so high that Jamaal Bowman, the New York lawmaker who was one of the most progressive members of the House and the Squad, went so far as to pull a fire alarm in a House office building, in what Republicans said immediately was an illegal bid to slow down the process.

Bowman had been working alone on the second floor of the Cannon House Office Building that Saturday with almost no staff around. With no one there to tell him it was time to walk to the House floor for votes, Bowman realized too late that he wouldn't make it at all if he didn't sprint. He rushed out of Cannon and found that the doors he typically used were locked. Without thinking too hard about the consequences, he pulled the fire alarm and ran out.

A series of unforced errors followed this original sin. After a surveillance camera picture of him pulling the alarm was leaked within hours of the incident (presumably by Republicans), Bowman's lawyers counseled him to say nothing in public about the incident while he was being investigated by the Capitol Police. If he played this wrong, they warned, he could be charged with a federal offense and maybe even end up in prison. Bowman, frustrated, stayed silent as the narrative was shaped by his political opponents that he had pulled the fire alarm expressly to delay the vote.

A junior staffer then accidentally blasted out talking points to the entire Democratic Caucus that Bowman later said were meant to be circulated internally to the team for editing. In the document, Bowman's office suggested to Democrats that they should defend him by reminding people to focus instead on the "Nazi members" of the Republican Party.

Bowman was swarmed by reporters after the incident. Usually, he loved engaging in self-promoting stunts. He was a former middle school principal, but also a former college linebacker who could bench-press more than four hundred pounds. Everyone knew this because, like Marjorie Taylor Greene, he enjoyed posting workout videos on social media. But this time, he had to heed the advice of his lawyers. "When you were a principal, did you ever punish any students for pulling a fire alarm?" a reporter asked him. He laughed awkwardly.

"At the end of the day," he told CNN's Manu Raju, "I wasn't trying to prevent a vote or shut down the government or do anything. It was a bad decision. That was a mistake, [I] took responsibility for it. I don't know why it's gotten this much attention."

Bowman was ultimately charged with a misdemeanor, censured by Republicans, forced to pay a thousand-dollar fine, and, a year later, defeated in his primary.

But he made it to the vote on time.

When the vote was called, 209 Democrats backed the bill, far more than the 126 Republicans who did. Both sides of the chamber cheered as McCarthy immediately tried positioning himself as America's great conservative savior. "I'm a type of conservative who wants to get things done," he said at a press conference immediately after the vote. "It's easy to be a conservative who wants to do nothing."

His closest colleagues understood the significance of what he had just done, though. Back in McCarthy's office, McHenry stared at the television catatonically. "Maybe we can negotiate that you can stay until the end of the year," he said.

"You're crapping out on me?" McCarthy shot back. He had danced his way through the debt ceiling deal, getting the majority of Republicans to vote for it by pure gut instinct. He thought he could keep dancing through another spending fight.

What bothered many of the hard-right members was that Biden hinted that he had made some gentleman's agreement with McCarthy to bring Ukraine funding to the floor at a later date, something they started referring to as "the secret deal." Ken Buck, the House Freedom Caucus member from Colorado, said what irked him most was that "there were all these side deals, at least in my mind. That was the straw that broke the camel's back."

For Gaetz, the straw that broke the camel's back appeared to be more personal—the funding deal simply provided him the right opportunity to finally make his move. For years, Gaetz had been running hot and cold with McCarthy, privately playing nice while publicly trashing him.

For instance, on August 8, 2022, when Mar-a-Lago was raided by the FBI, which was looking for the boxes of classified materials Trump had absconded with when he left the White House, McCarthy, then the minority leader, had immediately threatened to go after the Justice Department when Republicans took back the House. "The Department of Justice has reached an intolerable state of weaponized politicization," he wrote on Twitter.

Gaetz texted him the next day. "I know I give you a hard time a lot but your response has been strong and effective on this raid stuff," he said. "I even praised you on *War Room* this morning. As of now, I am suspending all my criticism of our team, which you do lead. It is time to unite now and I see that." He signed his text, simply, "Gaetz."

He offered his support again on June 12, 2023, the day McCarthy reached a deal with hard-right Republicans who had staged a weeklong blockade of the House floor as payback for the debt ceiling deal they hated. "I think today went well," Gaetz texted. "This is a bump, not a wall."

But the up-and-down relationship broke for good in September, thanks, in the minds of McCarthy allies, to Arthur Schwartz, a political consultant and informal adviser to Donald Trump, Jr., whom McCarthy had hired to help him win some MAGA bona fides. Schwartz had long been one of the more menacing characters in Trumpworld, a fixture at the Trump Hotel during the Trump presidency and part of a network of conservative operatives who had been compiling dossiers on journalists (including years-old tweets) in an effort to embarrass and undermine them. He was a more natural fit to be fighting shoulder to shoulder with Gaetz against the establishment. But this season, he was McCarthy's hired gun. "Stop blaming Kevin for your ethics investigation," he wrote to Gaetz on X. "Blame yourself for having threesomes with your staff." Schwartz had gotten over his skis.

On September 1, Gaetz sent the offending tweet to McCarthy with a foreboding message. "Your employee has made a very poor decision to lie about me," he wrote. "See you soon."

McCarthy shared Gaetz's text with his staff, some of whom tried to get Schwartz to take down his post—not that it would have done anything at that point. From that moment on, they were bracing for impact.

On October 2, Gaetz rose in the chamber as the House was almost done for the day. Wearing a fat gold tie that looked like it had been lifted from Trump's closet, Gaetz stood on the floor and finally went through with it: "Declaring the office of the Speaker of the House of Representatives vacant," he read off a piece of paper. "Resolved, that the office of Speaker of the House of Representatives is hereby declared to be vacant."

And that was it.

The clock was now ticking—the House had two legislative days to schedule and take a vote on ousting McCarthy.

"One of two things will happen: Kevin McCarthy won't be the Speaker of the House or he'll be the Speaker of the House working at the pleasure of the Democrats," Gaetz told reporters swarming around him after.

On social media, McCarthy challenged Gaetz: "Bring it on," he wrote. "Just did," Gaetz replied.

15

We're not going to let those guys throw you out.

—STENY HOYER

THE WEEKEND BEFORE THE VOTE TO OUST HIM, McCARTHY CALLED HIS longtime friend Steny Hoyer, the patrician Democrat from Maryland who served as Nancy Pelosi's number two in the House for two decades. Unlike most of his Democratic colleagues, Hoyer was actually quite fond of McCarthy.

"We're not going to let those guys throw you out," Hoyer assured him. That was good news. But Hoyer also had to remind his friend that he was no longer in charge. Hoyer, Pelosi, and Rep. Jim Clyburn of South Carolina had all stepped down from their top leadership positions together at the beginning of the year, making for a smooth transition for a new generation of Democratic leaders in the House to rise. "Ultimately, it will be Hakeem's call," Hoyer said.

McCarthy called Jeffries, too, but made it clear he wasn't going to negotiate with him for his help—he thought it was Democrats' duty to the institution of the House to save him. After all, in his mind, Pelosi had promised him just that back in January. This position confused even the most center-courting Blue Dog Democrats, those who bragged about an endorsement from the NRA, who could not fathom why McCarthy didn't even want to have a conversation about what it would take to get their votes to save him. He actually believed they were going to conclude that saving him was the right thing to do, with no assurances that he would change the House to function in a bipartisan manner? This did not make sense to them.

If there had been any shot at convincing Democrats to do so, McCarthy self-sabotaged it on October 1, the day after he passed the short-term government spending bill, when he went on CBS's *Face the Nation* and blamed them for everything.

"The Democrats tried to do everything they can not to let it pass," he told the program's host, Margaret Brennan, accusing Democrats of taking "dilatory actions" to prevent the bill from coming to the floor. "They did not want the bill," he insisted, a ridiculous claim when it had been Democrats who provided the bulk of the votes to pass it. "They were willing to let the government shut down, for our military not to be paid."

McCarthy's interview with Brennan turned out to be the most impactful television hit of the year. The ungrateful, untrue statement he made left Democrats who had been wrestling with a difficult decision—how to vote on a motion to oust the Republican Speaker—with complete clarity: Screw him.

McCarthy's team began planning for what was the most likely outcome: that his speakership was finally coming to its inevitable end. John Leganski pulled Patrick McHenry aside to give him a private heads-up that McCarthy had put McHenry's name at the top of a succession list that was stored in a secret envelope. It meant that if McCarthy was ousted, McHenry was set to become the "Speaker pro tempore."

Nobody in Congress understood much about the process of selecting the person for that job, or had a clear vision of what the job entailed. The "Speaker pro tempore" was a security put in place after the attacks of September 11, 2001, to keep business moving if the speakership was vacated for some reason. It was intended for an act of God or war—not for this historic event of a party removing its own Speaker by choice.

McHenry's name was not the one McCarthy had put in the envelope back in January, when he was elected Speaker. Back then, he had chosen a rank-and-file member who was not even informed that he had been selected. But later, McCarthy and his staff decided to switch it out and had been debating between Tom Cole, the cigar-smoking chairman of the House Rules Committee from Oklahoma; the ever-loyal Garret Graves; and McHenry for the top name on the list.

When Leganski told McHenry about the envelope, he made it clear it was not a big commitment. The job would be three days, max, he told

McHenry, maybe a fun opportunity for him to take his young kids for a ride in the security detail he would be awarded before returning to his normal day-to-day. He would have to schedule the conference vote for Speaker, and then he could return to committee work.

McHenry made a beeline for the House parliamentarian as he tried to understand what the job was and how he should interpret his powers. They agreed that the best route was to interpret them as narrowly as possible: His sole function, they concluded, was to call a vote to elect the House Speaker.

On the night before the vote to oust McCarthy, the outgoing Speaker called McHenry to offer him one last out. "I just need to know. If you want to be Speaker, you should not do this," McCarthy said. "I should make it someone else, and you can be Speaker. We can make that happen."

McHenry assured McCarthy that he did not want to be Speaker.

"Okay," McCarthy said. "Then I'll leave you at the top of the list."

Neither McHenry nor McCarthy thought that serving as Speaker pro tempore would be a job that lasted for weeks, or that during those weeks, McHenry would find himself back-channeling with Democrats on a secret plan to make him the acting Speaker indefinitely. In fact, McHenry seemed to be in denial that he was going to be taking center stage. An hour before the vote, he was wearing Allbirds sneakers when a staff member told him it would be inappropriate to approach the dais dressed so casually. Another staff member hustled to McHenry's home to bring him back a pair of hard-soled shoes.

16

The greatest Speaker in modern history.

—GARRET GRAVES

O N THE MORNING OF OCTOBER 3, 2023, BEFORE THE HISTORIC VOTE TO oust McCarthy, Republicans and Democrats were both scheduled to gather privately for their weekly party meetings. The outgoing Speaker texted Hakeem Jeffries at 6:10 A.M. ahead of a consequential day on the Hill to make it clear he would not be beholden to him.

"Just my opinion," McCarthy tapped into his phone, "don't split your conference, keep everyone united around you. This is my fight and my party. If I can't win now, the fight will just continue."

"Thanks, Kevin," Jeffries wrote back two hours later, texting in the same controlled manner in which he spoke. "Will approach the beginning of the caucus in listening-only mode and take it from there in terms of the unity of position on our side. All the best in your conference meeting."

At 10:40 A.M., Jeffries gave McCarthy the courtesy of an update. "Caucus is still ongoing," he wrote. "Sentiment is strongly opposed to supporting any procedural motion presented by the other side of the aisle. Republicans will have to work this out among themselves."

"Thanks, that's exactly what I texted you this morning," McCarthy replied. "Keep your conference united, it will help you in the future."

That was one of the final exchanges the two of them would have. Jeffries would later text McCarthy to wish him well on his departure from Congress and to express his condolences for the passing of McCarthy's mother the following spring. But what had started as an attempt at a working relationship and had at moments bordered on an actual friendship ended with raw feelings and a lack of trust on both sides.

Inside the meeting, Democrats were fired up about the *Face the Nation* clip and felt they owed McCarthy nothing. There had been some expectation that a handful of Democrats might not vote at all, a move that would help McCarthy by making the math work out for him to stay. But they emerged from that meeting united in their opposition to helping him. Even sympathetic Steny Hoyer was not going to break with his party to stand with McCarthy.

McCarthy arrived on the House floor trying to put on his happy face, as he always did. He sat in his usual seat toward the front of the floor, a passive observer of the vote to oust him, as his allies stood up to defend him and the small band of his enemies outlined why he had to go.

The chamber and the press gallery were packed; the mood was tense. It was one thing to make noise on social media about wanting to oust McCarthy. It was another to stand up in front of almost all 435 members of the House of Representatives and say it straight to his face.

Matt Gaetz had carefully teed up his caravan of detractors, with the goal of making it look like the effort was bigger than him. With that in mind, he had Bob Good of Virginia speak first. "We need a Speaker who will fight for something—anything—besides just staying or becoming Speaker," Good said.

Speaking in defense of McCarthy, Elise Stefanik rose to say that "this Republican majority has exceeded all expectations."

Her words served as an easy setup for Gaetz, who responded, "If this House of Representatives has exceeded all expectations, then we definitely need higher expectations!"

Garret Graves described McCarthy as "the greatest Speaker in modern history." It was a laughable statement, and it produced audible chuckles from the floor.

Gaetz pushed back against the notion that the Republicans ousting McCarthy were plunging the House into chaos. "Chaos is Speaker McCarthy," he said. "Chaos is someone we cannot trust with their word."

They volleyed back and forth like this for an hour as Democrats sat silently and listened. And then, the vote. The gallery was tense as the proceedings dragged into the late afternoon, with the House clerk reading out loud the alphabetical roll call and recording the votes by hand, just as she had done nine months earlier. The assumption was that Gaetz had the votes to oust McCarthy, but still, there was an air of uncertainty as the measure finally made its way to the floor.

The Republican rebels had a plan: Their safest members would be the first to vote to oust McCarthy. Lauren Boebert desperately wanted to vote "yes," but she couldn't afford to. Her staff was careful not to be seen as telling her what to do while they outlined the risks that voting "yes" would carry for someone who was barely hanging on as it was. They assured her they were praying for her to make the right choice for herself.

"No for now," she said, holding her grandbaby in her arms on the floor of the House. She had told Gaetz ahead of the vote that she was likely a no, but "if you don't have the votes, I'll be there."

The "yes" vote no one saw coming was from Nancy Mace. She hadn't been a part of the group text chain of members planning to oust McCarthy. She had not been one of the members who ever voted against McCarthy back in January, when she had described him as a helpful ally and described Gaetz as a sex offender. She had simply thrown herself into the fray. An audible gasp rippled through the chamber when she cast her vote.

Mace claimed she didn't relish the vote and that she was texting her consultants the green vomit emoji as she headed to the floor. She did not anticipate exactly how isolated her vote would make her in Washington, but the immediate reaction gave her a taste of her new pariah status.

"Fuck off," a Republican member said to her after she'd voted. Mace got up and walked out of the chamber. The floor was silent for an awkward two minutes as the vote stood at 216–210, with 8 Republicans joining all Democrats present in voting to remove McCarthy and members getting one final chance to change their votes. The tally did not change. Patrick McHenry stood on the side near the dais with his arms crossed, having finally changed into his hard-soled shoes and accepted his fate.

"The office of the Speaker of the House of the United States House of Representatives is hereby declared vacant," said Arkansas Rep. Steve

Womack, a McCarthy ally who had been overseeing the proceedings. McHenry took to the dais as the clerk announced that he would serve as Speaker pro tempore. He slammed the gavel down with force as he made his first pronouncement: The House was now in recess.

With that, Kevin McCarthy had made history. Doomed by just eight of his colleagues and a united team of Democrats, he became the first-ever House Speaker to be deposed by members of his own party. Like the cancer diagnosis you were daring to come for you after you never tried to quit smoking, events that have been inevitable for a long time can still have the power to shock when they finally arrive. McCarthy had tried to survive on a Ponzi scheme of promises to various factions of the House, thinking he could control the ungovernable wing of his party by empowering it. The moment had seemed a foregone conclusion but still hit hard when it finally arrived, throwing the House into even deeper dysfunction.

The hard right had enough power to break things, but not enough to run them. It was not clear who could get the votes needed to be elected Speaker, or whether anyone else could fare better than McCarthy had. The members who had ousted him had no plan for whom they wanted instead. This moment of collapse was where their plan ended.

McCarthy went down claiming he had been fired for doing the right thing twice: pulling the country back from the brink of economic collapse and then avoiding a government shutdown. "I don't regret standing up for choosing governance over grievance," he said at a press conference that night. His loyal friends stood and watched: Graves was there, of course, and so was Jeff Miller, a Washington über-lobbyist who had been close friends with McCarthy since the 1990s. "It is my responsibility. It is my job. I do not regret negotiating; our government is designed to find compromise."

But McCarthy was not in the mood to take the higher road and leave it at that. What happened to him, he thought, was unfair, and though he was smiling as usual, he was pissed. "You all know Matt Gaetz," he told the reporters at a news conference. "You know it was personal. It had nothing to do about spending. It was all about getting attention from you." McCarthy insisted he wasn't blaming anyone. But he went on,

"We're getting email fundraisers from him as he's doing it. 'Join in quickly.' That's not governing. That's not becoming of a member of Congress. I've seen the texts. It was all about his ethics, but that's all right." McCarthy was completely convinced that the only reason Gaetz had come for him was because of McCarthy's refusal to kill the House Ethics Committee's investigation into allegations of Gaetz's sexual misconduct and illicit drug use.

Former President George W. Bush called McCarthy that day to offer his condolences, as did leaders from Israel and Jordan. But McCarthy had taken an unprincipled approach to life, and many lawmakers thought he simply got what was coming to him. He may have made a responsible decision twice, but so many more times he had made the decisions that empowered the beast that ultimately came to eat him. "He's a totally untrustworthy partner in governing," Katherine Clark, the number two House Democrat, said. "It was about a pursuit of power, and the rest of it didn't matter. That inherently made him a dangerous and ineffective leader. There are absolutely no regrets about not having Speaker McCarthy."

Ken Buck, one of the eight Republicans who voted to oust him, called it "pain aversion."

"If I have to tell you something right now, and I have to deal with the consequences in six months, nine months, that's fine," he said. "As long as I get what I need right now. I get your vote on this bill right now. Over and over and over again, Kevin did that."

McCarthy was not at peace with how it had ended for him. Livid at the Democrats for not saving him, he ordered McHenry to evict Pelosi and Hoyer from the coveted offices in the Capitol he had awarded them back in January as the standard courtesy to the outgoing leadership team. It was petty, but Hoyer, at least, understood it. He had promised McCarthy that Democrats would save him and then had voted to do just the opposite. Hoyer packed up his stuff and moved out feeling guilty about the whole thing. Pelosi was less forgiving. "This eviction is a sharp departure from tradition," she said in a tersely worded statement. "Office space doesn't matter to me but it seems to be important to them."

But that was all child's play. What McCarthy truly wanted was political retribution against the lawmakers he really blamed, the Republicans who had voted against him, whom he tried, unsuccessfully, to brand as "the Crazy Eight."

All his political ambitions and goals had now been whittled down to one: Take them out.

17

Who's got the stones to take on the apparatus?

—STEVE BANNON

THE MORNING AFTER McCARTHY'S OUSTER, NANCY MACE AND MATT Gaetz made the well-worn trek to Steve Bannon's nineteenth-century brick townhouse and huddled with him for a meeting in the cluttered sanctuary of his recording studio before making a triumphant joint appearance as guests on *War Room*.

The mood in the room was charged and it felt like no one had slept much the night before. For months, Bannon had been propping up the GOP rebels who wanted to oust McCarthy, offering them unlimited airtime on his show and creating more incentives for them to wreak havoc on the House floor. He had been strategizing with Gaetz, offering himself up as a sounding board as the congressman carefully plotted his moves and counted his votes and tended to the Kevin haters.

Now Gaetz and Mace were there for a victory lap. Gaetz in particular was still pulsing with the adrenaline of the previous day, eager to rehash the events with Bannon, who was simply in awe of what Gaetz, his star pupil, had pulled off.

"It was a perfect way to start," Bannon told Gaetz of the decision to have Bob Good speak on the House floor first. They discussed it as if they were dissecting the opening play of a football game. Having others speak first, they said, made it seem like it was about something bigger than what they saw McCarthy trying to frame it as—a "Matt Gaetz grudge fuck."

Mace looked shocked at where she had found herself, taken aback by the extreme vitriol that had been directed specifically at her, the most unlikely member of the group of eight and the only woman. Now the trio huddled together before showtime and decided it would be classier not to "dunk" on the man they had successfully removed from power, but to use their time on the show to look ahead.

The problem was there wasn't much to look ahead to. None of them had a plan for whom they wanted to be Speaker instead of McCarthy or any idea of what the path forward should look like. "I'm just going to see how it develops," Bannon said. "Who's got the stones to take on the apparatus?" For Bannon, who catered only to listeners, not voters, it was easy to unapologetically root for peak chaos. What he wanted was for Trump to be Speaker, and second to that, he wanted people to talk about Trump being Speaker.

For the others, however, who harbored political ambitions beyond serving in the House, it wasn't a particularly great look to be viewed by voters as pure agents of chaos. Gaetz and Mace preferred to look like people who had taken a hard vote and done the right thing out of principle. This wasn't about getting attention or dethroning a man they personally despised. This was simply about single-subject spending bills!

Gaetz, in particular, could be prickly about his coverage. After participating, with reservations, in a *New York Times* profile that presented him as the leader of the resistance to the stopgap funding measure McCarthy was trying to pass to avoid a shutdown, he texted, "You don't get me." He was unhappy with the story, he said, because it portrayed him as, in his words, "some sort of shutdown enthusiast with no plan and a nihilistic energy."

(For this and other reasons, he would remain incensed at one of this book's authors, Annie Karni, for months after. Appearing inebriated at Trump's Des Moines victory party in January 2024, after Trump had won the Iowa caucuses, Gaetz berated a reporter there, *The Wall Street Journal*'s Molly Ball, who was confused and tried to extricate herself from the uncomfortable situation. Gaetz soon realized his mistake. "I just screamed at Molly Ball," he told another reporter. "I thought she was Annie Karni." After that, Gaetz refused to speak to us further for this book.)

After ousting McCarthy, Gaetz was willing to support almost anyone for Speaker simply to prove his point that what he did was right, that

McCarthy was the problem, and that he wasn't rooting for chaos and did not have nihilistic energy. Even Patrick McHenry, he said, would be palatable. "He has an ideology, unlike the last person who held the position," he said. Still, looking ahead meant contemplating an uncertain future.

In Bannon's lair, between segments, the guests chatted about their options.

"Want to go meet with any of them today, together? Like Scalise or Jordan or anyone?" Mace asked Gaetz, who demurred. "This has been the most unproductive Congress we've had in years, right?" Mace said. On the previous Monday, they noted, the House had renamed two post offices.

As a tech set them up with earpieces and microphones, Bannon and Gaetz reminisced about the old days, when the podcast first started and they would just hang out in the basement together for hours, talking about the stolen 2020 election or railing against federal mask mandates or what they called a criminal invasion of the southern border, or whatever else was on their minds. (Bannon once had Gaetz's wife, Ginger, on his program to discuss the *Barbie* movie. She didn't like it.) They joked about how Gaetz used to just knock on the door, come on the show, and stay as long as he wanted. Now he had to be booked by real producers and sometimes ended up on the D block.

Bannon chuckled. At this moment, however, Gaetz was no D-block guest. He was a platinum member of Bannon's cadre, ever since Bannon had made Capitol Hill his main obsession of the year.

Bannon compared Gaetz to Daniel Webster, a nineteenth-century lawmaker known for his great oratorical skills. "That shot of you at the Capitol yesterday, did you see that?" Bannon said, referring to a picture of Gaetz on the Capitol steps, the nucleus of cameras and bodies all shoving microphones and tape recorders closer to him. "It was tremendous."

Three days after the recording session at Bannon's house, on October 7, Hamas launched a massive terrorist attack on defenseless Israeli citizens, leaving Congress impotent and leaderless at a time when a key democratic ally might imminently need financial support. Some 3,000 terrorists killed more than 1,100 people, causing an international crisis and underscoring how reckless it was for one branch of the American government to be rendered inoperable. But at the table in Bannon's base-ment that day, the group was certain they were the main players in a story that would continue to be the biggest news event in the country.

The *War Room* audience was still wary of Mace, who had voted to hold Bannon in criminal contempt for defying a subpoena from the January 6 Committee. In the past, she had also called Gaetz a "fraud" and accused him of opposing McCarthy because the Speaker wouldn't defend him against "allegations that he sex-trafficked minors."

But Bannon and Gaetz viewed Mace as a gift. Her vote to oust McCar-thy had allowed him and his cohorts to push back on the notion that it was only an angry group of ultra-MAGA hard-line men who had lost faith in the Speaker. "Nancy is not a hard-right intransigent lawmaker," Gaetz said on the show. "Nancy is a fiscal hawk."

"You gotta be at the ramparts today because K Street is coming hard," Bannon said, describing what had happened as a "tectonic plate shift here in the imperial capital."

Mace tried to frame herself as a maverick. And every time she spoke, she hit her talking points: working mom, Citadel graduate, small-business owner. "The knives are out for me," she said. "When I was at the Citadel, when I went through that, they teach you about duty, doing the right thing no matter who is watching. What we did last night was decentral-izing that power and giving it back to the people. It's about broken prom-ises."

As the program broke for commercials, the group discussed that there would likely be a motion to expel Gaetz from the Republican conference. "They need to poll your favorability in their districts against their own and then make that expulsion vote," said Caroline Wren, a Trump fund-raiser who had popped in ahead of her slot on the podcast.

Ultimately, no one ever moved to expel Gaetz, despite McCarthy's prodding. McCarthy and his allies pushed for it, briefly, but they were ultimately convinced by enough members they trusted that doing so would only turn Gaetz into a martyr and play into his hands.

On the show, Gaetz tried to temper the enthusiasm of the base. "Do not allow the posse to get punch-drunk," he said on the program. There was still more work to do. He left after recording three segments of the show.

"I'll talk to you later today," Bannon said as Gaetz showed himself out.

Mace, meanwhile, tried to embrace her new pariah status. At the next conference meeting, she walked past the cameras camped outside wearing a tight white T-shirt with the letter *A* emblazoned across her chest: the scarlet letter. "I like telling people to fuck off when they're wrong—and they did persecute me," she said later, discussing the T-shirt stunt. "My consultants told me not to do it, they thought it would make me look like a victim, but I was doing it to feel empowered."

And she still had VP aspirations rattling around in her mind. "I think he's going to pick someone that he likes on TV," she said of Trump. "I go on the radio shows he likes and the TV shows he watches. That's my theory. And if I end up getting something else out of it"—she paused—"I'm trying to play this long game also." She added, as if test-driving a line we never heard her use again, "If Trump wants to win women, go with the gal who wore the scarlet letter?"

As Mace slurped up the attention, both positive and negative, Lauren Boebert was getting backlash from the base because she had not voted to oust McCarthy. Bannon, once her lifeline after the *Beetlejuice* episode, now had no interest in having her on. "If it came to another round, I was probably going to vacate him," she said later. But voting to oust McCarthy would likely have spelled the end of her career in Congress.

18

The cleanest thing for everyone here is for me to want nothing.

—PATRICK McHENRY

I N SELECTING PATRICK McHENRY FOR THE UNTESTED ROLE OF SPEAKER pro tempore, McCarthy, it would turn out, chose wisely for what would end up being an incredibly difficult job, one requiring a deep understanding of House rules; the backbone to stand up to the increasingly plaintive demands of Speaker candidates who were falling short; and some bigger idea of what was in the best interest of the party and the conference writ large. It helped that McHenry recognized that his superpower in the dysfunctional Congress was not wanting anything and thereby allowing no one to have leverage over him. "The cleanest thing for everyone here is for me to want nothing," he said. It was a bonus that he was a reformed rabble-rouser himself, one who still, despite having matured, relished a confrontational fight.

(After the dust had finally settled, the two longtime friends would joke that McHenry should be included in McCarthy's Speaker portrait, perhaps a framed picture on McCarthy's desk in the official oil painting, an Easter egg to mark the untested role McCarthy had thrust McHenry into, the strange coda to his short reign.)

There were issues that McHenry could have tried to deal with, like a fairly uncontroversial (at the time) resolution in support of Israel after October 7. But McHenry thought trying to move ahead with anything, even a nonbinding resolution, would only serve to elongate the process of electing a Speaker by showing that there were ways to make the floor work without one. The best way forward, he decided, was to leave the House completely frozen until it elected a Speaker and continue that narrow definition of his role—that his job was to call a new vote for Speaker and nothing else.

The job was immediately eye-opening for McHenry, who at various times in his career had toyed with the idea of running for Speaker himself. As he sat in the back of his armored SUV one morning, the words of former House Speaker Paul Ryan rang in his ears: The speakership was a prison. Surrounded at all times by people but always fundamentally alone, he was getting a rare glimpse of the uncomfortable isolation of power. He was grateful for the parents at his children's school, who couldn't have cared less whether he was the Speaker of the House or unemployed, who just shouted, "Come on, McHenry!" if his detail double-parked in the drop-off line and made them late for work.

The only member of leadership not eyeing the speakership during this time was Elise Stefanik, who decided she was unlikely to win and would do better for herself by checking her own ambition and simply helping McHenry run a smooth process to elect someone else. You can't fake your real passion, and Stefanik was locked into a different goal: serving in the Trump administration.

She went on NBC's *Meet the Press* and referred to the January 6 prisoners as "hostages." She deleted all old press releases from her official website, whitewashing the fact that she had called the violence at the Capitol on that day "anti-American" and "tragic" in real time. She said she would not commit to certifying the 2024 election results if Biden won. "We will see if this is a legal and valid election," she said. In April 2024, she was the only Republican member of leadership to vote against Ukraine aid.

Stefanik was not in the true believer category, like Marjorie Taylor Greene and Matt Gaetz, politicians who had never been anything but Trump acolytes. When she was elected to Congress in 2014 as its youngest woman, she was a proud moderate millennial Republican who counted Paul Ryan as a mentor and had an elite résumé that included her Harvard University diploma and a stint on the Domestic Policy Council in the George W. Bush White House. Ryan described her in a 2019 *Time* magazine spotlight as "the future of hopeful, aspirational politics in America."

Like everyone else in Congress, she had done her private hair-pulling about Trump, venting about "dumb" decisions the White House made that put House Republicans in a bad spot. (She now denies this.)

But by 2024, she counted as an early adopter in a Republican Party that unfailingly bent the knee to Trump. By then, she had been a MAGA warrior for almost as long as she had been a moderate Bushie before. The party had completely transformed itself, and Stefanik remained the face of its future.

Still, she was firmly in the "you should know better" category of lawmakers who underwent a metamorphosis while chasing power. The Elise Stefanik who first landed in Washington after college was described as a sweet young woman with liberal college friends she went out of her way to stay in touch with, who liked sharing literary fiction recommendations and was eager to take advantage of what the city had to offer.

One of the perks of a junior position in the White House was that she often got free tickets to sit in the president's box for performances at the Kennedy Center, or was allowed to invite friends to the South Lawn to watch a Marine One landing. But mostly, young Stefanik liked doing regular twenty-something things. She hosted viewing parties for *The Office* and *Grey's Anatomy* at her apartment and made pizza for her friends. She eagerly sought reassurance from them about whether someone she was interested in romantically was reciprocating. She was kind, often checking in with her college crew via email, asking friends, "How's the new jobby?" as she and her ambitious fellow Harvard grads started their careers. She was a diligent worker who put her career first, but she also had a bit of a wild streak. Despite having a job that often kept her at work till after 10 P.M., Stefanik was always eager to go out and socialize with her friends and potential romantic interests, most of whom worked on Capitol Hill.

By 2024, the fun streak, the sweet friend, and the "hopeful" future were difficult to find in the hardened character into which Stefanik had transformed herself. "One of my killers," Trump liked to call her, a moniker earned from her role as his chief defender on the House Intelligence Committee during his first impeachment trial. Stefanik was not a natural politician—she was guarded and lacked any warmth or humor she was willing to show publicly. She was also not a natural bomb thrower, always scurrying away from reporters on Capitol Hill and sticking to scripted talking points. She didn't engender any great affection from her colleagues, who described her, alternately, as a "nice-seeming lady" or nothing at all. Where she had stood out from the pack was playing the prosecutor in high-profile committee hearings, first acting like a Trump defense lawyer during his first impeachment trial and then taking apart the presidents of Ivy League universities, two of whom were forced to resign because of their feeble responses to Stefanik's line of questioning about anti-Semitism on campus.

Stefanik knew her strengths, and running and winning a Speaker's race wasn't one of them. Her bet would pay off. After Trump won the 2024 election, one of his first personnel announcements was his nomination of Stefanik to serve as ambassador to the United Nations.

19

Long live Speaker Scalise.

—MATT GAETZ

WHILE ELISE STEFANIK HUNG BACK, TWO MEN IMMEDIATELY WENT into overdrive to try to win the speakership: One, Jim Jordan, the Trump ally whose investigations were targeting President Biden, was the favorite of the hard right. The other, Steve Scalise, was the favorite of the establishment.

Scalise was the natural heir to the House majority that McCarthy had spent years building. If McCarthy was the chief executive of the company, Scalise was the vice president who expected the promotion. (Conversely, many members argued, if the company is failing, why would anyone want to promote the number two to run it?) He tried pitching himself to his colleagues as a man uniquely positioned to unite them in desperate and demoralized times. After McCarthy, he was the best fundraiser in the House. And he had the experience, and the leadership staff, to hit the ground running.

All year, Scalise had been frozen out by McCarthy, who was animated by a years-long rivalry with his number two, which boiled down to two people with similar skill sets who were in each other's way for the same jobs for too long. It's not clear that anyone was right or wrong, but McCarthy was viewed by the other team as a sensitive grudge holder and Scalise as a secretive backstabber, so the relationship had calcified into its permanent state: hatred.

The antipathy was so intense that McCarthy was looking for a way to make sure Scalise would not be his successor—he privately told Tom

Emmer that *he* was the natural heir to the speakership, a private endorsement McCarthy hoped would motivate Emmer to challenge Scalise for the post. Emmer, however, bowed to Scalise when the number two House Republican called to tell him he was running and wanted Emmer's support.

The shadowboxing between Scalise and McCarthy, two ambitious climbers with different regional power bases in Congress, was not a unique dynamic in leadership. On the Democratic side, Steny Hoyer, the longtime number two Democrat, operated in Pelosi's shadow for decades, his frustration about that dynamic sometimes barely concealed. In 2001, after Pelosi beat Hoyer for the position of House minority whip, Hoyer said that "if she hadn't been a woman or from California, I think we would have been okay. Gender and geography in this case were overwhelming. C'est la guerre." In 2006, when Democrats won back the House and Pelosi became the first woman Speaker, she backed her friend Rep. John Murtha of Pennsylvania for majority leader over Hoyer, who ended up winning that race. Hoyer made the best of it, conceding that over the years, when they were both vying for top jobs, "there were no public attacks and no public assertions—I don't mean there weren't some private elbows thrown; we both wanted to win."

But any resentment Hoyer may have felt was tempered by the fact that eventually he came to see Pelosi as a historic figure who was, at the end of the day, just better at politics than he, however difficult it was to come to terms with that. "I think Nancy is the best Speaker we've had, so I was the number two," Hoyer told us in an interview for *The New York Times* in 2022, after he had made the decision to step down from leadership at the same time she did. "But I was the number two to someone who people think is, in history, one of the five top Speakers who we've had. What am I going to offer?"

With McCarthy, there was no Pelosi-like record that you had to eventually hand it to, no foundation of respect for his abilities that tempered the rivalry. Even the attempts to mask their rivalry were half-hearted. In April 2023, after *The New York Times* reported on their mounting tensions, Scalise appeared on ABC's *This Week,* a prestigious Sunday show, where he was asked about it and tried to downplay the story. "We don't always agree on everything, but we have a very candid relationship," he said. Candid, perhaps, in that they both knew they disliked and distrusted each other.

On the night of McCarthy's ouster, members of his inner circle were distraught and looking to cast blame for what happened. Some of them claimed to have witnessed Scalise's crew, who worked from a suite of offices on the third floor of the Capitol, one floor above McCarthy's office, wheeling champagne into their conference room, clinking glasses and giving toasts. Scalise staff were appalled that anyone would think that they would hold a festive gathering on such a high-stakes night, when what they were really doing was huddling in tense meetings to figure out how Scalise needed to proceed. But they weren't surprised that McCarthy's staff would accuse them of such behavior: On the Hill, rivalries between principals can be outdone only by rivalries among their staffs.

The fact that Scalise hadn't been anywhere near the room where the debt ceiling deal had been negotiated—as hard as it was to stomach at the time—was now looking like a gift. Hard-right members who might naturally have favored Jordan, he thought, wouldn't see Scalise's involvement in the deal that ultimately ended McCarthy as a reason not to support him as their second choice.

Scalise had arrived in Washington in 2008. A political animal since childhood, he was eager to take advantage of all that his new position had to offer him. He joined the Bible study group and the congressional baseball team, where he would play in a Louisiana State University baseball jersey and buy tickets for all his staff members and their kids. He found his desired policy platform on the Energy and Commerce Committee, where he became an ally of the oil and gas industry. And he kept a foot in politics, serving as the recruitment chair of the National Republican Congressional Committee and then chairman of the Republican Study Committee, at the time the largest group of conservative House Republicans. By 2014, he had played all his cards right and risen to the number three position in the House.

Scalise was viewed as a stock Christian conservative character from the Deep South until 2017, when he was gravely wounded after a gunman, distraught over Trump's election, opened fire on members of the Republican congressional baseball team at an early morning practice in Virginia. Scalise was in critical condition, with shattered bones, ruptured organs, and major internal bleeding. Three months and multiple surgeries later, he made a triumphant return to the Capitol walking with two canes. "I'm definitely a living example that miracles do happen," he said on the House floor, where he was greeted with an extended standing ovation from colleagues on both sides of the aisle. He was now a figure of resilience.

Scalise still limps and walks with a lift in one shoe but otherwise has made a remarkable and complete recovery. He claimed that the experience changed his perspective on life. "If you look on paper, I shouldn't be here," he said. "I don't feel like I've been through anything that anyone should feel sorry for. I'm lucky to be alive."

For the most part, he tried to keep hold of that almost-died perspective that can make all of life's quotidian frustrations seem like daily gifts. But it's impossible for anyone to hold on to that perspective all the time, and he could still get enmeshed in the petty politics of Capitol Hill. As the majority leader, a position he held beginning in 2023, it was basically part of the job to do so.

As he mounted his bid for Speaker, Scalise pointed out to his colleagues that his rival for the position, Jim Jordan, had supported the primary opponents of twelve sitting members of Congress. How would Jordan be able to help them win their districts, and raise money for them, if he had actively worked against them just one cycle earlier? Jordan had also refused to make a commitment ahead of time that whoever came in second would support the winner.

But right off the bat there was a big optics problem for Scalise. He had recently been diagnosed with a rare blood cancer, multiple myeloma, and was undergoing aggressive chemotherapy sessions for treatment. He assured his colleagues that his doctors had cleared him to work and run for the bigger job—but that meant appearing in the Capitol in a heavy-duty, medical-grade mask that looked like a ventilator, and often social distancing himself from his colleagues at news conferences and internal party meetings. Masking had always been a loaded political statement for Republicans. Scalise himself had refused to wear a face covering throughout most of the Covid-19 pandemic and had publicly denounced federal mask mandates as "political theater."

Some of his colleagues had real concerns about his health, and some simply didn't like the optics of the House Republican conference being led by someone who looked sick and weak and whose appearance now served as a walking advertisement for the efficacy of face coverings that they had dismissed as a political charade.

Marjorie Taylor Greene said she liked Scalise so much "that I want to see him defeat cancer more than sacrifice his health in the most difficult position in Congress." (She really did prove to be a loyal friend to McCarthy until the bitter end.) Scalise said Greene was wrong that he was making any choices between his health and his ambition; he had been fully cleared by his doctors. But Trump, who endorsed Jordan, went on Fox News to say that Scalise "is in serious trouble from the standpoint of his cancer." Scalise's team was also convinced that Garret Graves, serving as McCarthy's henchman, was responsible for spreading rumors that Scalise had only six months left to live. Graves denied doing so. But those who harbored doubts about whether Scalise was giving a full picture about his health felt somewhat vindicated for holding his cancer against him when, in January 2024, he announced he would be working remotely for weeks while receiving a stem cell transplant. How would that have worked if he had been Speaker? they wondered in front of reporters. (Scalise made a full recovery.)

In the first Republican conference meeting where the two candidates for Speaker fielded questions from their colleagues, Ken Buck stood up to ask them to address what had become one of the defining issues of the party.

Buck was a right-winger's right-winger. The AR-15 he kept mounted on a wall in his office had become a Hill celebrity in its own right: Constituents often came by, even when Buck wasn't there, to take a picture with the gun (locked and stripped of parts to make it inoperable). A former federal prosecutor, Buck often advocated for the most conservative policy positions possible, and he didn't like to see GOP leaders find compromise with Democrats. But he wanted to see Republican leaders fight for conservative causes, not live in a fantasyland of lies about a stolen election.

"Will you unequivocally and publicly state that the 2020 election was not stolen?" he asked both Scalise and Jordan. It was notable that a question like that—one they could have expected in a televised interview on MSNBC—would come up in a closed-door meeting of a party that had been subsumed by Trump and his Big Lie. It was something like the final flash of an immune system that was being overwhelmed by a virus it could not defeat. In response, Scalise and Jordan both dissembled, rambling about discrepancies and the Pennsylvania secretary of state, about how Arizona hadn't done a good job of certifying the signatures. Neither would give a hard "yes" or "no" answer to the question.

Buck wasn't surprised by that. What did surprise him was the reaction he got from some of his colleagues for even posing the question. Rep. French Hill, a traditional conservative from Arkansas, publicly backed him up. "I'm going to rephrase Ken's question," Hill said. "Did Trump lose the election?" Again, no answer. Republicans in the room started getting fidgety. Privately, more Republicans told Buck they were happy he'd brought it up and thus voiced a rare dose of reality in the collective madness on the subject of election denialism. "[Pennsylvania Rep.] Brian Fitzpatrick comes up to me and says, 'Thanks for asking that question,'" Buck said. "Six or seven people said the same thing. I thought, *There's more people here that are quiet but feel the way I do,* which is a big problem in life, when you are the one who puts your head up and gets it shot off and everyone else says, 'I'm glad he did that.'"

It can also be a good problem in life when you're already looking toward your next move and want to be employable. Raising objections over election denialism may not make you popular in the House Republican conference, but it's a solid way to be palatable down the line as a cable television commentator, a paid speaker, or someone who can sit on corporate boards.

Mace, in classic Mace fashion, decided to zig while everyone else was zagging: She went on cable television and called Scalise a racist. "I personally cannot in good conscience vote for someone who attended a white supremacist conference and compared himself to David Duke," she told CNN's Jake Tapper.

She was referring to a scandal from Scalise's past that had almost derailed his career once before. In 2002, when he served as a state legislator in Louisiana, he spoke at a meeting of a white nationalist group founded by Duke. A blogger broke the story in 2014, and at the time, Scalise called it a mistake, claiming he didn't know the group's background and quickly condemning its views. At the time, he leaned on a Black Democrat in Congress, Cedric Richmond, to serve as a character witness. "I don't think Steve Scalise has a racist bone in his body," Richmond said then.

Scalise had also once described himself, according to a local columnist, as "like David Duke without the baggage." He survived the scandal and the calls for his resignation and had put to bed the entire incident years earlier. In 2020, he voted to remove Confederate statues from the U.S. Capitol, breaking with the majority of his party on the issue. And in a conference where members like Marjorie Taylor Greene proudly claimed that Muslim lawmakers like Rashida Tlaib and Ilhan Omar weren't "really official" members of Congress because they did not take the oath of office on the Bible; where Rep. Troy Nehls, a Texas Republican, referred to the Black husband of a Democratic woman of color, Cori Bush, as a "thug"; and where bigoted attacks had become part of the everyday discourse, Scalise's decades-old brush with racism seemed rather quaint by comparison.

If anything, Scalise and his advisers were consumed with the opposite problem: appearing too mainstream to the far-right crowd. But they were confident that there were still more mainstream Republicans in the House than there were hard-right members. The math, they thought, was on their side.

On October 11, 2023, in an anonymous internal vote of 113 to 99, Scalise beat Jordan for the title of Speaker-designate. The problem with the vote breakdown was that it was close enough to leave Jordan and his allies thinking that the position could still be theirs.

In an earlier era in Congress, such thinking would have been inconceivable. The rules of the game had long been understood: The person who wins the vote in conference is the Speaker-designate. That was that. It was now the duty of the rest of the Republicans who had voted against Scalise to rally around him and vote for him on the floor.

But that tradition was from the pre-Trump era, when election results weren't a matter of opinion. In denying the results of the 2020 election,

Trump had set a new standard for the party. If your opponent wins, that new Trumpian standard was to keep fighting anyway, to say the election was rigged, to make up any excuse to keep fighting—but, by all means, to keep fighting.

Scalise's wife stood next to him as he thanked the conference for selecting him. His speech notably did not include a single word about McCarthy, who sat in the audience and noted it. When Scalise got the votes, Patrick McHenry and his team thought their role was over: McHenry's chief of staff, Jeff Butler, huddled with Ben Napier, a top adviser to Scalise.

"Let us know when you're ready," Butler told him. Napier said they would likely be ready to go to the floor before 5 P.M. that day.

McHenry and his team went out to Hank's Oyster Bar for a long celebratory lunch, checking their phones to see when Scalise's team would notify them that it was time to schedule the floor vote. *So long, security detail,* McHenry thought. It wasn't until after lunch that McHenry and his staff started scrolling X and noticed that members were not fully behind Scalise. When Butler checked in with Scalise's team later in the afternoon, he was told they needed more time. Things were not going well with their whip count.

It was clear by 5 P.M. that this wasn't going to be a normal process, wherein the conference at large supported the member who had won the majority. What was also clear was that Jordan thought he still had a shot at becoming Speaker.

Jordan, who had once been nicknamed a legislative terrorist, had decided he wanted to be the Speaker of the House, a job that required passing bills (not just blowing them up) and bringing people together. The decision surprised some longtime Hill staffers. For years, Jordan's position as the thorn in leadership's side meant he wielded all the power and none of the responsibility. Why would he want the responsibility that came with actually having to govern and cut unpopular deals?

Later, he said that he had never planned on running for Speaker and had done it only because "I thought someone has to try to bring the team together. I thought maybe I could do it."

"The good Lord's been kind to me," he added.

It was true that in recent years Jordan had become more of a team player, in large part because the team catered to him. McCarthy brought him into the tent by offering him a powerful gavel—Judiciary Committee chair—meaning he had a seat at the grown-ups' table and no longer voted with fringe groups like the Twenty to blow things up all the time. "He's standing next to me now instead of shooting at me," McCarthy told *The Washington Post*'s Paul Kane of Jordan's strategy. Indeed, Jordan had been a team player through the Speaker fight and the debt ceiling debate. But when the opportunity to seize more power came his way, it was the old Jim Jordan who reared his head.

Immediately after Scalise finished his speech, Jordan stood up to address his colleagues. He told them they shouldn't leave the room until Scalise was able to get 217 votes in support of his bid.

Jordan was making it clear he did not plan to support the person who had just won the vote. Instead, he was, after the fact, raising the threshold Scalise would need to cross to win. This was interpreted by many members in the room as an attempt to overturn the will of the majority, who had just voted to elect Scalise as Speaker-designate. Five Jordan supporters stood up to tell their colleagues they would never vote for Scalise— enough holdouts to effectively block his bid. And it wasn't lost on Scalise supporters that Jordan did nothing to push back on them. Still, McHenry was unconcerned enough to head off to lunch thinking his duties were soon to be over.

"It was a real election, a winner was declared," Rep. Mario Díaz-Balart, a more moderate Florida Republican, said one day in the ornate Speaker's Lobby outside the House Chamber, under the gaze of Speakers past, who looked down on us from oversize oil portraits hanging on the walls. "The guy who loses the election basically says, 'no.' To me that was a really sad moment. That created a major, major problem."

The coalition that wanted to take out Scalise was different from the one that had ousted McCarthy. Gaetz, for one, was no longer a problem, under the age-old truism that the enemy of an enemy is a friend. "Long live Speaker Scalise," Gaetz proclaimed as he exited the Republican conference meeting in the Longworth House Office Building.

Mace, however, was continuing to be a stick in the wheel. The David Duke incident had been flagged for her by Fitzpatrick, notably a close ally of McCarthy's. Mace texted Scalise to let him know she would not support him on the House floor. "Last night it came to my attention your comments about David Duke and attending a white supremacist event," she wrote. "In my district, I represent families from Mother Emanuel. I didn't know about those previously."

Scalise texted back that what she had said wasn't true and he wanted to talk to her about it.

Mace fired back, "If it isn't true then why apologize for attending a white supremacist event?"

Later, when thinking further about it, she said, "If I wasn't who I was and I had more seniority, I would run for it and say this is what we're going to do and we're marching to war. It's just one big circle jerk," she said.

Mace's house was a classic Capitol Hill brick row house directly across from the office building where she worked. In the front hall, she displayed an oversize photo of the Kennedys, Jackie as the focus, a surprising choice for a Republican. The living room included few personal touches; it looked like an Airbnb. In fact, it was. Mace would sometimes rent the place out and sleep in her office.

The practice was rare for women, and rarer for a lawmaker who owned a multimillion-dollar house a block away from work to do it so she could bring in a little extra cash—rare because it was prohibited. A Mace enemy even filed a complaint with the House Ethics Committee alleging that the congresswoman had overcharged a reimbursement program for members by $23,000, even though she owned her own home in Washington and was not allowed to seek reimbursement for mortgage payments.

Mace's paying guests would have had no reason to know they were staying in a congresswoman's second home. But when the place wasn't rented out, it offered Mace a nice refuge to escape the Capitol and her colleagues. On stressful afternoons, she would sometimes unwind there in yoga pants, with a glass of sangria and takeout Indian food. The blinds were often drawn.

The truth was, Mace had been in a bit of a downward spiral since her vote to oust McCarthy. In the month following that vote, she had fired all her D.C. staff who hadn't quit. She had parted ways with her fiancé in an ugly and traumatizing breakup, had lost thirty pounds from an already slim frame, and had acquired a primary challenger as well as nine tattoos, up from zero. She now had her kids' names on her ribs, a Robert Frost quote on her left side, the famous first sentence of Virginia Woolf's *Mrs. Dalloway* on her torso ("Mrs. Dalloway said she would buy the flowers herself"), and Bible quotes on her fingers, tattooed in red to make them less visible. For lucky number ten, she was planning to do a goat with some flowers, the goat representing the "Greatest of All Time." (Some of her detractors were eager to share this fact with Trump, who hated tattoos.)

"I have no trust in humanity right now," Mace said of all the personal and professional trauma she was working through. "It's going to be a long and painful and arduous recovery."

In the good-news column, she would go on to score an endorsement from Trump for her re-election campaign now that she had gone all in. "I told him, 'I'm bilingual, I can speak MAGA, I can speak suburban mom,'" she said of campaigning with Trump in South Carolina ahead of the presidential primary there.

McCarthy held a particular chip on his shoulder about Mace. He helped recruit a candidate to run against her, and groups aligned with him would end up spending more than four million dollars in attack ads trying to beat her. "I hope Nancy gets the help she needs—I really do," McCarthy told reporters on a visit to the Capitol. "I just hope she gets the help to straighten out her life. I mean, she's got a lot of challenges."

Mace wanted to win her primary mostly as a fuck-you to McCarthy. "I hope to embarrass him tonight," she said on Election Day as she visited a Waffle House. "I want to send him back to the rock he's living under right now. I hope I drive Kevin McCarthy crazy." It was a primary about nothing except revenge. With no real policy differences between the candidates, it was a multimillion-dollar exercise in forcing voters to weigh in about something that had nothing to do with them.

Mace won that night by twenty-seven points. When Trump visited Capitol Hill two days later, she told him it was thanks to his support that she had walloped an opponent by double digits for the first time in her career.

In Washington, Mace's reversals had made her prime fodder for ridicule, but at home, they were paying off and winning over voters in a district whose new lines had turned it from purple to red. Lynn Fontaine, the southern regional director of the Beaufort County Republican Party, said most of her friends and neighbors in Hilton Head couldn't stand Mace, because she had criticized Trump after January 6—the exact move that had made Mace, for a moment, a shining star in Washington. Fontaine was still a Mace supporter, and so was her husband—mostly because she was so pretty, she said, laughing. But voters like Fontaine's neighbors were people Mace needed if she wanted to keep her seat. "Mace's vote against McCarthy was a redeeming moment for her," Fontaine said.

Mace's victory would change her stature in Washington. She was still viewed as an erratic person, but now she was heading toward being a three-term congresswoman, and the embarrassing stories and the smear campaign driven by McCarthy hadn't been able to stop her. And now she had Trump on her side. She was less the butt of a joke—or, at least, the joke was now on someone else. "I'm not going to change a damn thing," she said of how she planned to act going forward. In November 2024, after the election of Rep. Sarah McBride from Delaware, the first openly transgender person in Congress, Mace found a new animating issue: the bathroom. She led the charge to ban transgender women from using women's restrooms and changing rooms in the Capitol complex. Of course, Mace had previously called herself a lawmaker who was "pro-transgender rights."

When Jordan went through the motions of saying publicly that he was with Scalise, his body language, all shuffling feet and downcast eyes, told a different story. There was no joint press conference, just some mumbled comments from Jordan that he would give the nominating speech for Scalise on the floor.

In a one-on-one meeting with Scalise in his office, Jordan delivered an ultimatum. "I'll support you publicly for one vote on the floor," he said. "But if you don't win, you have to endorse me."

Scalise, typically soft-spoken in public, blew up at Jordan. "The conference just made a choice," he said. "You're going to give me one round, so you can tell all of your guys to hold off, that all we need to do is get through this one vote. Do you think I'm that stupid?"

In Jordan's telling, there was nothing inappropriate about the ultimatum. "I said, 'I'll support you, but if you don't make it, will you support me?' He wouldn't do it."

Scalise was right that the deal was a loser for him. Jordan was right that he deserved a shot if Scalise didn't make it through. The plain reality was that neither one of them had the votes to be Speaker.

Scalise said hell no to Jordan's deal, still hopeful that the conference would come together to back him. But in the larger group meetings he held in the same conference room where his staff had been accused of clinking glasses as McCarthy was ousted, the reality of the situation became clear to Scalise and his team: There were about a dozen holdouts; the math wasn't changing. If they squinted to see if it was moving at all, it was changing for the worse.

"If we had a twelve-seat majority, it would have been a different story," Scalise said. "Then, you can go to the floor and see what the numbers are. If it's twenty 'no's, you can narrow it down. But if you can afford to lose five and you're at twelve, and you've met with them multiple times and you know these people—I knew where it was. We got close, but we didn't get close enough."

A mere thirty-six hours after being elected Speaker-designate, Scalise dropped out without ever taking a floor vote. The abrupt ending surprised members, who figured he would stick it out through the weekend and work to win over the holdouts. Some of his supporters pushed him to stay in and fight, saying he had won, fair and square. "I'm not going to put the conference through that," he told them.

The official end came in a brief statement delivered in the basement of the Capitol. "Our conference still has to come together and is not there," he said. "There are still some people that have their own agendas. I was very clear: We have to have everyone put their agendas on the side and focus on what this country needs."

Scalise tried going out on a classy note, saying he wasn't going to let his own ambition hold up the process of the House reopening. "I never came here for a title," he said, while also noting that he still very much enjoyed his title of majority leader and planned to keep it.

McCarthy's head had already rolled. Scalise, too, was now deposed.

The strange scenario put Republicans in a situation that upended their entire structure of governance. The majority leader had been dealt a blow by his conference, but he had no plans to step down as leader. The person he had already defeated in a secret ballot was now on his way to becoming the party's nominee for Speaker, despite having had fewer votes than the guy who had just dropped out.

A day after Scalise ended his bid, on a Friday night, the beleaguered Republicans went back to the dreaded Longworth House Office Building conference room to take another secret ballot vote to elect a new Speaker-designate. This time, Jordan won over a virtually unknown rival, Rep. Austin Scott of Georgia, who threw his name in the mix simply as a vessel for protest votes from members who opposed Jordan.

But Jordan now had his own unique set of problems with a different group of members.

20

My brand is "fighter."

—JIM JORDAN

F OR DON BACON, THE FOLKSY CENTER-LEANING REPUBLICAN FROM
Nebraska, Jim Jordan's behavior the day Steve Scalise won the internal
party vote was, in one word, "dishonorable."

Bacon didn't have any serious moral objections to Jordan. He thought
he had done a decent job as chairman of the Judiciary Committee, and he
would have supported Jordan "reluctantly" if he had emerged from the
secret ballot with the support of the majority of the conference. But he
hadn't.

"The way he treated Steve Scalise wasn't right," Bacon told people. It
was a reminder that so much of what happens, or doesn't, in Congress
comes down to its being a large body of people simply having human,
emotional reactions to one another. That wasn't necessarily new, but it
took on greater prominence in people's thinking when there was no substance to mitigate the personal grievances and petty fights that can easily
consume all of us.

"I can't get past the fact that those five guys said they wouldn't back
Scalise, and you were in the room and said nothing. It wasn't right," Bacon
told Jordan when he asked him for his support. "I don't think it's honorable."

Another holdout was Ken Buck, who said he could not vote for Jordan on the House floor because of Jordan's deep involvement in the
planning and execution of the effort to overturn the 2020 election,
which had resulted in a deadly riot at the Capitol on January 6. Buck

prepared for a meeting with Jordan by taking a copy of the House January 6 Committee's final report and marking it up with all the references to his involvement on that day.

Trump and Jordan had spoken for ten minutes on the phone the morning of January 6 and again later that day. On January 5, Jordan texted Mark Meadows, then the White House chief of staff, to tell him that Vice President Mike Pence should "call out all the electoral votes that he believes are unconstitutional as no electoral votes at all." (Jordan says he was merely passing on advice from a conservative lawyer.)

Sitting with Buck in his office now, trying to win him over, Jordan didn't have much to say in response to these charges. "He said, 'Well, that's not true' and 'That's only partially true' and 'That's kind of true,'" Buck recalled of the meeting. "I said, 'Okay, but the bottom line is the perception out there is more than anybody else on the Hill, you are the Republican who was interacting with the Trump administration.'"

Buck was firm in his rejection of Jordan, who had also sidelined him on the Judiciary Committee. "I can't support you," he told him. "I will vote 'present' if I'm the deciding vote, but I just can't vote for you on this."

The opposition was dug in. But unlike Scalise, Jordan was not one to drop out without a fight. Doing so would cut against his public persona, and it's not how the MAGA base expected him to conduct himself. "My brand is 'fighter,'" he insisted to his colleagues.

Jordan's team worked hard that week, but the more they tried to work the holdouts, the more ground they lost. They came back to Bacon with poll numbers from his district that were meant to convince him he needed to support Jordan. The numbers showed Bacon's own favorability at 52 percent in his district, Jordan's at 38 percent, and Trump's at 36 percent. The argument from Team Jordan was "We don't hurt you. You're strong."

Bacon guffawed. "I take the opposite view of those numbers," he told them.

As the House prepared to leave for the weekend, Jordan's plan was to hold off on going to the floor until he had secured enough votes to win.

And his allies had a strategy: Unleash hell.

They started a public pressure campaign aimed at the holdouts, unleashing the party's angry MAGA base against the lawmakers standing in the way. Jordan allies shared their phone numbers on social media, and Fox News host Sean Hannity and his producers called members and their staffers to press them to support Jordan. On television, Hannity blasted the "few sensitive little snowflakes in Congress" who were standing in the way of Jordan's speakership.

The result was an intense and ugly pressure campaign that at times turned to violent threats that were referred to the FBI and Capitol Police—and it all had the exact opposite effect Jordan had hoped it would have.

Jordan called Bacon again and asked him where his head was if they proceeded to a floor vote.

"I'm still a no," he said. Within thirty minutes of his call with Jordan, he was barraged on social media by people calling him a traitor, a RINO (Republican in name only), and worse.

Over the following week, Bacon's office would receive thirty-one thousand threatening and bullying calls, up from the average of three hundred constituent calls it fielded in a typical week. For a week straight, the office phones rang at two-second intervals. Bacon's wife received threatening text messages and voicemails that had to be referred to the police.

Bacon gave one of them to CNN, which played it on air in full. "Why is your husband such a pig?" the anonymous caller said. "Why would he get on TV and make an asshole of himself? Because he's a deep-state prick? Because he doesn't represent the people? So, what we're gonna do is we're gonna fucking come follow you all over the place. We're gonna be up your ass. Fucking nonstop. We are now Antifa." The threatening caller said he demanded a Speaker who was "Jim Jordan or more conservative, or you're going to be fucking molested like you can't ever imagine. . . . You must be a bitch to marry a fucking ugly motherfucker like that."

Bacon was still in Washington that night. Back at home, his wife slept with a loaded gun on the pillow next to her.

In the Jordan camp, the complaints about harassment were greeted with a dramatic eye roll. Death threats were part and parcel of being a member of Congress in 2023, was their thinking. Their general reaction to members complaining about threatening phone calls? Grow a pair.

This was in dramatic contrast to Scalise, who took the threats seriously. "I had a guy try to kill me. It's real," he said. "I don't take it lightly when we get death threats."

Meanwhile, Jordan decided to go to the floor knowing he didn't have the votes to win, hoping it would serve as part of a pressure campaign to "smoke out" the defectors.

Ahead of the Monday vote, he received an unexpected text message from Paul Ryan, the former House Speaker and prototypical think tank conservative whose life Jordan had made miserable when he was in leadership. "Looks like things are going well," Ryan wrote to him. "Call me if I can ever help."

On the floor, 22 Republicans voted against Jordan, which made Bacon feel relieved and protected. If he had been part of a small handful of "no" votes, he had feared, it would have been hard to hold up the election of the Speaker. But the "smoke them out" strategy had smoked out a broad coalition of anti-Jordan members who were enraged by how they were being treated.

"When we came to the floor, I thought there were five of us," Mario Díaz-Balart recalled. "I was fine if there was one. We never talked until after that first vote."

One night the following week, Bacon was having a drink at the Capitol Hill Club, a Republican members-only establishment across the street from the Capitol. There, he ran into a colleague who was one of Jordan's allies, who asked him how he was doing.

"That was a rough week," he admitted.

The colleague shook his head. "I told them not to do that to you, but they said they thought you'd melt under the pressure. They said, 'We'll see what he can take.' "

Bacon was stunned, even if the admission wasn't surprising. "I have no doubt his team was pushing this," he said. "Did anyone harass when Kevin McCarthy was under the gun? Did it happen with Steve Scalise? Jim Jordan brought this out."

Bacon wasn't alone. Buck's office received twenty thousand angry and threatening voicemails, and the landlord for one of his two district offices in Colorado was so livid with him for refusing to support Jordan that he evicted him, a move that had the effect of shuttering the office that handled constituent work for veterans and seniors.

Jordan's team firmly denied that they'd had anything to do with the threats, and they balked at the idea that they would have had the power to control how the congressman's supporters across the country would react. "We don't do that, we don't try to gin up people against our colleagues," Jordan said.

But he didn't have much else to say on the subject of threats or violence. He didn't condemn those who did it, in real time or later, when pressed about what had happened. He simply said that his team wasn't directly responsible for what had been unleashed.

Following his failed floor votes, Jordan asked Patrick McHenry, who was still presiding as the temporary Speaker, to convene a meeting with the 22 "no" votes. McHenry convinced 17 reluctant holdouts to take the meeting by telling them that the purpose was to help Jordan understand he was never going to be Speaker—not to have them hear him out.

Jordan asked McCarthy to come, too, to demonstrate that he had some backing from the establishment. What followed was one of the most professionally run meetings on Capitol Hill—and the most violent. No one raised their voice. No one became emotional. It was a perfectly polite business meeting that was effectively a political guillotine.

Rep. Carlos Gimenez of Florida set the tone. "Look, I don't want anything, okay?" he told Jordan calmly. "There's nothing you can do for me, there's nothing that I'm asking for, okay? There is nothing you can give me, take away from me, okay? If I'm here, not here, it doesn't matter to me. I can go home. I'll be just fine. But you're not going to be Speaker."

If Jordan didn't show surprise, it was because he had received a very similar message from Díaz-Balart two days earlier in a meeting with House Republican leadership, delivered in the same chillingly calm tone. "I like you," Díaz-Balart told Jordan. But then he calmly reminded him that his family members had faced a firing squad. That was a formative experience. "Because you threatened me," he explained calmly, "I can never, ever vote for you."

Rep. Drew Ferguson, a Georgia congressman close to Scalise, noted that Jordan hadn't called his wife to apologize for the death threats she had received.

At one point, Warren Davidson, the only Jordan ally in the room, piped up to note that McCarthy had been given fifteen rounds of votes to win the speakership and that Jordan should be given the same amount of time and votes to win his colleagues over.

But in January, McCarthy had had bargaining chips that his detractors wanted. Jordan had nothing to offer. McCarthy had also worked for multiple election cycles to help raise the money and recruit the candidates to help Republicans win the majority. There was no sense that Jordan had done any of the work that would have given him the right to badger these mainstream Republicans into supporting him.

For over an hour, there was one clear message: There was nothing Jordan could offer them, and they were going to act as an immovable bloc. McCarthy had joined the meeting late, sitting in the back and listening with his loyal chief of staff, Machalagh Carr, a respected conservative lawyer, at his side.

Jordan listened politely until every member had said their piece and left. He then hung back to confer with McHenry, McCarthy, and some aides.

"Well, that was pretty clear," McHenry said.

"How do you want to proceed?" McCarthy asked Jordan.

"Well," Jordan answered, "I'm making progress with the New Yorkers."

His "brand," after all, was "fighter." He was off to the floor for another vote.

The Speaker's race is an internal election among colleagues. But part of what kept Jordan in was the pressure he was getting from the public, who had no vote in the contest but whose collective voice was hard to tune out. His office was also being flooded with calls. That week, it fielded about eighteen thousand calls from people telling him some variation of "Keep going. You cannot stop. This is the one chance to get a conservative guy."

At the next conference meeting, McHenry warned against prolonging the process with floor votes that would fail. The risk was in losing control and accidentally allowing Hakeem Jeffries to be elected Speaker. House rules required that the Speaker receive a majority—not a plurality—of the votes cast. It was a liberal fever dream, and it was unlikely, but it was still a real risk. Nancy Pelosi had alerted Jeffries about it back when McCarthy had been struggling in January. If just a handful of members happened to be away from the Capitol when the vote was happening, Jeffries could be elected Speaker.

"Each time we go to the floor, it's a risk," McHenry told House Republicans. "And I don't think we should take that risk unless we have confidence we can elect a Speaker." It could often feel like getting a solid whip count was like herding cats. Members of the House view themselves as individual entrepreneurs, and they don't feel it is a requirement to tell anyone where they're going to be or when they're going to be there.

Rep. Darrell Issa, a California Republican who often bragged that he was the richest member of Congress, for instance, was spotted at Dulles Airport ahead of one vote. When a leadership aide tried to ask McCarthy's team if this was true, the answer was, "Who knows? Issa never even responds when we ask him where he is." Reps. Cory Mills of Florida and Derrick Van Orden of Wisconsin both went to Israel for a stretch while the House was still trying to elect a Speaker. In a tight majority, it was always possible for floor votes to go wrong.

Jordan, however, felt he had to keep fighting.

As is often the case for Republican lawmakers who show some public backbone and stand up against bullying, bad behavior, and the tactics of Trump's MAGA base, Bacon received a lot of private attaboys from more senior colleagues who were publicly supportive of Jordan. "I had two committee chairmen come up to me and say, 'Don, thank you,'" Bacon recalled. "I said, 'Chairman, I need you. I'm getting the shit kicked out of me. You would help spread out the pain.'" The answer was that they couldn't do it because of backlash from "the base." He added, "I had two that said, 'I have smaller kids. I don't want the threats.' I said, 'My wife's being threatened. You have to stand up for what's right.'"

Publicly, Jordan vowed to stay in the race for as long as it took to win over everyone—in other words, to continue the beatings until morale improved. Steve Bannon and others were pushing for him to keep the House in session all weekend and just run back-to-back votes for Speaker, wearing people down.

But in every failed floor vote, the number of Republicans voting against him grew. On a third and final attempt on the floor, 25 House Republicans voted for someone else. That Friday, Jordan approached McHenry and asked him to move a resolution in conference to empower him as Speaker pro tempore. McHenry immediately saw what Jordan was trying to do: Aware that he had no immediate path to victory, but unable to accept defeat, he wanted to create a contrast between himself, the MAGA fighter, and McHenry, the establishment stooge who would be able to win such a vote but only with the support of Democrats. The move would allow Jordan to continue his war against the Republicans who had voted with Democrats to empower McHenry, framing them as RINOs while continuing his own bid for the speakership and never having to officially drop out or play against his "brand" of "fighter."

In McHenry's view, such a move would only tear the Republican Party apart. The only beneficiary would be Jordan, who would be able to save face.

"I'm not going to do that," McHenry said bluntly.

Jordan pressed him again.

"There's no fucking way I'm going to do that," McHenry responded.

Jordan insisted that if he, as Speaker-designate, was asking him to do so, McHenry was required to do so.

"I don't think you understand," McHenry responded a third time, leaning forward in his chair. "There's no fucking way I'm doing that."

When they went back to the floor, Jordan approached McHenry on the dais to make the same request again, telling him he needed to call up the resolution. "We have to vote on it," Jordan insisted.

McHenry, enraged, knew the rules and knew that he had the power to stop Jordan. "No, we don't," he said.

"You have to recognize me," Jordan insisted.

"No, I don't," McHenry responded again. "You don't even know what the fuck you're talking about."

Out of options, Jordan went to his Republican colleagues and asked them to take an anonymous, internal vote about whether they wanted to keep him as Speaker-designate or move on to someone else. He asked for unanimous consent.

Privately, Jordan knew he was defeated and wanted the secret ballot vote to end his bid for him. The fact that it was secret would allow him to protect his status as a martyr and say the conference had taken the title from him.

Before the vote, he did something that was unthinkable for a man who had won 150 high school wrestling matches and two NCAA national championships and nearly made the Olympic team in a grueling and unforgiving sport: He prayed to lose.

The worst-case scenario, Jordan thought, would be a close victory—one that would keep him in the race with no path to victory. Even though nearly 200 Republicans had voted publicly for him on the House floor, when given the choice of how to proceed secretly, they voted him out.

There would be no Speaker Scalise. And there would be no Speaker Jordan. After the conference kicked Jordan out as a candidate, "No one was happier than Jordan," one of his close advisers said.

"The most popular Republican in the United States Congress was just knifed by a secret ballot, in a private meeting, in the basement of the Capitol," Matt Gaetz said after the vote. "It's as swampy as swamp gets, and Jim Jordan deserved better than that."

Jordan was reflective about the entire episode and the quiet death of his newly discovered dream of becoming Speaker. "I got to know so many people; that's a healthy thing," he told the conference in the private meeting. "Everyone said, 'This is not personal.' It sure kind of felt that way."

But it is hard to give up on a dream. After failing to win the speakership on his own, Jordan thought of one more gambit, one final way to have a chance at running the House. In a private room, he proposed to McCarthy that they launch a power-sharing agreement in which he and Jordan would join forces and together lead House Republicans as something akin to co-Speakers. Maybe McCarthy could return as Speaker and a new leadership position could be created for Jordan.

"Kevin, is there any way we can try to get you back in there?" Jordan asked him.

No one was sure how such an arrangement would work. But the two men and their aides circulated it on Capitol Hill to see if it could gain traction.

"I thought Kevin was the right guy for the job," Jordan said. "I went and talked to people. 'If no one can win, maybe we should go back to the guy who should have never gotten out of the job.' We were trying to work something out."

McCarthy loved being Speaker and was open to the idea, but only if he was drafted. When Jordan approached him with his power-sharing proposal, he was lukewarm to it, but he said he was happy to do it if Jordan thought it would help him. Ultimately, the co-speakership idea didn't get much further than conversations between Jordan and McCarthy.

Jordan suffered little political blowback for his failed bid for Speaker. He was quickly back to a regular diet of Fox News hits, chugging along running the Biden impeachment inquiry from the Judiciary Committee just as he had before. And there was always the next Congress.

Voting for a Globalist RINO like Tom Emmer would be a tragic mistake!

—DONALD TRUMP

NEXT UP FOR PUBLIC AND PRIVATE HUMILIATION WAS TOM EMMER, whose Speaker candidacy lasted not much longer than it takes to read this chapter. It went worse than any of the bids that preceded it and served as a signal to Democrats of how little appetite there was among Republicans to find some common ground.

Rep. Dean Phillips, a Minnesota Democrat who at the time was mounting a longer-than-long-shot primary challenge against Biden, went on a local radio show to say that Emmer was a Republican Speaker he could get behind, one who could build a "bipartisan bridge to the future."

Whoops. "Our phones lit up," Democrat Katherine Clark recalled. The message was "Are you trying to kill Tom Emmer's candidacy?" In a party driven by a group who held an extremist ideology, that's how little it could take to derail someone—even to get themselves out of their own civil war.

After Jim Jordan was deposed, a free-for-all broke out among Republicans. Some nine candidates threw their hats in the ring. Emmer was the most mainstream politically of any of the men who had run for Speaker. He had voted in favor of same-sex marriage, and the right wing of the conference viewed him with deep suspicion.

Despite his status as the third-highest-ranking House Republican, Emmer had to battle through five rounds of closed-door votes just to secure the nomination, eventually edging out Mike Johnson, that little-known lawmaker who had seemed so interested in the maneuverings on the House floor all those months earlier.

After Emmer secured the ill-fated title of "Speaker-designate," he gathered the exhausted Republicans in the conference room in the Longworth House Office Building and vowed to do things differently than those failed candidates who'd preceded him. He said he would keep them there until he had the 217 votes necessary to win the gavel on the floor. "We are going to go out on the floor tonight, and I'm going to be the Speaker of the House," Emmer shouted at them. Then he did what none of the candidates had done yet: He asked for an alphabetical roll call vote in the room to test whether he had the support to move straight to a floor vote that night. His problem became clear by the time the roll call hit the *B*s.

Rep. Rick Allen, an evangelical Christian from Georgia, said he was supporting Johnson, the like-minded, deeply conservative Christian lawmaker from Louisiana. Indiana Rep. Jim Banks, who had despised Emmer since losing the whip race to him late the prior year, said he intended to keep voting for Jordan. Oklahoma Rep. Josh Brecheen, another hard-right lawmaker, said he, too, would be for Jordan on the floor. By the end of the roll call vote, Emmer was close to 30 votes short of the 217 votes needed to win the gavel.

Instead of taking a break to re-evaluate, Emmer approached the microphones again and told his colleagues he didn't want to cut backroom deals. He wanted to work everything out together, in public, in the room. "If people have issues with me," he said, "I want you to come to the mic and explain."

It was a nice idea, in theory: He planned to stand there and take on his critics one by one, in a cinematic show of leadership. But he was unprepared for the avalanche of criticism that followed. A long line began to form behind the mics.

Allen was first up. He said Emmer's support for a law that mandated federal recognition of same-sex marriage—which passed with strong bipartisan support in the House in 2022—was antithetical to his faith and that he couldn't support a candidate who had supported it. Allen spoke on behalf of a small group of religious conservatives who saw the same-sex marriage vote as a red line. Their opposition should not have come as a shock to Emmer—they had voiced the same concerns a year earlier, when he was running for the number three position of House whip and they had lined up behind Banks instead. Within the conference, Emmer was well liked and more popular than Banks, and he had squeaked through in the race for whip. But when you wanted to be the Speaker, all you needed was a handful of hard-liners to derail you.

It was an extraordinary dynamic. Same-sex marriage was broadly popular across the country and across party lines. It would be tricky for any Republican presidential candidate to run opposing it. Trump supported it. And yet, for House Republicans, where that small group of hard-right lawmakers wielded outsize influence over the group as a whole, the dynamic was turned upside down. Because of the makeup of the House, you couldn't be elected Speaker in 2023 if you had taken a vote for an issue that was broadly popular across the country, even among Republicans.

Emmer, growing more aggressive, shot back that when he served in the Minnesota state legislature, he had introduced an amendment forbidding the state from recognizing same-sex marriages. He claimed that he hadn't voted to support same-sex marriage, which he noted was already legal, but had voted "yes" because the bill in question provided religious protections to churches. And he reminded the room that the party leader, Donald Trump, also supported same-sex marriage.

Famous for his red-faced rage, Emmer grew mocking in tone and told Allen, "I hope you can find it in your heart to forgive me for my policy positions."

Allen shot back, "You don't need to get right with me, brother. You need to get right with God."

The mood in the room grew increasingly uncomfortable as more members approached the mic to say the same-sex marriage vote was a deal-breaker for them. All the attacks on Emmer pointed to the same problem: Enough of his colleagues viewed him as insufficiently conservative to award him the speakership.

Lauren Boebert accused him of working for billionaire George Soros, the longtime political bogeyman of the right, referencing Emmer's work over a decade earlier as a spokesman for the National Popular Vote initiative, which was funded by Soros and sought to end the electoral college and institute a nationwide popular vote to elect the president.

"That's bullshit!" said Emmer, erupting in a rage.

Rep. Ronny Jackson—Trump's former White House physician, who in that role had predicted that the McDonald's-gorging president would live to two hundred because he was blessed with "incredible genes"—now represented one of the reddest districts in Texas and had kept a surprisingly low profile throughout the Congress. But when Jackson got up to the mic, he raised concerns about the fact that Emmer was not close enough with Trump. Others questioned Emmer's 2019 vote for an amendment that blocked the Pentagon from using funds to implement Trump's transgender military ban.

At one point, Matt Gaetz tried to come to Emmer's rescue, eager for the chaos to end in order to prove that ousting McCarthy had been a righteous goal, that the House would function better without him. "Tom, you called President Trump over the weekend. Can you tell us about it, because it's really important that the Speaker has a good relationship with the leader of the party," he said, trying to help Emmer position himself as a Trump loyalist.

Emmer agreed that he would act as a great partner to Trump.

Gaetz prodded him again, asking if he was endorsing Trump, which Emmer had yet to do publicly.

"Yeah, he's going to win, he's going to be the candidate, and I support him," Emmer said. It did little to help him win over any holdouts.

Eventually, Emmer called for a two-hour break in the uncomfortable meeting, telling the group that he would stay and continue having conversations with anyone who wanted to talk it out more. But many of those opposing him simply left.

It was during this break that Trump posted a statement on Truth Social calling Emmer a "Globalist RINO" who was "totally out-of-touch [*sic*] with Republican Voters" and whose election as Speaker would be a "tragic mistake" for the party that he, Trump, controlled. Members who had left the meeting read the statement on their phones from their offices and naturally started to gravitate back to the conference room, where they assumed Emmer would now drop out. The Trump statement effectively ended a bid that had already been on life support.

For his part, Emmer, a former ice hockey player, had worked himself up into a lather even before the Trump statement torpedoed him. He was comparing what was going on in real time to the bombing of Pearl Harbor. "We're going to get through this," he told his allies. But after the Trump statement, he had to accept that it was over.

Trump had recently spoken to Emmer in a round of conversations he had with all the Speaker candidates. But the following day, when Emmer was asked about supporting Trump, his answer was deemed insufficiently loyal. "I'm focused on the House" was all Emmer was willing to say publicly. If the goal was to have Trump on his side, it was a misplay, one that was flagged for Trump by Emmer's enemies and enraged him.

"I'm the whip. I can count votes. Obviously, I don't have them," Emmer told his colleagues when the group reconvened. He then stormed out of the room, literally sprinting past reporters in the hallway and hopping into an SUV idling outside. He had been Speaker-designate for a total of four glorious hours, a tenure that made Scalise's thirty-six-hour-long reign look downright Elizabethan.

It was back to the drawing board for the fourth time.

Most Republicans assumed that night that Emmer's career in politics was over, thanks to Trump, and that he would never rise higher than his current post. This didn't stop Emmer from endorsing Trump on January 2.

"They always bend the knee," Trump told people of Emmer's submission. In April, Trump endorsed Emmer's re-election campaign on Truth Social, calling him a "fantastic representative" who was "doing an incredible job" as whip.

Emmer had earned Trump's "Complete and Total Endorsement!"

22

We're playing with fire.

—MIKE McCAUL

IT HAD NOW BEEN ALMOST THREE WEEKS SINCE McCARTHY'S OUSTER.

There was an ongoing war in Ukraine, an escalating war in Gaza between Israel and Hamas, and a branch of Congress that was not functioning while Republican members spent day after day rejecting one another for the position of leader.

Committees did not meet. Democrats, who had to stick around but had no insight into how long this was going to take, were frustrated that they didn't know when they could go home. And the parents at Patrick McHenry's children's school had accepted as a permanent fact of life the security detail clogging up the morning drop-off line.

"We're playing with fire," Texas Rep. Mike McCaul, the well-respected chairman of the Foreign Affairs Committee, fumed at his colleagues. "Our adversaries are watching this, and they see weakness and dysfunction. And it plays right into their hands that democracy doesn't work."

McHenry, the temporary Speaker, agreed. He had rejected Jim Jordan's idea that he empower himself, but as time went on and the conference exhausted all their options, he spent hours trying to figure out what it might look like if that eventually came to pass.

Three days after McCarthy's ouster, Pete Aguilar of California, the number three Democrat in the House, had reached out to McHenry via text. "Hey, Mr. Speaker. If you have a few minutes to connect, I would love to catch up," he wrote.

Aguilar, forty-four, a former mayor of Redlands, California, who had risen to become the highest-ranking Latino in Congress, was known on Capitol Hill as an affable guy who had the best relationships with Republicans of any of the new generation of Democratic leaders. McHenry, who needed to be able to say that he never negotiated with Democrats, never responded to Aguilar's text. But an ally did.

Dave Joyce, an Ohio Republican who chaired the middle-of-the-road Republican Governance Group, responded to Aguilar and made it clear he had been empowered to speak with him on McHenry's behalf—because McHenry, through Joyce, did in fact want to catch up.

House Republicans were in crisis, and in the middle of it all, McHenry sat in a position that had no real power. Joyce had been trying to get traction with his colleagues for the idea of making McHenry more than a seat-filler—he wanted to empower him to stay on as Speaker through the end of the year while tensions cooled and the conference got its act together to unite behind a permanent leader.

Joyce told reporters that he had been consulting with the House parliamentarian on how such a plan could work. What he never said out loud was that with McHenry's blessing, he was also working closely with Democrats, who (unbeknownst to McHenry) had written the resolution to empower him.

Democrats were alarmed by what they were watching and deeply concerned that somehow Jordan was going to muscle his way into the speakership. To them, Jim Jordan as Speaker represented a worst-case scenario: It would mean Ukraine funding never coming to the House floor; no chance of extending a terrorist surveillance program known as the Foreign Intelligence Surveillance Act, which the Biden administration deemed essential; and more bitter fights ahead anytime the government needed funding. So, they embarked on a secret plan to craft a deal with Republicans to back a resolution that would empower McHenry to stay on as Speaker for a designated period.

On October 13, Aguilar met with Joyce in his office to look at the proposal he had drafted. The idea was solid, but the language in the legislative text needed work, and Aguilar's chief of staff, Becky Cornell, ended up rewriting it herself. The lawmakers then outlined a plan that could get a significant number of Democratic votes.

The resolution they came up with would keep McHenry in the chair for ninety days, with an agreement to push through a few critical legislative issues by the end of the year. The House would pass the funding bills at the levels that had been agreed to in the debt ceiling deal, and it would move ahead on a national security supplemental package that would send aid to Israel, Ukraine, and Taiwan. The deal also outlined a path for getting legislation to the floor that had around 300 members supporting it. In other words, it created a way for the House to fast-track legislation that had broad bipartisan support or the Senate had already voted on.

"If you do this, we effectively have a suspension House," McHenry told Joyce, meaning that everything would be done by suspending the rules and getting two-thirds of members to back legislation to pass it off the floor. It would mean he would effectively be a nonpartisan Speaker.

The assumption was that Republicans would continue to fight it out for Speaker during McHenry's ninety-day reign, but it left open the possibility that in January he would be renewed for another, perhaps longer, period.

Democrats liked the plan. It would allow them to clear the decks of all the major legislation before entering the political season of 2024, when lawmakers rarely did more than posture for voters with messaging bills. McHenry was unwilling to entertain the plan until it felt like all other options had been exhausted, and he wasn't willing to give Democrats anything in return for their votes, other than the gift of a functional government.

As they pushed ahead, Aguilar saw a social media post about rumblings that McCarthy was looking for a way back. "Is this real?" he asked Joyce in a text.

"He is not interested, but would not rule it out if drafted," Joyce responded. "He should talk to Hakeem, but the wound is still raw."

McCarthy never did.

For the plan to work, McHenry wanted to have an even number of Democrats and Republicans voting for Joyce's resolution: The hope was for 110 members of each party to get on board. But that was always going to be difficult. John Leganski, McCarthy's floor director, had a theory of Congress that year: On any bill or resolution, you got either around 20 Democrats or 200 of them. There was rarely an in-between.

Throughout the failed floor votes for Speaker, Joyce and Aguilar agreed not to make eye contact or speak to each other where anyone could see them. But the entire time, Joyce held in his hand the folder with the resolution written by Aguilar's chief, waiting for the right moment to introduce it.

McHenry, however, continued to have deep reservations about moving ahead, so the resolution stayed tucked inside Joyce's folder. How would a coalition Speaker, a guy elected with more Democratic than Republican votes, he wondered, work leading into an election year when it's the Speaker's job to be both the chief fundraiser for the House and the chairman of the Republican National Convention that would nominate Trump? How would he effectively go raise money to defeat the people who had elected him?

If McHenry wanted to ensure that the reasonable people who made up what he called the "governing coalition" of his party made it through Republican primaries, this was surely not the way to make that happen. He could picture the hard right burning him in effigy. The only way it would work was for McHenry to leave in January, but it was not clear that anything would be resolved by then.

On October 20, after Jordan's turn had passed, McCarthy stood in front of the conference and told his beleaguered colleagues that it was time to take a pause. "You're all emotional," he told them. It was going to be impossible for anyone to win, and McHenry was totally capable of performing the job, he said.

McCarthy's advice was in line with the Joyce–Aguilar plan: Empower McHenry for three months and come back and address the issue of electing a Speaker in January. McCarthy had the room ready to vote when Mike Johnson—who has been mentioned in only two scenes in this book so far and who was sitting in front—ran up to the microphone.

Many people in the room that day had no idea who he was.

The low-profile congressman rose to pose a series of constitutional questions about empowering McHenry. "This is untested," Johnson said.

"How can we be sure that any bills we pass would become law and not be challenged in the courts? We need to talk about this as a group and know whether there is a constitutional basis for this," he said.

Johnson's longtime chief, Hayden Haynes, was standing against the wall on the side of the room watching when a top McCarthy aide hissed at him, "You fucking Speaker wannabe."

It was clear to everyone that something unexpected was afoot.

23

Maybe it's my time?

—MIKE JOHNSON

MIKE JOHNSON ANNOUNCED THAT HE WAS RUNNING FOR SPEAKER shortly after his lunge at the mic. "I have never before aspired to the office," he claimed. "However, after much prayer and deliberation, I am stepping forward now."

Of course, no one rises to the pinnacle of politics through prayer alone, without a detailed plan for getting there. And even though he liked the pose of a humble public servant who had been drafted against his will to run in the middle of a crisis, the reality was that Johnson had a plan in motion before he rushed to the mic with his constitutional questions. There were rumors that Johnson had been quietly eyeing the speakership since January, when John Leganski noticed him sidling up to McCarthy's staff and taking mental notes as they struggled through fifteen painful rounds of votes.

McCarthy's obvious weaknesses had Johnson's top staff asking themselves, "Why not Mike?" He was conservative enough for the House Freedom Caucus but had no personal beef with any of the moderates. Everyone who knew him thought he was a "nice guy." His low profile might actually work to his advantage.

Johnson held a minor leadership position as the vice chairman of the conference, essentially serving as Elise Stefanik's understudy. His role didn't carry much power, but it allowed him and his wily chief, Hayden Haynes, to sit in every leadership meeting, where they studied the dynamics of McCarthy's dysfunctional leadership team. These people all hated one another, they observed. Johnson's staff called the House Republican leadership meetings a "petty party."

After McCarthy was ousted, the internal talk of a Johnson speakership flared up again. Haynes quietly took the temperature of members of the House Freedom Caucus and senior appropriators, those members on the Appropriations Committee known as "cardinals," who for decades had wielded influence on the Hill. He was convinced there was a path for his boss.

"You gotta run," he told Johnson.

"I can't run against Steve," Johnson said, shooting the idea down. "We've been friends for years."

"But what if he doesn't get it?" Haynes replied. "Let me put together a plan and be ready to go." Johnson gave him the green light.

Johnson's team had watched as Scalise failed. Haynes wasn't surprised. He figured McCarthy's folks would need a scalp as revenge for their boss's demise, and what better scalp was there than that of his longtime nemesis? Then Scalise would need a scalp as revenge for *his* failure, and that scalp would be Jim Jordan, who had tanked Scalise's bid.

Johnson considered Jordan his mentor, but not a "brother" like Scalise, and he considered challenging him after Scalise withdrew. "Maybe it's my time?" Johnson asked Haynes.

This time Haynes urged his boss to take a beat. "Let's think about it," he cautioned. "Steve still needs his scalp. Jim's not gonna get it. You know that. I know that. Sit it out. There's still time to get into this race. It's not over yet."

It was after Jordan's failure that Johnson's staff decided the circular firing squad was over and the party was primed to pick a leader. They targeted Tom Emmer as a soft opponent and decided it was finally time to jump in. Johnson's staff knew Emmer had a problem on his right flank and, at the time, a Trump problem that would prevent him from getting the votes he needed to become Speaker. A handful of right-wing members were also throwing their hats in the ring and would be fighting one another for the limited number of votes from House Freedom Caucus members.

Johnson's plan was to target the middle of the party, those lower-profile but deeply conservative members whose names no one knows—in other words, people just like him. His plan to beat Emmer was to outlast him. He didn't have to win any ballot, but he needed to come in second, to position himself as the next logical option when Emmer's bid inevitably collapsed.

Other candidates in the race went on TV and gave out gifts to their colleagues. Rep. Kevin Hern of Oklahoma, who had made a fortune owning McDonald's franchises, handed out McGriddles (bacon, egg, and cheese on a pancake). Johnson didn't give out gifts, and he didn't go on TV, not for an internal party election. Every television hit would have been time away from personally winning over members. "They don't want a Happy Meal," Haynes scoffed.

Haynes figured Johnson needed just 30 to 40 votes on the first ballot to get second place. Rather than assembling a large whip team to make five-minute phone calls, Johnson ran a targeted operation. He focused on specific low-profile members whose votes he believed were in play and then talked to them each for at least thirty minutes and sometimes up to an hour. "They all hate each other," Haynes said. "Let them vent."

When Johnson got 34 votes on the first ballot, his staff was ecstatic. Haynes framed the whip card and hung it in his office. He knew from that moment Johnson was on the path to victory. After Emmer predictably imploded, Johnson was next in line. Other members who had been in the race approached him and offered to drop out, but Johnson pressed them to stay in.

"We need a race," he said.

Johnson had one final hurdle to overcome. McCarthy's allies had organized a shadow campaign for him in which his supporters (who were growing fewer by the day) would refuse to vote for Johnson and would write in "other" on a secret ballot—hoping to prevent Johnson from securing enough support, in order to keep alive McCarthy's hopes of returning to the speakership.

But Johnson's team had Drew Ferguson, a Scalise ally from Georgia, move to make public the names of those voting "other" on the next ballot. "Either run or get the hell out of the room," Rep. Trent Kelly, a Mississippi conservative, yelled.

With that threat, the opposition to Johnson faded away, much to the disappointment of members who favored the McHenry plan.

"We were one ballot away from McHenry," recalled Rep. Max Miller, a first-term congressman from Ohio who had worked as a top adviser to Trump in the White House. "It almost worked."

Miller, a self-described "piddly freshman," had a little more stature than the average piddly freshman because of his close association with Trump. He had been making the case to his colleagues that the process was too emotional and too rushed and that they needed a few months to choose a Speaker.

When Johnson emerged as a candidate, Miller recalled being mostly confused. "Somebody asked me, 'Will you vote for Mike?'" he recalled. "I said, 'I guess?' That's how half the conference felt."

On October 21, the day after Jordan was removed as Speaker-designate and the day Johnson announced he was running for Speaker, Pete Aguilar texted Dave Joyce to check in on their McHenry plan.

"How are you feeling?" he asked.

"Johnson can never be Speaker," Joyce responded, still eager to empower McHenry. That sentiment was shared by many Republicans, who were googling "Mike Johnson Congress" and wondering how Johnson would be able to raise any money.

"Can we do this? Can we run this play?" Aguilar asked him.

"We have to," Joyce said.

"We're ready to go whenever you are," Aguilar told him.

"I'm working Patrick," Joyce responded.

But then, on October 25, Republicans called Aguilar to tell him Johnson appeared to have the votes. The Democrats had missed their shot.

After three weeks of ugly infighting and paralysis that left them no choice but to go with someone no one knew well enough to harbor any major personal objections to, Mike Johnson was elected to be the fifty-sixth Speaker of the House by a unanimous Republican conference. Everyone was worn down, embarrassed, and worried that prolonging the situation any further would make their own paths to re-election that much harder.

Trent Kelly, who had called out McCarthy's gamesmanship in the closed-door meeting, told a group trying to figure out a way forward, "What we need is someone unassuming, uninspiring, and unknown."

So, Mike Johnson it was.

"Everyone was exhausted, frustrated, angry, upset, divided, and beside themselves," said Marjorie Taylor Greene. "That's how Mike Johnson became Speaker."

Never had someone with so little experience come into a position of power so vast at such a critical juncture. On social issues like same-sex marriage and abortion, Johnson's views were in line with where the Republican Party had been in the 1990s and where America had been in the 1950s. He had referred to homosexuality as "inherently unnatural" and a "dangerous lifestyle" and had called abortion a "holocaust." On fiscal matters, he was a standard-issue conservative. On Trump, he was a sycophant who still had to prove himself with ring-kissing trips to Mar-a-Lago and the Manhattan Criminal Courthouse, where Trump was standing trial, and, of course, by advancing the lie that the 2020 election was stolen. It was on foreign policy where Johnson, an isolationist from the hard-right wing of the party, would be tested as a leader and prove to be a throwback more in the mold of Ronald Reagan than anyone anticipated.

"The Bible is very clear that God is the one that raises up those in authority," Johnson said from the dais as he accepted the gavel, reading from a speech he had written himself the night before. "I believe that God has ordained and allowed each one of us to be brought here for this specific moment."

Johnson didn't think he was coming into a job with a lot of perks. "He had a very sober idea of what the job would be," his wife, Kelly Johnson, said.

Johnson added: "I thought I would be a caretaker, to try and heal the institution and be done, and do it for as long as I could caretake." Johnson may have been untested, but he could be more charming and fun to be around than his earnest Christian caricature would lead one to believe. He often did spot-on impressions of his colleagues and Trump and joked about the worst instincts of his broken party even while he encouraged them. Those skills helped to allow him to hang on for longer than McCarthy did.

Johnson would go on to pass funding for Ukraine and a $1.2 trillion bipartisan package to fund the U.S. government, one that included none of the deep cuts or policy changes that ultraconservatives had demanded. He would pass the Foreign Intelligence Surveillance Act reauthorization on his third try. And he would do all of it with Democratic votes, just as

McHenry would have done under the plan Democrats wanted and just as McCarthy would have done had he still been Speaker.

It would take Johnson five months to get through it all. The following June, when Biden met with Ukrainian president Zelenskyy in Paris, he personally apologized to him "for those weeks of not knowing what's going to happen in terms of funding." He added, "Some of our very conservative members were holding it up."

If Aguilar and Joyce had been successful, it all would likely have happened on a faster time line. Ukraine aid would not have been delayed for months, a period during which the country lost "territory, lives, and infrastructure," as Anne Applebaum wrote in *The Atlantic* after the House finally passed an aid bill in April 2024. "If Ukraine had not been deprived of air defense, the city of Kharkiv might still have most of its power plants. People who have died in the near-daily bombardment of Odesa might still be alive. Ukrainian soldiers who spent weeks at the front lines rationing ammunition might not be so demoralized."

IF JOHNSON WAS KNOWN at all in Congress, it was for the role he had played in the aftermath of the 2020 election, when he recruited House Republicans to sign a legal brief supporting a lawsuit seeking to overturn the results. But the most defining trait of the Southern conservative was his evangelical Christianity—many detractors said his views were a perfect example of Christian nationalism—which he placed at the center of his political life and policy positions. He was viewed by Democrats as a true believer.

"This is the wrong guy," said Katherine Clark weeks after his election. "He's not going to dial back on the national abortion ban because it is part of what he feels his divine mission is."

Clark also imagined Johnson would have "tremendous power" to whip Republicans to vote as a bloc against certifying the 2024 election or to pull other procedural levers to overturn election results if Republicans were in control of the House. "I have a real fear of that," she said.

Ken Buck did not. He ultimately voted for Johnson, despite his previously stated concerns about having an election denier running the House.

His explanation sounded like hairsplitting because it was hard to see a meaningful difference in Jordan's and Johnson's levels of involvement in the gambit to overturn the election results. Johnson recruited Republicans to sign the legal brief in support of a Texas lawsuit, rooted in baseless claims of widespread election regularities, that tried to throw out the election results in four states Biden won. He told House Republicans that Trump was "anxiously waiting" to see who would have his back and sign on to the brief. In a radio interview, Johnson claimed that a software system used for voting was "suspect because it came from Hugo Chávez's Venezuela." (Chávez had died a decade earlier.) Even the conservative-leaning Supreme Court ultimately rejected the suit, saying it "has not demonstrated a judicially cognizable interest in the manner in which another state conducts its elections."

No matter. At the end of the day, Buck said, he was happier with a Speaker Johnson than with a Speaker McCarthy. "To me," he said, "Mike was the best of the election deniers we could put in that position."

Johnson's election seemed as if it would cement the party's rightward lurch, putting in place a MAGA warrior and election denier, another victory for the party's far right. In fact, it underscored how the far right would make it impossible for anyone, even one of their own, to govern and would force Johnson to act just the way his predecessor had, turning to Democrats for votes to be able to pass any bills.

"He's going to do a great job," Trump said.

I got my mojo back.

—MIKE JOHNSON

A NY MIRAGE OF REPUBLICAN UNITY THAT HAD ELECTED SPEAKER JOHN-son faded as quickly as it appeared—a reminder that shifting alliances, personal feuds, and chaotic maneuvering were as much part of the modern-day GOP as any ideological or policy position.

Israel was at the beginning of what would be a long war, and Johnson saw in it an opportunity to score some chits with the right. He brought to the floor a bill with $14.3 billion in aid to Israel that would be paid for with cuts to the IRS—a poison pill Democrats would never vote for.

"I got my mojo back," Johnson told colleagues of his plan.

It didn't buy him much.

He then passed the exact same stopgap funding measure that had been the reason for McCarthy's downfall, a bill that passed with more Democrats voting for it than Republicans. The following day, a bloc of far-right Republicans protested by sinking a major spending bill and voting against the rule. It was *Groundhog Day* all over again.

"The Swamp won, and the Speaker needs to know that," Chip Roy said.

The question of whether the Swamp was winning was one that seemed to bedevil the right. "The Swamp is on the run," Matt Gaetz said on *War Room* just after Johnson won the speakership. "MAGA is ascendant. If you don't think that moving from Kevin McCarthy to MAGA Mike Johnson shows ascendance of this movement and where the power in the Republican Party truly lies, then you're not paying attention."

But "MAGA Mike" was acting differently now that he was in leadership. In trying to tamp down the growing anger on the far right, Johnson had long conversations with Tucker Carlson and conservative political activist Charlie Kirk, under the theory that it was harder to beat up on someone if you knew them.

He stopped by a Freedom Caucus meeting with a message that went over like a gift of socks on Christmas morning. "Look," he told the group, "I'm doing this for your own good." The members who opposed the funding bill on principle stared back at him like he had lost his mind.

"I can't stay long," Johnson told them, "because I have to go pick up a two-million-dollar check to get you guys elected." Again, the hard-right members shot one another confused glances. They were on solid footing in their red districts. It was for those vulnerable Republicans representing blue and purple districts that Johnson was out there raising money.

Johnson was aware of his thankless position. "If I were king, we would do things a lot differently," he said. "But I'm a leader of a disparate body in a very turbulent time, when there is an open debate about the direction of the party itself."

And as for the deposed Speaker? Well, the life of a rank-and-file member was a painful existence for a man who had been in leadership for more than a decade. McCarthy stopped attending the weekly conference meetings he used to enjoy presiding over. He had been booted from the Speaker's suite and now occupied a lesser hideaway office down the hall. In a basement hallway one afternoon, Tim Burchett, one of "the Crazy Eight," accused him of elbowing him in the kidney.

McCarthy complained that he was getting no special attention from the new Speaker, who he said wasn't reaching out to seek his advice. In reality, Johnson knew he had to cater to a deeply wounded ego, and he regularly texted and called.

"Kevin, I could really use your counsel," Johnson would tell him in calls that were sent straight to voicemail. "We're praying for you, we love you and Judy." But for the first five months of Johnson's speakership, McCarthy gave him the cold shoulder. And Kelly Johnson, who had been close friends with Judy McCarthy, also lost a friend.

"What Kevin went through is a Greek tragedy," Mike Johnson said later. "It was so wrong in so many ways. He worked his whole life for that position. It meant the world to him, and then it was so abruptly taken away like that. He was understandably upset at a lot of people, but he can't hold it personally against me."

Friends came by the office to try to cheer McCarthy up, knowing how much he hated to be alone, but even they noticed he didn't laugh at their jokes as he used to and appeared distracted and glum.

McCarthy briefly considered doing what he had always done—raising massive amounts of money to gain more seats in the House and maybe coming back as Speaker. He considered himself the king of the comeback story. But when he thought it through, he couldn't make it work: If he was out there raising more money than Johnson, people would assume he was undercutting the new Speaker. If he failed, it would be too humiliating. The truth was, there was no good resting place for him in Congress. The only move, while waiting for the next opportunity, was to leave and try to take down the people who had taken him down.

By the end of the year, McCarthy had resigned.

Now unemployed at fifty-eight, McCarthy was hung up on the fact that he was the same age his father had been when he died. He was ready for a next act, possibly in the shape of a cabinet post in a potential Trump administration, and he viewed this gap year as his golden chance to build up a nest egg if he was to return to a government salary.

The easiest way to do that, he figured, would be to spend his time giving paid speeches and writing a book. But that plan didn't unfold quite as he expected. He paired up with Pilar Queen, a powerful literary agent at United Talent Agency, and discussed the possibility of a million-dollar book deal. That figure was not connected to reality, and on top of that, McCarthy didn't have a good sense of what he wanted to say. The topic that really interested publishers—dishing on his private interactions with Trump—was off-limits for a guy whose two-year plan included possibly working for him.

Editors who met with McCarthy described him as an affable blank slate who arrived at the meetings with no formal proposal, hoping his name slapped across a cover was enough to pop him into a different tax bracket. "You guys tell me," he said to editors who asked him what his book would be about. "You're the experts."

He had the additional problem of occupying a no-man's-land in the political ecosystem: He was reviled by the hard right overtaking his party; he was equally detested by Democrats, who viewed him as the embodiment of what had happened to the Republican Party under the influence of Trump. He received one offer in the two-hundred-thousand-dollar range, but that wasn't the kind of "wealth" he was looking to generate in what he hoped was only a short sabbatical from politics. He turned it down and eventually dropped the book idea altogether.

He signed up with the Harry Walker Agency to handle requests for paid speeches offered in the form of "a fireside chat with Speaker McCarthy" or "the 'Happy Warrior' leadership mindset." But McCarthy wasn't in happy warrior mode. In his public speeches, he continued railing against Gaetz, saying the only reason he had been removed was that Gaetz "wanted me to stop an ethics complaint because he slept with a seventeen-year-old." Gaetz, for his part, always claimed that the years-long inquiry into his conduct was a smear campaign driven by McCarthy and his allies.

What really animated McCarthy was his revenge tour, in which he tried to unseat the eight Republicans who had ousted him. He played a barely behind-the-scenes role, pushing Trump to endorse candidates challenging those seats and directing millions of dollars in PAC money to undermine them.

"I just traveled to your district," McCarthy told Bob Good, the hard-right Virginian who had voted to oust him, when McCarthy happened to be standing near him on the House floor during his final days in Congress. "It's a really nice district."

"Why don't you come down and spend money there?" Good taunted him in response.

"Oh, I'm going to," McCarthy shot back. "I might spend five million there, too."

In that case, he was as good as his word: He poured more than $6 million into the race to unseat Good in Virginia and more than $4 million to attempt to defeat Nancy Mace in South Carolina. And still, the results were underwhelming: Mace won by a bigger margin than ever; Good's race was a virtual tie that ended up as a recount that took weeks to resolve (though Good did eventually lose); and Gaetz had a primary challenger no one in Florida had ever heard of, whom he beat by forty-five points.

McCarthy had no public-facing job anymore, but he continued popping up on television, sometimes making nonsensical statements. "Has Hillary ever said she lost the 2016 election?" McCarthy said on Fox News. Howard Kurtz, the television host, noted that Clinton had conceded to Trump. "She never in the press ever says that," McCarthy said.

After Trump was convicted of thirty-four counts of falsifying business records in the hush money case, McCarthy chimed in to note that Trump's only "crime" was running against Biden in 2024. "The American people see right through this weaponization of the legal system," he said.

Meanwhile, back in the land of the employed, the right was rebelling against Johnson, like clockwork, even starting to use his devout faith against him. "Don't tell me you're Christian. I don't want to hear more Bible verses when you've allowed all of that demonic trash throughout the defense budget," Bannon railed after Johnson passed the annual defense budget that excluded the restrictions the far right wanted on abortion access, transgender care, and racial and diversity inclusion policies at the Pentagon. "We don't need a Speaker that's Paul Ryan with a Bible," Russell Vought said, claiming that the only reason Johnson was even still in the speakership was because he had agreed to tie Ukraine funding to border security measures.

But Johnson had one hard-right ally deeply invested in his success: Matt Gaetz, who wanted to prove that House Republicans had a better leader in the new guy than the guy he had tossed out. "He's let us down on a number of fronts," Gaetz told CNN's Jake Tapper. Still, Gaetz had no intention of leading any charge against Johnson. He needed him to succeed. "We're not worried that Mike Johnson's lying to us," Gaetz said, trying to explain why Johnson was any better than McCarthy. "We're worried that he's changing his views on things."

Gaetz was a good ally to have: Unlike some of the other high-profile hard-right members like Marjorie Taylor Greene and Lauren Boebert, Gaetz was jazzed by the process of negotiating and had the relationships to bring votes along with him if he was in the mood to play a productive role.

The most prominent example of Gaetz playing against type and acting as a dealmaker was on a critical vote to reauthorize a portion of the Foreign Intelligence Surveillance Act, the expiring warrantless surveillance law that Trump was urging Republicans to "kill." National security officials said the bill was crucial to gathering intelligence and fending off a potential terrorist attack. In April 2024, the hard-right flank of the House blocked legislation to extend it, arguing in favor of more restrictive limits on the government's spying powers. Publicly, Gaetz was part of the group that tanked the bill and delivered Johnson an embarrassing defeat.

Privately, he was trying to help.

On the evening of April 10, the day the five-year extension was blocked, thanks in large part to Trump's railing against it, Gaetz met with Johnson and his top staff members in the Speaker's office, where he was now a welcome guest.

"I told you, Mike," he said. "A five-year bill won't work."

But Gaetz, the nihilistic rabble-rouser, was in a constructive mood that night. After all, Johnson's success was his success. "How are we going to make this work?" he said. "I would love for it to be repealed, but how can I get something my folks want?"

Johnson was of the more traditional view that the legislation known as FISA, which allows the government to collect the communications of targeted foreigners abroad without a warrant, played a key role in the country's national security.

Trump's opposition was part of the former president's distrust of the shadowy "deep state" and law enforcement and intelligence agencies generally, more a political statement than one based in a real understanding of the law or policy. "KILL FISA, IT WAS ILLEGALLY USED AGAINST ME, AND MANY OTHERS. THEY SPIED ON MY CAMPAIGN!!!" Trump wrote on Truth Social ahead of the vote. (Never mind that the part of the bill he took issue with was not the part up for re-authorization.)

But "MAGA Mike" thought FISA was more critical to saving lives than even Ukraine funding. And he was open to the idea Gaetz was pitching him that night: changing it from a five-year extension to a two-year extension, which he could sell to the hard right by telling them that in two years, Trump would be in office and could do whatever he wanted with the law. Gaetz also insisted on a vote on an amendment to require the government to have a warrant, which Johnson opposed, but Gaetz was adamant that including it was the path forward. "If you can agree to a two-year extension and the warrant amendment vote," Gaetz told the Speaker, "I can bring the votes."

With a green light from Johnson, Gaetz got to work and gleefully delivered. "Mike, you won't even believe what these guys are saying to me," he called excitedly after putting out feelers. "They're saying if they could vote twice for it they would! This deal is going through like a knife through butter!"

Ultimately, the warrant amendment failed dramatically when Johnson voted against it on the floor. But, more important, the two-year extension passed. Johnson's team credited Gaetz with helping to move the 19 Republicans who blocked consideration of the bill off their opposition. When Johnson brought up the two-year bill two days after his stinging defeat, they all voted to let it move ahead.

Meanwhile, Gaetz leaned into a new persona: dealmaker. "The belief among House Republicans is that if you preserve an at bat for President Trump, there's an opportunity for more change than we could achieve without him," Gaetz said after the vote.

Mr. Gaetz, look me in the eye.

—HUNTER BIDEN

AS HE SETTLED IN, JOHNSON DECIDED TO TARGET ALEJANDRO MAYOR-kas, the Homeland Security secretary whom McCarthy had vowed to impeach months earlier.

Republicans in this case weren't even pretending there were high crimes and misdemeanors or allegations of corruption against Mayorkas. They were simply charging that he had breached the public trust by "willfully" refusing to enforce border laws.

Congress had not impeached a sitting cabinet secretary since 1876 and had never even attempted to impeach one without some evidence of personal corruption. But the Trump era and the MAGA Congress it spawned were one long experiment in discovering the difference between norms that could be easily shattered and laws that served as sturdier guardrails. Lawmakers' refusing to impeach cabinet secretaries for political purposes was a norm, not a law.

Right away, three Republicans said they would not vote to impeach a cabinet secretary based on policy differences. One of them was Ken Buck, who watched in confusion as his friends and colleagues in the House Freedom Caucus introduced impeachment articles against various Biden cabinet secretaries.

The defense secretary? The secretary of state? The U.S. attorney in D.C.? Did they want to impeach everyone?

Buck had been one of the founders of the Freedom Caucus, but he also was a former federal prosecutor who didn't support the Constitution's being twisted for political purposes. He, too, phoned Jonathan Turley, the law professor who told McCarthy he could move ahead investigating President Biden. "He spent forty minutes on the phone and went through a long analysis of why it wasn't impeachable," Buck recalled of their conversation regarding the Mayorkas impeachment. "And so I decided based on the Constitution—not a TV contract in the future, not a corporate gig somewhere, but based on the Constitution—this was wrong."

When Johnson finally brought the Mayorkas impeachment to the House floor for a vote, he sat in the chair at the front of the chamber to oversee the proceedings, assuming center stage for this historic vote. With only 3 Republicans refusing to support the impeachment, Republican leaders thought they had enough votes for a 1-vote victory.

They hadn't counted on the presence of Rep. Al Green, a Texas Democrat who had been absent from Capitol Hill while recovering from abdominal surgery. Green had been absent for votes earlier that same evening. But for the impeachment vote, he showed up in a wheelchair, still dressed in a blue hospital gown, tan socks, and no shoes, to cast a deciding "no" vote, tying up the vote at 215–215 and dealing Republicans a humiliating defeat.

In a sleight of hand, Hakeem Jeffries had arranged an Uber to pick Green up from the hospital and then kept him waiting in the attending physician's office ahead of the vote, to keep Republicans guessing. Green went straight back to his hospital bed after the vote. It was cinematic and mortifying for Republicans: an ailing lawmaker putting his party over his own recovery in order to save a vote that he thought was wrong. Republicans were livid.

"They hid one of their members," Marjorie Taylor Greene complained after the vote, "waiting to the last minute, watching to see our votes, trying to throw us off on the numbers." It was called counting votes, but, yes, she was correct: Democrats had outfoxed Republicans on their sham impeachment.

Republicans tried again the following week, when Steve Scalise had returned from his stem cell transplant and they were certain there would be no more "hidden Democrats" to foil them again. This time they succeeded and impeached Mayorkas, who reacted to this news with a yawn. It was a piece of Off-Off-Broadway political theater that would be dead

on arrival in the Senate. Johnson waited two months even to send the articles of impeachment over, and when he did, they were dismissed within
hours without a trial even taking place.

Impeachment had become a political charade, a kind of super-censure,
and nothing more. The GOP inquiry into President Biden and his family
also marched on, with Republicans repeatedly seeking to question Hunter
Biden, the president's wayward son, only to be rebuffed. Finally, they
threatened him with contempt of Congress, and Hunter gave in and
agreed to an interview.

On February 28, 2024, the younger Biden strode into the Capitol
Complex's O'Neill Building dressed in a dark suit. He appeared confident
as he entered his closed-door interview. "You have trafficked in innuendo,
distortion, and sensationalism—all the while ignoring the clear and convincing evidence staring you in the face," he said. "You do not have evidence to support the baseless and MAGA-motivated conspiracies about
my father because there isn't any."

House Republicans attempted to question Hunter about deals in
Ukraine, Russia, and Romania, pressing him on text messages he'd sent,
on the state of his bank accounts and unpaid taxes. But they could not tie
any of his business deals in any concrete way to the president.

Finally, Matt Gaetz tried to get more direct with his questions. He
pressed the president's son on whether he had been "on drugs" while serving on the board of the Ukrainian energy company Burisma, a delicate
subject given that Hunter had been open about his struggles with addic-
tion, which many voters viewed as relatable.

"Mr. Gaetz, look me in the eye," Hunter said. "You really think that's
appropriate to ask me?"

"Absolutely," said Gaetz.

"Of all the people sitting around this table, do you think that's appropriate to ask me?" he pressed. It was a clear reference to the accusations
against Gaetz: that he had been involved in drug and sex parties and had
paid for sex with an underage girl.

Gaetz wouldn't back down.

"Yeah. Are you going to answer it?"

"I will answer it this way," Hunter Biden said. "I have been absolutely transparent about my drug use. Again, I spoke to you all earlier this morning about that. I'm sorry; I'm an addict. I was an addict. I have been in recovery for over four and a half years now, Mr. Gaetz. I work really, really hard at it. Let me answer. I work really hard at it, under an enormous amount of pressure. Was I an addict? Yes, I was an addict. What does that have to do with whether or not you're going to go forward with an impeachment of my father other than to simply try to embarrass me?"

In the end, after all the bluster and the calls of "Where's Hunter?" the interview turned up nothing.

Democrats gleefully pronounced the impeachment inquiry dead that day. But the death knell of the Republican impeachment drive didn't take place on Capitol Hill. It occurred in a federal court in California. There, the FBI informant whose allegations on that famous Form FD-1023 had been championed by Republicans was charged with fabricating claims that the president and his son had each accepted a five-million-dollar bribe from a Ukrainian company.

The indictment alleged that the longtime informant, Alexander Smirnov, forty-three, falsely told the FBI that Hunter Biden had demanded money from Burisma to protect the company from an investigation by the country's prosecutor general at the time. But his claims were easily disproved, prosecutors said.

It was over. There would be no Biden impeachment.

James Comer privately told allies that even if there was no impeachment, he had been successful. Polls now showed many Americans believed President Biden was corrupt, and that, he said, was a political win.

Not long after, Comer was in Florida and had a chance meeting with Trump. The two discussed how to proceed now that they had found themselves at a real dead end. If impeachment was not available to them, maybe criminal referrals could be? Comer sent out a fundraising message calling for criminal referrals, not impeachment, which amounted to nothing more than glorified letters.

Many Republicans thought this idea was stupid. If there wasn't enough evidence to impeach Joe Biden, how could you refer him for prosecution?

Even Jim Jordan privately distanced himself from the criminal referrals. Still, he and Comer sent referrals against Hunter Biden and his uncle

Jim Biden to the Justice Department, accusing them of making false statements. There was no such referral to send against the only person who mattered, Joe Biden.

Jordan would never admit that it had all been done for political reasons. There was enough stink around Hunter Biden's actions that he could always justify investigating the prodigal son and whether any wrongdoing reached up to his father. But he acknowledged that House Republicans' own dysfunction had destroyed any chance they had of building a case that was strong enough to persuade GOP members from swing districts to vote for impeachment.

Sitting in his office, Jordan laid out why he believed they had failed. The three weeks of chaos following McCarthy's ouster derailed their momentum and knocked them off track, he argued. And as members resigned from the dysfunction of the 118th Congress, Republicans' voting advantage dwindled, making it harder to win close votes.

But, in his mind, it was Smirnov who had really tanked the case. His lies weren't central to the allegations, Jordan argued—even though Jordan had previously said on TV that Smirnov's claims were the best corroborating evidence they had—but because of how Republicans had hyped those lies on TV directly after reading them in that FBI document, the public and lawmakers now believed they were foundational.

When your case is built on lies, it's hard to move forward.

Even Gaetz conceded that the allegations against President Biden in some cases were "oversauced." Alexandria Ocasio-Cortez believed Oversight Democrats deserved the credit for the Republican case falling apart. At every turn, they had countered the Republicans' claims in a way that the Democrats on the Homeland Security panel had not done when it came to the impeachment effort targeting Mayorkas. "That kind of shows the stakes of when you're not able to stop the momentum of one of these impeachment hearings," she said. "You had Secretary Mayorkas impeached by the House on absolutely no grounds whatsoever. But that is the consequence of what happens when the momentum doesn't get stopped."

Lacking evidence for impeachment, Republicans decided to pivot to the final stage of any failed political investigation, one that Democrats on the Hill jokingly referred to as the "please obstruct me" phase.

Republicans would spend some of their final months before the election asking for anything and everything they could think of related to the Biden family, hoping agencies would deny them and they could find someone to accuse of obstruction or hold in contempt. They would accuse Attorney General Merrick Garland of contempt for declining to provide audio recordings of Biden's interview with the special counsel who investigated his handling of classified documents. But as with their other criminal referrals, that recommendation went nowhere. They viewed it as their job to keep the drumbeat of negative Biden headlines alive through the election.

Bleach-blonde, bad-built butch body.

—JASMINE CROCKETT

THE REPUBLICAN PUSH TO PURSUE CONTEMPT CHARGES AGAINST someone—anyone!—in the Biden administration ended in the only logical place it could: an embarrassing, juvenile food fight in the House Oversight Committee, one that underscored how much Democrats had changed during the Trump years. (Whether they had evolved or devolved was a matter of opinion.)

The members of the panel gathered in their hearing room after eight on a cloudy evening in May 2024 for a debate that was ostensibly about whether to hold Merrick Garland in contempt of Congress. The committee had gaveled in so late that evening because Lauren Boebert, Anna Paulina Luna, and other members of the panel had spent their workday in front of the Manhattan federal courthouse where Trump was on trial on charges related to his hush money payments to a porn star. They said they were there to speak on the former president's behalf because a gag order prevented him from speaking for himself. Outside the courthouse, Boebert was greeted with a *Playbill* from *Beetlejuice* to sign, which she pretended not to see as a security guard ran interference.

Most people never knew, or would soon forget, the official purpose of the session, which would live on in congressional lore as the infamous "Oversight After Dark" meeting. Marjorie Taylor Greene, who hadn't joined the group in New York City that day—she had already made her pilgrimage days earlier, thank you very much—kicked things off by bringing up the trial and asking whether any House Democrats had hired the judge's daughter, who had ties to a marketing firm that had worked for Democratic candidates in the past.

"Please tell me what that has to do with Merrick Garland," Jasmine Crockett, the freshman Democrat from Texas, responded. "Do you know what we're here for?"

"I think your fake eyelashes are messing up what you're reading," Greene replied.

This may have seemed very low on the list of offensive and ridiculous things Greene had said over the years, but it violated one of the few rules that existed in the House of Representatives to guide behavior. Anyone could talk about anything they wanted to, but one hard-and-fast rule was there could be no face-to-face ad hominem attacks, known in parliamentary jargon as "engaging in personalities."

"That's beneath even you, Ms. Greene," Jamie Raskin, the top Democrat on the committee, snapped at her.

Alexandria Ocasio-Cortez, the committee's number two Democrat, demanded that Greene's words be "taken down" from the record, an official rebuke that would mean Greene would be barred from speaking for the rest of the session. "How dare you attack the physical appearance of another person?"

"Are your feelings hurt?" Greene responded, her voice dripping with sarcasm as she peered at Ocasio-Cortez over her glasses.

"Oh, girl, baby girl, don't even play," Ocasio-Cortez shot back. To avoid being muzzled for the rest of the session, Greene agreed to have her words stricken from the record, but she pointedly refused to apologize to Crockett.

"Well, then you're not striking your words," Ocasio-Cortez said.

This counted as gold for Greene, who had long tried to get Ocasio-Cortez to engage with her in order to elevate herself. Greene for years had been calling for the New York progressive to debate her, which Ocasio-Cortez had refused to do because she claimed it was beneath her but also because there was no purpose to their ever needing to debate.

Ocasio-Cortez knew that Republicans often wanted to get into it with her so they could coast off her slice of fame, and she tried to be restrained about letting them get to her. One evening, Jamaal Bowman, the progressive from New York, exited the Capitol and seemed unable to contain himself as he walked by Greene on the steps. "No more QAnon, no more MAGA, no more debt ceiling nonsense," he yelled at Greene.

"She ain't worth it, bro," Ocasio-Cortez said, dragging him away.

But this evening, Greene had finally gotten Ocasio-Cortez to take the bait. "Why don't you debate me?" Greene said.

"I think it's pretty self-evident," Ocasio-Cortez replied.

"Yeah, you don't have enough intelligence," Greene shot back.

Later, reflecting on the episode, Greene said that she had once begrudgingly respected Ocasio-Cortez. But as she had watched her mature into her role and act less like an agitator and more like an insider, Greene said she respected her less. "She has no life experience, really," she said, sounding a lot like Sen. JD Vance of Ohio, who at the time was defending the resurfaced comment denigrating "childless cat ladies" he had once made during an appearance with Tucker Carlson. "She doesn't have true life experience. She doesn't have a family. That changes your perspective."

She added, ostensibly as proof of how much Ocasio-Cortez did not know, that "'baby girl' is a term of endearment in the South. My whole family calls me baby girl."

Crockett, the target of the attack that had set off all the heated cross talk, sat quietly studying Greene's appearance while she argued with Ocasio-Cortez. She gave Greene a slow once-over, taking in her bleach-blonde hair falling flat over her shoulders and the muscular arms she showed off in her sleeveless blue blouse. The entire package of Greene brought to mind an insult Crockett's grandmother used to use that had lodged itself in Jasmine's brain as a child: "bad-built." Crockett also found Greene's energy to be very masculine, and she figured that describing her as "butch" would get under the skin of a lawmaker who had called for the end of Pride Month and publicly fretted that straight people could face extinction.

Crockett scribbled six words on the notepad in front of her before turning to address James Comer, the panel's chairman, who was defending Greene's conduct.

"I'm just curious, just to better understand your ruling," Crockett said. "If someone on this committee then starts talking about somebody's bleach-blonde, bad-built butch body, that would not be engaging in personalities, correct?"

"A what now?" Comer said, in way over his head.

The late-night audience in the room burst out laughing, and Crockett turned away from Comer to hide her smile. But she had framed her clapback as a proper parliamentary inquiry, in order to make a cutting point: If Greene could get away with a throwaway comment about eyelashes, what was next? It was the moment that perhaps best encapsulated the new ethos of the Democratic Party: They were no longer putting up with any nonsense because they felt obligated to take the high road.

The internet erupted. Crockett's line sounded like a Cardi B lyric, and by the next day, there were hip-hop, country, and gospel songs all made in tribute to Crockett's "bleach-blonde, bad-built butch body" dig. The internet was having fun, never a great sign for the functionality of Congress.

Crockett said the eyelash dig from Greene was more annoying than hurtful. "I knew what she was trying to do: intentionally be racist toward me," she recalled. Long before Greene's comment, Crockett had seen the digs about her eyelashes online, memes calling her a "ghetto girl," and Greene, as was often the case on the right, was elevating that ugly online discourse in a congressional hearing room. "It's always been racist, this attempt to act as if this is something only Black girls do, and only a certain type of Black woman, and it's just not true," she said of the eyelash extensions she wears.

Democratic Sen. John Fetterman of Pennsylvania, hardly the paragon of congressional decorum in his gym shorts and hoodies, decided to throw himself into the mix online. "In the past, I've described the U.S. House as *The Jerry Springer Show*. Today, I'm apologizing to *The Jerry Springer Show*," he wrote on X.

But Crockett had no time for him. "He can kiss my ass," she said of Fetterman. "I didn't sign up for getting attacked. One of the reasons that you punch a bully back is to get the bully to stop punching or to think twice before they punch you." Crockett noted with some satisfaction that Greene had been scarce in committee hearings since their run-in and hadn't dared challenge her since.

Crockett immediately started selling "B6" merch and said all proceeds from her "Crockett Clapback Collection" would go to help elect Demo-

crats that November. She brought on a Black-owned local business to produce her "B6" T-shirts, and she trademarked the term.

The White House took notice, with senior aides passing video of the
exchange around the office. The Biden campaign enlisted Crockett to
send out a fundraising email for the president with the subject line
"BBBBBB." Crockett herself greatly elevated her profile: The Biden
campaign later relied on her as one of its official surrogates in the spin
room after the debate that would end the president's re-election campaign.

"We're benefiting off of her back," Crockett said about Greene. "The
money we make goes to the campaign, and those dollars go to vulnerable
Democrats. It feels like a Robin Hood story."

Greene didn't disagree with the fact that Democrats were benefiting
from her, although she was not particularly introspective about why that
was. "There's Trump, and then there's MTG," she said. "I'm their villain.
I think there are quite a few of them that really respect me. But they're
not going to be my friends. They can't; they raise too much money off
of me."

In the moment, Comer had no idea how to wrestle back control of a
meeting that had gone off the rails. "I have two hearing aids. I'm very
deaf!" he shouted. "I'm not understanding—everybody's yelling. I'm
doing the best I can." No one seemed to care.

"I think my body's pretty good," said Greene, a CrossFit devotee. (She
later posted a photo of herself in a bikini, to which George Santos replied,
"50 and fabulous.")

Boebert, gasping for political air, saw an opening to position herself as
the one who was finally above it all, but most specifically, above Greene.
She was the only Republican to vote with Democrats to have Greene's
words stricken from the record.

"I just want to apologize to the American people," she said. "When
things get as heated as they have, unfortunately, it's an embarrassment on
our body as a whole."

Later, Boebert said that if Democrats hadn't moved to discipline
Greene, she would have done so herself. "I thought that was one of the
most vile and disgusting things that have ever come out of Marjorie's
mouth," she said. "That was embarrassing."

Raskin couldn't believe his eyes. He generally enjoyed himself on this committee and even got along with some of the same Republicans he publicly railed against as deranged fanatics and betrayers of democracy. He and Boebert, of all people, had become buddies. She showed him pictures of her grandson in the hearing room, and he beamed. "I'm jealous," he told her as she scrolled through her photo roll. "I'm sixty, and I have no grandchildren." One day, Raskin showed up at the Capitol with a present for her, a onesie he had ordered online that read, "I May Take a Lot of Naps but I'm Still Woke." Boebert cackled. The two texted regularly.

(Unlike Greene, Boebert actually developed some close friendships on the Hill. She valued her relationship with Raskin. And the Speaker's race had made her close friends with both Ginger and Matt Gaetz, with whom she developed a feisty rapport. "He's big on endangered species and wildlife," she said. "I'm ready to go into these wolf dens and make hats.")

But that day, Raskin wished Comer could get the committee under control, and he didn't blame Crockett, Ocasio-Cortez, or any of the Democrats for standing up to Greene's bullying. The bad behavior, in his eyes, began all those months ago when Comer refused to check Greene after she displayed the nude photos of Hunter Biden in the committee room. "The major problem was that we allowed pornography in this committee, and we've gone down a bad road," Raskin complained. "I do blame it on Comer, because he simply refused to stand on principle," he said later. "Marjorie was basically threatening him that if he simply enforced the one major rule of decorum that we have, that she would unleash the MAGA hordes on him. He backed down. So, he was ultimately responsible for all of the chaos that took place."

But Raskin was pleased with both Crockett, whom he called his "prized pupil," and Boebert, who had voted with the Democrats to silence Greene for the rest of the meeting. "It's like the Beatles and the Rolling Stones," Raskin said later. "You've got to pick one as your favorite, and we're all Lauren Boebert people."

If Crockett had once had reservations about joining the committee known for its partisanship and fighting, she harbored them no longer. She had fully embraced her role as the Democrats' brawler, and she was proud of it. Privately, she said, many Republicans were, too. After her takedown of Greene, Crockett was surprised by the number of GOP lawmakers who showed her support. One gave her a quick thumbs-up. Another winked at her in the hallway. Some texted her privately to thank her for pushing back against Greene.

One Republican confided, "I like your lashes."

To hell with this place.

—GEORGE SANTOS

THROUGHOUT 2023, KEN BUCK HAD BEEN SICK OF CONGRESS. IN FACT, he claimed he had been sick of Congress since the day he got there in 2015. "This is a miserable existence," he said one afternoon in October, a few weeks before he publicly announced he wouldn't be running for reelection. Some lawmakers make a life in Washington and move their families to the District. That's most common for senators, who have stable six-year terms and a job for life if they represent solidly red or blue states.

Someone like Sen. Kirsten Gillibrand, a New York Democrat, was a fixture in her Washington neighborhood on the weekends, often spotted grocery shopping in workout clothes, like every other Capitol Hill mom, or taking her dog to romp at the Congressional Cemetery, where residents have to spend years on a waitlist for their pets to become tagged as part of the "K9 Corps" and earn the privilege of roaming off leash across the thirty-five-acre grounds. But House members with their two-year terms are never not running, and most of them don't have the privilege of simply becoming tony Washingtonians.

Buck had certainly never done that. Every Thursday afternoon after votes he was on a plane back to Colorado for some local event he was privately dreading. One weekend, it was the retirement of a Chinese restaurant owner, a fixture of the state's Chinese American community, and Buck was a guest of honor at the event. "There's always something in the district," he said, sighing. "There's a two-hour time difference; every week you fly twice. It's not a pleasurable job."

He was right: The life of a modern-day House member was pretty awful. The travel was exhausting, the fundraising demands relentless, the partisan attacks a psychic drain, not to mention the surge in threats and violent political speech against members of both parties, which made the job downright scary.

Take Marie Gluesenkamp Perez, a thirty-five-year-old auto shop owner from Washington state who in 2022 flipped her district blue in one of the country's most competitive House races. She represented a district that Trump had won twice and that she had won by less than one percentage point—or, to put a finer point on it, by just 2 votes in each precinct in the district. She was considered the most vulnerable Democrat in the entire House. There was no way she would be spotted walking her dog, Uma Furman, in D.C. on a weekend anytime soon.

Perez, the daughter of an evangelical pastor, lived in a house she and her husband had built with their own hands in the middle of the woods in Washougal, Washington, on top of a hill that was a forty-five-minute drive from anything. The stylish home had gorgeous views of the mountains and a sauna they built in the backyard, and it had all been lovingly designed for an idyllic DIY lifestyle that hadn't anticipated Perez holding a job on the other side of the country. On the few weekday mornings when she was home, Perez left her house around seven to drive an hour to drop her toddler off at daycare. Every week, she had to catch a plane from Portland, Oregon, back to Washington, D.C., where her only social life was the 6:30 A.M. members-only gym scene and two Republican Bible study groups she joined in part because she thought her party was embarrassed that she was a Christian.

"It is very lonely, working all the time," she said, sitting in her auto shop back home, in what used to be her office before she was elected. "You go back to your apartment and eat some fucking frozen peas. It's so emotionally taxing that at the end of the day you eat some peas and go to bed."

Perez is a moderate Democrat from a red district, with blunt-cut bangs and fashionable vintage clothes she hunts down on eBay and from bins at local thrift shops. She looks like a progressive Bed-Stuy hipster, but her voting record is far from it: After she voted against Biden's student loan relief initiative, progressives around the country began review-bombing

Dean's Car Care, the auto shop named after her husband that they own and run together.

"This place is horrible," wrote one anonymous reviewer. "They charge interest that compounds daily. Ohh wait, that's student loans. This place really is the worst."

"Awful company with terrible owners," another wrote. "Pay back your PPP loan you frauds."

It all drove Perez crazy. "There's a lot that has to come together to keep a good reputation as a shop," she said as she drove her Toyota Tundra through rain and snow across her district, from daycare drop-off to a ride-along with a local EMS. "Which is why all those fucking one-star reviews were so obnoxious. I had to work my ass off for that rating. Someone named John Doe is doing it. It's like reputational arson."

So, much of the job in 2023 was a downside. And Perez was not a household name like Alexandria Ocasio-Cortez. Since the New York representative had been elected to Congress in 2018 and become a national obsession—equal parts adored and reviled—threats had been a very difficult and defining part of her life. One year at the Pride Parade in Queens, a man followed Ocasio-Cortez back to her office and tried forcing himself into an elevator with her. Another man tried barging into her district office, breaking a bottle and threatening building staff. One afternoon, security alerted her that a person who had traveled across the country had been sitting in a bakery across the street from her office all day, waiting for her to come out. In Ocasio-Cortez's case, harassment sometimes happened right out in the open, on video. "See my favorite big-booty Latina, AOC!" one man yelled at her as she walked into the Capitol while he filmed her. "She wants to kill babies, but she's still beautiful."

When Ocasio-Cortez was first elected, her staff provided her with sheets of photos of all the people who had been flagged that day for making threats against her. Every morning, she would try to memorize the faces on the sheets in case any approached her. But they all became an overwhelming blur, and eventually she stopped asking for the sheets at all.

It was all too hard to process. Who were these people, she often wondered, and why did they all call at the same time, repeating the same types of phrases? The threats would surge after Tucker Carlson singled her out on his show, she noted. *Who would want to work for me?* she thought as she watched interns answer abusive calls coming into her office. *Nobody deserves this.*

"It's such an all-encompassing aspect of the experience," she said. "It's hard." There was no protection from the Capitol Police, which provided security only to the top four congressional leaders. At one point, Ocasio-Cortez requested an escort to protect her from harassment at the airport, and she was turned down. Two and half years into her congressional career, Capitol Police finally assigned her extra protection. But it was only for a few days and only after one specific threat. Then she was back on her own.

"I don't know how seriously people are going to take this until someone gets hurt," she vented to colleagues. "My experience has been that I am responsible for my own security. I have to fundraise for my own security."

After the Capitol came under attack on January 6 and Ocasio-Cortez hid in the bathroom of her inner office, thinking she was going to die, she spent fifty thousand dollars in a single month on round-the-clock security. There were periods when there were so many threats that she couldn't stay in her own home and times when it overwhelmed her and all she could do was repeat to herself the phrase "It's messed up. It's messed up."

At other times, the threats were just background noise she ignored. During the January 6 Committee investigation, the panel released a video of a man marching on the Capitol who pledged to drag Ocasio-Cortez out by her hair. "When I saw that video, it wasn't even particularly shocking to me, because it's like—another Wednesday," she said.

Even Marjorie Taylor Greene was shaken by the threats she got. She blamed Democrats—who used her as one of their top fundraising tools and plastered her face across districts far from her own—for driving up the death threats she received. Her home in Rome, Georgia, was regularly "swatted"—when someone calls 911 to falsely report a serious crime at someone else's address. She said she came home one evening to find a syringe with hospital stickers in her mailbox and sent it to the FBI for testing. "If someone comes to my house, I'm just going to tell you, I'm going to shoot them," she said she told law enforcement. "I shouldn't have to be prepared like that."

It all made you wonder who besides young idealists, power-hungry climbers, narcissists, and sociopaths would actually want this job.

And then there was the question of for what?

When he was in Washington, Buck didn't feel like the House was doing anything worthwhile. He opposed the political impeachments that had become the norm. Add to that the election denialism that had gripped his party, and the January 6 mob attack on the Capitol, and he was finally ready to leave ahead of an election cycle that was directly related to those events.

Buck had no desire to be a hero fighting against those forces within his own party. "Why don't you just keep getting the crap beat out of you and stay? No thanks," he said one afternoon, an edge of anger in his voice.

During his final week in Congress, he was unceremoniously booted out of the House Freedom Caucus, a group he had helped found almost a decade earlier, because of his vote against the Mayorkas impeachment. "Sorry to have to call you under these circumstances," Bob Good, the group's chairman, told Buck by phone one night after he had been out to dinner with his brother. "The Freedom Caucus decided to remove you."

"Okay, have a good night," said Buck, before hanging up. He shrugged. His entire posture toward Congress by then was a giant shrug.

Perez, young and idealistic, was motivated to keep at it for exactly those reasons: The other side was too intolerable to cede ground to. And so were the progressives, who she said simply didn't understand or respect the desires and achievements of the working class. The bad reviews from the left and the extremism on the other side of the aisle all made Perez work hard to keep hold of her seat. "I have a two-and-a-half-year-old; we still run the auto shop. I'm not going to throw my life in a blender to be someone I'm not," she said. "It sucks, it's a burden on my child and my husband, but I also see that, like, God has given us a strong family network and good teeth. We're healthy, we're young. No one else is going to fix this." (In 2024, Perez won reelection, defying the odds as the Democratic Party suffered crippling losses across the country, with down-ballot Republicans being buoyed by Trump. She blamed her party for being condescending to working-class voters.)

Jasmine Crockett often fantasized about returning to a more anonymous and normal life. "Dude, I can go back to my other life," she said. "Where nobody really knows me, where I don't need security because some wack job is gonna try to harm me because of being stoked by the MAGA club. And I can date, and I can make money, and all the things." She wasn't quitting just yet—she took seriously the significance of being a Black woman succeeding in a role that few who looked like her had served in before. And part of her liked being famous. "But at the same time," she said, "I don't think that most people appreciate how much we sacrifice to serve."

Working in Congress was rough for everyone, but it was particularly trying for Republicans who didn't fall in line behind Trump. Maybe that's why there were so few of them. The thankless position Buck was in was apparent on November 1, the day he announced he wasn't running again. Trump weighed in on Truth Social, calling Buck an "ineffective Super RINO" and saying his decision to leave Congress was "a great thing for the Republican Party."

Buck usually didn't care much what Trump said about him online or anywhere else, but he was struck by the irony of the broadside coming while he was also in court testifying on Trump's behalf in a suit trying to kick him off the primary ballot in Colorado based on arguments that the Fourteenth Amendment would prevent him from holding office again. (A judge ultimately ruled that the former president could remain on the ballot.)

In more normal times, a rank-and-file congressman deciding not to seek re-election would not hold great interest to House leadership. But in a tiny majority, when one seat was still occupied by the fabulist George Santos, whom everyone assumed could be gone any day, Buck's announcement made leadership uneasy. He hadn't given them much of a heads-up: He called the new Speaker from the greenroom at MSNBC, where he was about to go on Andrea Mitchell's program and break his news. (In a little D.C. sleight of hand, Buck had chosen MSNBC as his preferred cable network that day to quell rumors that he had already been offered and accepted a job as a paid contributor on CNN.)

Steve Scalise and Mike Johnson asked if he could hang on until the end of 2024. Their pitch was that there would be exciting things happening this Congress. He was highly skeptical. In reality, that meant a political impeachment of Mayorkas in which Buck was one of 3 Republicans to break with his party and vote "no," helping to tank their first attempt in embarrassing fashion. It wasn't clear they wouldn't be better off without him.

"We're at a time in American politics where I am not going to lie on behalf of my presidential candidate, on behalf of my party," he said on MSNBC. "I'm very sad that others in my party have taken the position that as long as we get the White House, it doesn't really matter what we say."

Buck was already entertaining offers that were coming in and was making no promises of sticking around until the end of his term. In March, he announced he would be leaving a week later. "This place keeps going downhill, and I don't need to spend more time here," he told reporters in the hallway.

He spent his final day in Congress cleaning out his locker, downloading cell phone numbers of members and television producers from his communications director, and pretending to be surprised by a farewell party his staff had planned for him in the afternoon.

Retirements were skyrocketing in both parties in the House, but they were more imminently problematic for the shrinking Republican majority. Typically, lawmakers don't leave if they chair powerful committees or think they're going to stay in the majority or possibly grow the majority and gain more seniority. But this wasn't a normal Congress, and for all the positive spin about how Republicans intended to keep control of the House in 2024, their sprinting for the exits told a different story.

Rep. Blaine Luetkemeyer, from Missouri, was in line to be the top Republican on the powerful Financial Services Committee. In January 2024, he made a surprise announcement that he was retiring at the end of his term. He provided no reason for his decision, other than that it had come as a result of "a lot of thoughtful discussion with my family."

Rep. Greg Pence of Indiana, the older brother of Mike Pence, also decided he was done.

Drew Ferguson of Georgia had started the 118th Congress with hopes of rising in the ranks. He toyed with the idea of running for majority whip. In 2020, he had spoken out against Marjorie Taylor Greene, telling *Politico* bluntly that she "shouldn't have a place in Congress." Turns out, there was space for Greene and less room for an old-school Republican like Ferguson. He announced he was done with Congress in December

2023, a few months after receiving death threats for voting against Jim Jordan for Speaker.

Rep. Mike Gallagher, a fresh-faced forty-year-old from Wisconsin who served as chairman of the Select Committee on the Chinese Communist Party, announced in February that he was not going to seek another term and then, like Buck, that he wouldn't even finish his current one. He left and was immediately hired by Palantir Technologies to head up its defense business. Gallagher had also voted against the Mayorkas impeachment, but nonetheless, his early departure left the Republican majority with the slim margin of being able to lose only one vote on party-line bills. His unexpected exit underscored the frustration among Republicans who no longer wanted to serve in what they described as a completely dysfunctional governing body.

Prestigious posts such as Appropriations chair and Energy and Commerce chair weren't the powerful draw they had been in previous years. All told, at least four committee chairs would announce they were retiring, including Patrick McHenry.

McHenry wanted to leave with some level of dignity and respect intact. He thought about staying a few more terms and trying to become Speaker one day, but it was hard to picture contorting himself into whatever embarrassing posture the party was demanding of its leaders. "This is a very rewarding place when you're not obligated," he said. He had also had a revelation during the pandemic when he was regularly home for dinner with his family, something that hadn't happened in years. "I said to my wife, 'This is amazing. So, you all did this, like, every night?'" He got a taste of the normal life he had been sacrificing and realized it was pretty good. And in his three weeks as Speaker pro tempore, he got enough of a taste of the big job to know he didn't need more. "I got to try on the clothes, and I said, 'I'm good,'" he said.

It's easy to dismiss politicians who claim they are leaving powerful jobs to spend more time with their families as using their long-suffering wives and kids as an excuse. But the jobs really do take a toll on a functional family life, and if there's not much payoff, it becomes hard to justify such a sacrifice.

Rep. Brad Wenstrup, an Ohio Republican, a doctor, a former colonel, and a veteran of the Iraq War who chaired the subcommittee on the coronavirus pandemic, made the decision to leave Congress after more than a decade because he couldn't justify it anymore. "I got married late, my kids are little. I'm missing stuff; it's time to be home," said Wenstrup, sixty-five, who had served in Congress since 2013. He tried to FaceTime and be home on weekends. Still, it gutted him when his ten-year-old son told Wenstrup's wife that sometimes it felt like "Dad doesn't even exist." The chaos was not the sole factor that made him decide his time in Washington was over, "but it's making it easier," he said, laughing. His district also changed and became more Appalachian.

But certainly, being home to coach Little League seemed more appealing than being a phantom parent giving up those years to be in Washington as part of a party that couldn't even govern.

Wenstrup was a Catholic who said he was inspired as a young man by Mother Teresa. A card-carrying member of the "you can disagree without being disagreeable" caucus, he spoke about how fulfilling it was to work with colleagues across the aisle. When Anthony Fauci came to testify before his committee, Wenstrup had the doctor who had been so vilified by the right sign his son's science homework, a keepsake to take back home to Ohio. On the face of it, he looked the part of the exiting older guard of a once-normal political party. But in reality, he was an example of how far even center-leaning Republicans had been pulled to the right.

Wenstrup was one of 125 Republicans who signed an amicus brief organized by Johnson that was rooted in baseless claims of widespread election irregularities. The brief was presented to the Supreme Court and ultimately rejected. For Wenstrup, the impeachments of Trump were problematic, but the attempt to impeach Biden was not. "There are some real crimes that have been committed. This is a little bit different," he said. "What we're researching is really important." He also voted to impeach Mayorkas.

And then there was the one Republican member who left against his will, tossed out by his colleagues in a historic rebuke: the Tom Ripley of Congress himself, George Santos. During his brief and colorful stint in elected office, Santos was mostly treated like a pariah by his colleagues and a scandal-plagued curiosity by the media, when he wasn't simply being ignored altogether by everyone on Capitol Hill.

Santos had exaggerated or lied about everything there was to know about him, including his education (the Baruch College volleyball scholarship never existed), his career (he never worked for Citigroup or Goldman Sachs), his family history (his grandparents were not Holocaust survivors), the whereabouts of his mother (she wasn't in the South Tower of the World Trade Center, or even in New York, during the 9/11 terrorist attacks, as he claimed), and being a landlord (he wasn't), among other brazen tales he told.

At different times in life, Santos used different names: "Anthony Devolder," "George Devolder," "Anthony Zabrovsky," and his drag queen name, "Kitara Ravache," among others.

Santos was detested by the rank-and-file Republicans from New York, who worried that an association with the serial fraudster would tarnish their chances at re-election, and he was protected by leadership under McCarthy, who could not afford to go after him and lose a reliable vote.

Santos was an odd duck for the Republican Party—a former drag queen and the only openly gay Republican in Congress. But his attention-seeking spirit and loyalty to Trump made him, in other ways, a perfect fit for modern-day Congress. For months, he refused to address the allegations against him, encapsulating the ethos that had come to drive the Republican Party since Trump's rise, in which shamelessness in the face of attacks is rewarded and apologizing or admitting culpability is seen as a sign of weakness. He was the logical extension of the political con man that was Trump himself.

And, like Trump and the politicians he sought to emulate, Santos courted attention. His 2023 State of the Union confrontation with Sen. Mitt Romney was a striking juxtaposition to the party's transformation over the course of ten years. "You don't belong here," Romney, once the party's standard-bearer and the 2012 Republican presidential nominee, told Santos when he spotted him leaning into the aisle of the chamber, close enough to reach out for a presidential handshake.

"Go tell that to the one hundred forty-two thousand that voted for me," Santos, unrepentant, shot back.

Romney was appalled by Santos's brazen presence at the annual tradition of the president's address to a joint session of Congress. "He's a sick puppy. He shouldn't have been there," he told reporters later, the Mormon equivalent of a curse-filled diatribe. "Given the fact that he's under ethics investigation, he should be sitting in the back row and being quiet instead of parading in front of the president."

But Romney's sense of decorum was out of date. The following year, after Santos had been expelled from Congress, he showed up at the State of the Union again, wearing a Swarovski-encrusted collar and holding court. There was no point to his appearance except to remind everyone that he existed, and he was now greeted warmly by other Republicans. Beth Van Duyne and Rich McCormick came over to say hello. (That same year, Greene showed up dressed in a red MAGA cap to heckle Biden in the middle of his speech.)

Things got serious for Santos when federal prosecutors charged him with thirteen felony counts, mostly having to do with financial fraud. He was charged with spending campaign funds the way only a gay Zillennial would know how to—on Botox, Sephora, OnlyFans, Ferragamo shoes, and weekend trips to the Hamptons.

His crimes were serious, but his persona wasn't. He posted his own fashion reviews of the 2023 White House Correspondents' Association Dinner on X, and at one point, he walked around holding a baby for no apparent reason, adding to the weirdness of the scene by refusing to say whose baby it was. Was it his? "Not yet," he forebodingly told reporters tailing him. (The baby belonged to a staff member.)

As a freshman lawmaker who had voluntarily removed himself from all the committees he served on, Santos had so little power on Capitol Hill that his entire existence there was entertaining more than worrisome.

For him, being at the center of multiple scandals had been traumatic, but also exhilarating. Being a freshman can be a lonely, anonymous, frozen-pea-eating existence. But dodging cameras and walking with an attendant horde of reporters at least had given the committee-less congressman a purpose. The problem was that if the story wasn't about Santos's own issues, there was really no point in soliciting his opinion on anything. He voted with his conference—he needed leadership's protection and could not afford to align himself with the rabble-rousers blocking floor votes—but nobody really needed him to weigh in with his thoughts about the debt ceiling or government-funding measures.

So, he courted the press when he could, leaving donuts and Chickfil-A outside his office to feed the vultures often staked out there for a Santos sighting. "They looked hungry," he told his staff. "Some of them were skipping lunch because they were afraid of missing me."

But after the buzz around Santos started to die down, feeling invisible started getting to him. "I've been trying to go on *War Room,* and Bannon never puts me on," Santos vented to a confidante late one night. The confidante suggested he try to book a slot on the podcast with Bannon's co-host, Natalie Winters, a young woman Bannon had hired to broaden his appeal with younger listeners. "I want to go on with Bannon!" Santos whined. "They keep telling me they're working on it, but the day never comes! And to be honest, right now I don't even want to go on *War Room,* because Bannon is going to light me on fire because I'm going to vote for the CR," he said, referring to the stopgap funding measure that Bannon was constantly railing against.

In short, Santos still wanted to be a player in a party that wanted him gone. "I'm going to lose the general," he moaned. "I'll win the primary, but I'll lose the general. But if I win the general, I'm going to run for leadership." That thought made him cackle.

Months later, after a damning House Ethics report revealed he had spent campaign funds for personal use, Santos announced he would not seek re-election. He would last until December 2023—almost as long as McCarthy himself, surviving two efforts by New York Republicans to expel him—when the House finally voted to remove him from office. With that, the notorious fabulist had made a little bit of real history: Santos became the first person in Congress to be expelled without first being convicted of a federal crime or supporting the Confederacy. (In 1861, ten senators were expelled for "disloyalty to the Union.")

In the end, Santos had used Congress the way many of his colleagues had: to get famous. Leaning into the caricature, he tried to Anna Delvey his way into the future through branding and cashing in on his fifteen minutes of fame.

On his second-to-last day in Congress, Santos booked a conference room in the Longworth Building and invited a group of about a dozen reporters to listen to him speak. He wore navy Ferragamos that he promised had not been purchased with stolen campaign dollars ("Go on the website!" he said. "They're six years old!") and seemed to have no real agenda other than to be the center of attention in the waning hours of his influence. He knew most of the reporters seated around the table by name and was up to date on what they had said about him online. He complimented the women in the room on their skirts. These people, after all, had been his lifeline to relevance. He would miss them. They would miss him. Santos may have been a liar and an accused criminal, but he had also been a colorful distraction—he offered a break from more serious issues like debt ceiling negotiations, failed border talks, stalled funding for Ukraine, and politically motivated impeachment inquiries.

That afternoon, seated at the head of a long conference table, Santos acknowledged that he expected to be expelled in the next twenty-four hours and was scared to go to jail. "Wouldn't you be? Of course," he said matter-of-factly. "Everybody should be. These are serious allegations, and I have a lot of work ahead of me."

But he also claimed to have reached a state of inner peace. "I am done losing sleep. I am done stressing," he said. "I have just made peace with God in the best way possible and said that whatever comes my way, I will accept it. I am thirty-five, I have a lot of life left to live.

"I'm not sad," he insisted. "To be sad is to be miserable."

Santos got what he wanted out of the session: flattering questions about whether he might next consider running for governor of New York or mayor of New York City, about who might play him in the movie version of his life.

"This is a career-making move," he said, laughing. He insisted he was highly employable and that job opportunities were pouring in. When everyone was out of questions for him but he still sat there searching everyone's face for more, someone asked: Would he ever do *Dancing with the Stars*?

"Today, I would not do that," he said. "Maybe in the future, if I find the chutzpah to go on television and embarrass myself with my four left feet, maybe."

He said he would fight to prove his innocence, but he didn't deny that he had spent money on cosmetic work. "I use cosmetic Botox and filler. That's not a secret. Did anybody ever doubt that?" he asked the room, his lips full and slightly puckered, his forehead essentially wrinkle-free. "I've been doing it for years."

After leaving Congress, Santos tried to cash in on the platform Cameo, monetizing on his strange slice of infamy by charging hundreds of dollars a pop for his short personalized videos. He would later announce that he was running as an independent in New York's First Congressional District on Long Island, represented by the member of the Republican Party he hated the most and whom he blamed for his expulsion, Rep. Nick LaLota. A few months later, he announced that he was ending the bid.

On the floor of the House in the afternoon ahead of the debate about his expulsion, Santos sat in the middle of a mostly empty chamber, joined by a motley crew of allies who planned to speak up on his behalf: Matt Gaetz, the House's most famous problem child; Rep. Clay Higgins of Louisiana, a far-right conspiracy theorist; and Troy Nehls of Texas, a Trump loyalist who had pushed to nominate the former president to be Speaker of the House after McCarthy's downfall.

Gaetz, who had his own pending issues with the Ethics Committee, took the opportunity to say that expelling Santos because of the panel's report would do "grave" damage to the institution of the House. "Since the beginning of this Congress, there's only two ways you get expelled: You get convicted of a crime or you participated in the Civil War," Gaetz said. "Neither apply to George Santos. And so I rise not to defend George Santos, whoever he is, but to defend the very precedent that my colleagues are willing to shatter." He added, "Now there is no requirement of any conviction."

The arguments about due process would not be enough to save Santos. The following day, 105 Republicans joined 206 Democrats to vote in favor of his expulsion.

"Well, that's it," Santos muttered as he turned to walk out of the chamber, ending his brief congressional career and finalizing the expulsion that many Republicans would grow to rue as their numbers continued to dwindle until their majority was hanging on by a single vote.

"Why would I want to stay here?" Santos said as reporters trailed him out of the Capitol for the final time, anger having replaced the claimed serenity of the previous day. "To hell with this place."

They're burning this thing
to the ground tonight.

—CHRIS MURPHY

FOR MOST OF THE 118TH CONGRESS, THE MAGA CHAOS WAS A FEATURE more prevalent in the House. The more deliberate Senate, with its six-year terms, its statewide officeholders, and its filibuster, was, for the most part, still more functional and less feud-driven.

Lawmakers in both parties went out of their way to highlight when they got together to work on bipartisan legislation. Both parties seemed to get a kick out of the odd couples that teamed up to work on bills: Sens. Ted Cruz of Texas and John Fetterman of Pennsylvania working together to limit social media access in schools; Sens. Elizabeth Warren of Massachusetts and JD Vance of Ohio working on a bill to claw back executive pay in the event of a company failure.

When long-serving Democratic Sen. Dianne Feinstein of California died in 2023, Mitch McConnell, the Senate's top Republican, gave a speech on the Senate floor calling her a "truly remarkable individual." Such words for a member of the opposing party were hard to fathom in the modern-day House, where partisan warriors like Lauren Boebert screamed "We're gonna get you!" at their political opponents in the hallways.

But the Senate was certainly not immune from Trump: Republicans there, too, had long ago fallen in line. And when it came time for the Senate to tackle the biggest issues of the year, Ukraine funding and border security, Trump made it clear he would dictate policy even in the "cooling saucer" of the upper chamber.

On the afternoon of October 26, 2023, Jake Sullivan, the national security advisor, convened a bipartisan group of senators at the White House to discuss sending billions of dollars of aid to Ukraine. It was a productive meeting, in that it immediately became clear to the White House and to Democrats in the room that there was no path to getting Ukraine aid through the Senate if it wasn't paired with a hardcore border security bill.

Sen. Mike Rounds, a Republican Ukraine hawk from South Dakota, was a mainstream ally of McConnell, and here he was, telling Sullivan and other senior White House officials that there would be no Ukraine bill without legislation to secure America's border attached to it. If they were going to worry about other countries' borders, he said, they had to have something in there to secure their own. It wasn't a passing comment: The Republicans repeated it again and again in the room that day. It served as a wake-up call for Democrats.

Rounds was not a far-right isolationist like Vance, who became Trump's running mate. This was someone representative of a group of Republicans in the Senate who supported Ukraine funding but had concluded that they couldn't sell it to their colleagues if it wasn't coupled with tough border security measures. Because what was becoming clear to Republicans as time wore on was that the war in Ukraine was more identified with the Biden administration and, therefore, was a leverage point. Some Republicans wanted funding for Ukraine—McConnell, the long-serving Republican leader, for one, was staking out his legacy on fighting the isolationists in his party and making the case to support Ukraine in its fight against Russian president Vladimir Putin. But to most Republicans, politics were at the forefront. They wanted it, but clearly Biden wanted it more, so why give it away for free?

McConnell thought it was strange to link the two issues and was reluctant to do so. "I thought they were entirely separate issues, two different lanes," he said. "They just happened to happen at about the same time."

McConnell had long been known as something of a sphinx to his colleagues, even before the 2023 concussion that left him vastly diminished and occasionally freezing up in public. (After the incident, his doctors recommended he walk with a cane, which he stubbornly refused to do.) When Chuck Schumer took over as minority leader in 2017, after the retirement of Harry Reid, a group of Republican senators approached him in the Senate gym and asked him how he was getting along with McConnell. "Better than Reid," he told them. "He even laughs at my jokes sometimes." The Republicans looked at Schumer blankly, and one asked, "How could you even tell?"

McConnell had been watching political support for Ukraine crater within his own party, and for that, he primarily blamed Tucker Carlson, who repeatedly demonized the country and its president, Volodymyr Zelenskyy. Carlson's attacks on Zelenskyy, who is Jewish, were deeply anti-Semitic. He called Zelenskyy "sweaty and rat-like," "shifty," "dead-eyed," a "persecutor of Christians," and a "friend of BlackRock," the investment company.

McConnell was disgusted by this, but he understood the political reality those comments helped cause. If they were going to pass an aid package for Ukraine, they would need to pass a border bill, too. That didn't mean he had to like the situation.

Typically, Republicans flew down to the border to stage photo ops with law enforcement and talk about the dangers of bad guys crossing into Texas and Arizona illegally. Democrats, for their part, liked to tour shelters and talk about the treatment of migrants after they had already arrived in the country.

At the beginning of 2023, Sen. Kyrsten Sinema, the Democrat turned independent from Arizona, organized a bipartisan trip to the border and had the group do a little bit of each. "We did both," she said, "because both of those things are real."

This was exactly her kind of thing. Sinema liked to practice in the Senate what columnist Michelle Goldberg of *The New York Times* once aptly described as "aggressive centrism." Sinema thought of herself as a party of one who didn't fit into any box. The tight margins in the Senate in 2022 gave her a lot of power as a deciding vote—she was able to stop Democrats from closing the carried interest loophole while negotiating on one of Biden's signature pieces of legislation, the Inflation Reduction Act, a wide-ranging climate, health care, and tax bill. And she thought she played a key role in all bipartisan negotiations because Republicans trusted her.

That year, she switched her party affiliation to independent to remain relevant and keep her options open moving forward. She was unpopular with Democratic voters in her state (she had a 37 percent approval rating), unpopular among the Democratic senators in Congress (many viewed her as one of the major impediments to overturning the Senate's filibuster rule, which requires 60 votes to pass most legislation and is viewed by many Democrats as a roadblock to their agenda), and unpopular with reporters (she looked through them as if they didn't exist).

She mostly reserved her charms for her Republican colleagues. McConnell, who adored her for her intransigence on the issue of the filibuster, praised her as a true "dealmaker" in the Senate and called her the most effective first-term senator he'd ever seen in action. But one term was all she would have—in 2024, she would announce that she would not run for re-election, admitting that her experiment in trying to be above partisanship had failed miserably.

But in October 2023, Sinema saw a Kyrsten-shaped bat signal rise atop the Capitol when she heard there would have to be an intense, technically complicated negotiation on a border security deal to get Ukraine aid through the Senate. "When they said no Ukraine without border, I perked up. I thought, *This meets all of my interests,*" Sinema, a former immigration attorney, said in her hideaway in the basement of the Senate, a rose-tinted room furnished with midcentury modern burnt sienna–colored couches.

She was thrilled when McConnell selected Sen. James Lankford, a deeply Christian conservative from Oklahoma and her longtime friend, as the lead Republican negotiator.

On the Democratic side, Schumer asked Sen. Chris Murphy of Connecticut to get involved and work with Sinema. But he made it clear that, like McConnell, he had very low hopes of success. Work on an immigration bill for three or four weeks, he told Murphy and Sinema. Republicans would probably walk away from it, Schumer said, but that might pave the way for the Senate to pass a "clean" Ukraine bill—in other words, a bill to send the billions of dollars to Ukraine with no strings attached. And that, to Democrats, was the most important thing.

McConnell and Schumer had the same view of the exercise. Not sending the funding abroad would accelerate Chinese expansion plans, allow Putin to continue plundering Europe, and harm the United States' reputation on the world stage as a power that stuck by its allies. McConnell had considered all the anti-Ukraine arguments from the isolationists within his party and deemed them all "stupid." And he didn't think the amount of money they were debating sending abroad was a lot (it was something like 0.2 percent of U.S. GDP).

Neither McConnell nor Schumer had budgeted for the time the process would take. The negotiations that Schumer had expected to take three weeks ended up taking four months, a period that unhelpfully coincided with Trump's essentially locking up the Republican presidential nomination by winning back-to-back primaries from Iowa to South Carolina and ending the charade that had been the undercard Republican primary. Along the way, Trump railed against Ukraine aid and made it clear that the porous U.S. border (letting in "drugs, rapists, and murderers") was once again going to be the animating issue of his presidential campaign.

Biden, for his part, had been late to realize that immigration was a political killer for him. With ten thousand crossings a day, internal polls showed him to be underwater on the issue by more than thirty points—and yet the Democratic Party had for years been reflexively defensive about immigration, fearful of talking about border security and stemming the tide of undocumented immigrants, focusing almost entirely on how migrants were treated once they entered the United States. Biden only belatedly understood that what he most needed was the ability to shut down the border, something he would end up doing through executive action in June, keeping it closed to migrants at least through Election Day.

For months, the three senators met, often in Sinema's pink-hued hideaway, and discussed how to reach a deal. They brought in others, like Sen. Lindsey Graham of South Carolina, who was seen as a key representative of the Senate Republicans. Alejandro Mayorkas, the Homeland Security secretary himself, joined the discussions to go through the technical details of a deal.

They did not bring in anyone from the House, which Johnson would later blame for the bill's failure to launch. Johnson wanted Reps. Jim Jordan and Mark Green, House conservatives who chaired the Judiciary and Homeland Security committees, respectively, to be involved in crafting the bill.

"We've got real conservatives at the table," McConnell assured Johnson.

"You need *House* conservatives at the table," Johnson replied. "You can't spoon-feed them and just send something over." But McConnell viewed Johnson as a novice and swatted away his concerns, assuring him that his members would be happy with the final product.

It was clear to everyone involved that Trump would have an interest in blowing up the deal and opposing anything the senators came up with. Ever since he descended the golden escalator at Trump Tower in 2015 and burst onto the national political stage by warning about rapists who were bringing drugs and crime into the country, immigration had been the beating heart of his political persona.

Eight years later, after all the crazy things he had said—from "covfefe" to "very fine people on both sides" to "when you're a star they let you do it" to his recommendation to inject disinfectant to treat Covid—one refrain had outlasted them all: "Build the wall." No one involved in the negotiations thought Trump was going to allow Congress, in an election year, to actually start fixing the problems at the border and rob him of the main issue on which he wanted to run. Still, as the negotiations dragged on, more Republican senators started to actively help the group and give them some hope that maybe, against all odds, there was a path forward.

Eventually, the contours of a deal emerged: funding for thousands of new border patrol agents, personnel, and technology to catch drug smugglers. The new personnel would help crack down on border crossings, which Republicans liked, but it would also help eliminate the huge backlog of humanitarian asylum cases, which Democrats advocated for. Many more people would be deported, but fewer people with legitimate legal claims to be in the country would be left in limbo. It was a win-win. To sweeten the deal, Democrats agreed to something that would have been unthinkable months ago: an immediate shutdown of the border as soon as encounters reached a certain threshold. The level they agreed to—five thousand over the course of the week—would mean the border would be completely shut down the very first day the legislation was signed into law.

On the afternoon of Sunday, February 4, 2024, hours before the senators decided to finally release their final text of the bill, they had between 20 and 25 Republican votes in the "yes" or "maybe" columns, according to informal conversations they had with colleagues. Could it really be that in one of the most dysfunctional sessions of Congress in history, they were about to move ahead with an incredibly difficult deal? Occam's razor dictated no, not even in the more functional chamber.

From the minute the text was released, there was a full-blown assault led by Stephen Miller, a former Trump adviser on immigration, to set the narrative about what the bill did and didn't do. Within hours of its release, that support had completely evaporated.

The MAGA forces called it an amnesty bill that "erases our borders." And House Republicans went into overdrive, bashing the bill. Elise Stefanik immediately branded it the "Joe Biden/Chuck Schumer Open Border Bill." But, mostly, they focused on the number five thousand. The bill set a threshold of five thousand encounters at the border, a number at which the administration would be mandated to shut the border down. With border encounters often topping ten thousand a day, the new emergency authority would have been triggered immediately.

Republicans should obviously support that.

But, led by Trump, they opposed the deal and tried to create the impression that the bill would increase the number of undocumented immigrants entering the country by five thousand a day. "We're concocting some sort of deal to allow the president to shut down the border after five thousand people break the law," Speaker Johnson said. "This is madness."

Immigration policy is complex and easy to demonize in sound bites, especially when the charge is led by people who want zero immigration, legal or illegal.

"They're burning this thing to the ground tonight," Murphy texted Sinema as he watched it all unfold on social media with a fury he had never witnessed before. They had assumed Trump would oppose the efforts, but the swiftness of the campaign against the bill left them stunned.

"It was so clear that Trump's entire universe was going after this, and you were going to pay a price with them if you supported it," Murphy recalled.

Lankford tried his best to counter the misinformation about the bill. He booked as many conservative media hits as a human being could fit into a day, repeating the fact that the legislation "is not designed to let five thousand people in. It is designed to close the border and turn five thousand people around." But his was a lonely voice against Trump's anti-immigration machine.

At one point, Lankford had a conversation with a Republican Senate colleague who had originally been in the "yes" column to explain to him the fallacies being spread about the bill and, in particular, the "five thousand immigrants" talking point. "Oh, I understand it, but I don't care," the senator told Lankford bluntly. "What matters is what they're saying about it, not what it does." The writing was on the wall when Sen. John Cornyn, a Republican from Texas who had been updated about the bill throughout the negotiations, released a statement saying he had "questions and serious concerns" with the legislation.

It was over, and it wasn't much more complicated than the top-line fact that Trump had killed it. Politics won over policy: In the end, only 4 Republicans voted for the bill.

McConnell, for his part, was relieved that they could stop trying to do the impossible and focus on halting Putin's aggression. Meanwhile, they had lost critical months to the process.

"Had we gotten this done in November, before Trump was unquestionably the candidate, maybe we would have had a chance to survive," Murphy said. "We ended up writing a very big, complicated bill that took us four months. By the time it came out, his party was not willing to cross him." Murphy is always a pessimist in the middle of negotiations but an optimist in the big picture. One has to be to keep devoting every waking hour to hashing out complicated details of a bill that ends up dead on arrival.

Democrats, in Murphy's mind, had made a fatal error in assuming Latino voters cared only about a pathway to citizenship, when it turned out a lot of them also wanted a tough border and thought the asylum system was too generous. Many Black voters, meanwhile, felt they had been waiting in line for a long time and recoiled at the idea that undocumented migrants were somehow skipping in front of them. It was naïve to think that all Black and brown voters had a monolithic and progressive view of immigration. And there seemed to be less backlash against Democrats for voting for strict border security proposals—the progressive left was consumed with other issues, like the humanitarian crisis in Gaza, and was less focused on the issue of immigration than it had been during the Obama administration. "With some of our base, our position on immigration has been really problematic, and it's taken us way too long to figure that out," Murphy said.

Sinema was a more complicated character and had a less rosy view of what all her hard work had led to. "A member of the Democratic Caucus came up to me a few days after it all fell apart and said, 'I'm just so glad you did this, because now the Democrats have something to run on,'" Sinema recalled. "I felt inexplicable rage. I was just so enraged. It was very deeply painful, because that doesn't do shit for my state."

Sinema soon after announced her decision not to run for re-election, a race she would likely have lost. "The system is not designed to support or reward stepping outside of the partisan comfort zone," she said. "If you want to survive, you can't do it." Her underlying message: She was better than all this, and the voters were not in a place to reward her for it.

And as for the Ukraine aid, it now headed back to the chaos chamber, its fate uncertain.

29

They're deep state, too.

—MARJORIE TAYLOR GREENE

BIDEN AND CONGRESSIONAL LEADERS HAD BEEN PRESSING JOHNSON for months on Ukraine—a dynamic that frustrated Johnson, who thought they did not understand that he did not need convincing on the merits. At one February 2024 meeting at the Oval Office, Biden, Kamala Harris, Chuck Schumer, Hakeem Jeffries, and Mitch McConnell all took turns making the case that aiding Ukraine was existential.

"I find myself in the same position as the president and the two Democratic leaders," McConnell said in the meeting. "Time is a-wastin' here, and we need to get this done sooner rather than later." Privately, he urged Johnson, "Put it on the floor and let's see where the votes are. Let everybody vote."

Johnson had already explained to McConnell and Jeffries that he understood the necessity of sending money to Ukraine but that, politically, he had to thread a very small needle.

"It's going to take quite a bit of time," he told them. "You're going to have to trust me on this." The problem was that McConnell didn't, really. And with good reason. When Johnson was elected Speaker, McConnell had no idea who he was. "I can't name many three-term congressmen," he told people. What he did know was that Johnson had voted against Ukraine aid in the past, and that concerned him.

In the Oval Office, Johnson told them: "I understand everything that's being said here. It doesn't change the reality that I have to get the votes to do it. And under the current circumstances, we're going to have to recon-figure this." These were tense times.

McConnell blamed Biden's decision to leave Afghanistan for Putin's invasion of Ukraine. He couldn't prove the connection, but he thought it had given Putin the impression that the United States was pulling up its tent stakes around the world and going home. He also blamed Biden for not providing weapons to Ukraine earlier.

But even more than Biden, he blamed the isolationist forces in his own party, led by Tucker Carlson and Trump, for opposing aid to Ukraine, and he was concerned that this no-name red-state congressman with no experience in leadership was under the sway of those voices. As a rank-and-file member, Johnson had opposed efforts to fund the war in Ukraine, and early in his speakership, he was part of the "no Ukraine without bor-der" caucus. This all worried McConnell tremendously.

What McConnell, Schumer, and Jeffries didn't know at the time was that Johnson's staff had already begun working directly with the White House on a sensitive plan to move legislation to aid Ukraine. Only a hand-ful of people knew that Johnson's team had opened these back-channel negotiations. Paranoid that the hard right would discover their talks and tank them, or oust Johnson, they tried to put nothing in writing and avoided meeting during work hours. Johnson's chief of staff, Hayden Haynes, would sometimes meet Shuwanza Goff, the White House direc-tor of legislative affairs, in the dog park in their neighborhood at ten thirty at night to trade folders of proposals, as if they were characters in *The Americans*.

The talks started with Haynes and Goff, at Johnson's direction, before they slowly added others, one at a time, emphasizing how important it was that no word of the negotiations leaked out. Johnson himself was speaking regularly with Jake Sullivan, the national security advisor; An-tony Blinken, the secretary of state; and Steve Ricchetti, Biden's main conduit to Capitol Hill.

The two camps reached a secret deal in principle more than a month before Johnson would bring the measure to the floor. As Johnson ago-nized over how to do so without losing his job, Haynes sat in the Speaker's office one afternoon reviewing public polling on Ukraine. One number in particular stood out to him: a Pew poll that said 8 percent of Americans had confidence in Putin.

"Who are those people?" he wondered out loud.

It was after Johnson's first substantive meeting with Marjorie Taylor Greene that Haynes may have answered his own question. Personally, Haynes did not support sending billions more to Ukraine and thought there were more pressing issues, like the fentanyl crisis, to deal with. But he never let his own views color the information he made available to his boss, and even from his vantage point, he was sometimes stunned by what he heard from Greene.

For months, she had been warning that her "red line" for moving to oust Johnson would be if he brought to the floor any legislation to send more funding to Ukraine. Democrats had tried to counter that threat by signaling publicly and privately that if she moved to do so, they would vote to save Johnson. That wasn't an ideal situation for "MAGA Mike," but it was better than losing the job altogether.

"The same classified information was that there were weapons of mass destruction in Iraq, and there weren't any," she told him in one of their hours-long meetings, which grew heated. "You need to be able to take things with a grain of salt and use your own judgment when you're being fed information from the intelligence community, because they have goals."

Johnson was frustrated. "Marjorie, the briefing is provided by a four-star general—our general, not European generals. Our guys. The Pentagon. You don't trust anyone at the Pentagon?" he pressed her.

"Once you get in leadership at the Pentagon you're part of the deep state," she said.

"What about Ratcliffe, O'Brien, Pompeo, Nunes? Trump guys who say if we don't do this, we're going to start World War III?"

"They're deep state, too."

Johnson threw up his arms in frustration. "What are you talking about? Those are Trump cabinet members!"

"Once you go to the intel space," she said, shaking her head, "you just sell your soul."

Johnson paused to try to collect himself and remember the biblical admonition that one was supposed to be forgiving.

"Remind me, respectfully—you never served in the military?" he said.

"No."

"Have you ever been to Europe?"

"No."

"Okay, but you want me to take your gut feeling on this and defy all the intel?"

There was simply no convincing Greene. "The American people know, and you ought to know, if you weren't such a coward," she said.

Johnson did this for ninety minutes because he had to. "I spend half my day as Speaker of the House and the other half of the day as a mental health counselor," he would tell donors. "That's what the 118th Congress has been. We cannot be at odds with anyone. I spend so much time on the couch, just leaning in, like, 'How can we help you be successful and get you back on the team?'"

He viewed Greene, in particular, as more sympathetic to Putin than anyone else he knew. He would come home sometimes and joke with his wife: *Sure, you're supposed to bless those who persecute you, but every hour of every day?*

Johnson told Greene he believed the briefings were accurate: that Putin was a great threat who would steamroll across Europe after taking Ukraine.

"Have you seen a speech where he said that?" Greene pressed him, defending Putin. "Did they show you evidence of that?"

Moving forward with Ukraine aid would be the most consequential decision of Johnson's political career to date. It was true that he had voted against an earlier Ukraine aid package when he was a no-name Louisiana congressman, in part because it was fashionable to do so in his district and because it was essentially a messaging vote to signal to the White House that fiscally conservative Republicans wanted to see more information about a strategy and an endgame. The bill was certain to pass without him and he knew that.

But in private and since becoming Speaker, he had always expressed concerns about what would happen if Ukraine fell. The intelligence at the classified level had become "alarming," he told people, and he was personally convinced that Putin had the resources to take Kyiv, which would set him up near the border of Poland.

These concerns grew exponentially as he sat through security briefings and secure calls where NATO protocols were outlined for him, and the reality of the cost of putting some four hundred thousand U.S. troops on the Polish border set in.

"I think it's just made up," Greene challenged him at a Republican conference meeting where Johnson presented what the intelligence officials had told him.

"We can arrange a briefing for you," he said.

Greene never showed up to receive it. Nor did many of the other holdouts in his conference, which he found inconceivable and depressing.

In late April, Johnson finally announced that he was moving ahead despite the pressure campaign from Greene and having failed to convince the majority of House Republicans that it was the right thing to do. "I can make a selfish decision and do something that is different, but I'm doing here what I believe to be the right thing," he told reporters once he had publicly announced his decision to bring the bill to the floor for a vote. "To put it bluntly, I would rather send bullets to Ukraine than American boys."

The night before he brought the bill to the floor, Johnson and his wife stayed at the Pendry, a boutique hotel overlooking the Potomac River. Johnson spent most of that night in the living room of the hotel suite, praying.

"He was in turmoil," Kelly Johnson recalled. "He was just trying to find a way to make it all work. I went to sleep and things were not good." The Johnsons thought they had come to the end of the road. "We assumed we were done," Kelly Johnson said. "I was saying, 'Well, it's been great. It's been a nice but short little ride.' We thought we were going home."

On April 20, the House passed a $95 billion foreign aid package for Ukraine, Israel, and Taiwan. The vote in favor of aid to Ukraine was 311 to 112, with a majority of Republicans opposing it. (In addition to the 112 Republicans who voted against it, 1 voted "present.") Speaker Johnson was stunned by the number of holdouts who took one of the most consequential votes of their lives having refused his pleas to at least sit through an intelligence briefing before voting to oppose the package.

"I was convinced that if everyone had access to the information I had, it would change their minds," Johnson said. "I pushed it as far as I could, and we got the vote tally as high as we could."

In the modern-day Republican Party, Johnson's decision to do the bare minimum required of his job—bring to the floor a critical piece of legislation that had the needed votes—could pass for a remarkable moment.

Strange new respect poured in from around the world. Richard Branson, the English business magnate, sent an email full of praise for the new Speaker. Israeli prime minister Benjamin Netanyahu called him with congratulations. The decision left McConnell impressed and somewhat hopeful. "I'm optimistic that he's evolved from being a red-state congressman to being the Speaker," he said.

Greene, however, was unenthused and in a box. She had started needling Johnson a month earlier, filing a resolution calling for his removal after he pushed through a $1.2 trillion bipartisan spending bill. At the time, she called the resolution "more of a warning than a pink slip" and left Johnson some room to negotiate with her—and some weeks to keep the "will she or won't she?" spotlight trained on herself.

With McCarthy gone and no one in leadership paying her any special attention, she resumed a posture that felt more like her and went right back to where she had been when she first arrived in Washington: being a provocateur and the subject of derision by Republican colleagues who now also counted on her for fundraising help.

The problem that Greene posed for her colleagues was that there was no political downside for her in trying to oust Johnson, even with everyone from Donald Trump and Jim Jordan to Kevin McCarthy privately urging her to stand down. The more extreme Greene was, the more popular she became in her deep-red district in Georgia. Trump-loving voters loved their Marjorie, and she had some reputation building to do after having been kicked out of the House Freedom Caucus.

She fed off the hate she received from Democrats and "RINOs." "Trump is a rapist!" a heckler yelled at Greene while she campaigned in Goochland, Virginia, trying to unseat Bob Good, the chairman of the House Freedom Caucus who was seen as insufficiently loyal to Trump because he had made the political error of endorsing Ron DeSantis.

"Biden is a rapist," Greene shot back without missing a beat. "Ask Tara

Reade." (During the 2020 campaign, Reade, a former Senate aide to Biden, accused him of sexual assault. Biden said the incident never happened. Reade later applied for Russian citizenship, claiming she felt safer there.)

Jordan thought he could get through to Greene to stand down when it came to Johnson. When the House Freedom Caucus had voted to expel her after her public "little bitch" fight with Lauren Boebert, Jordan had been one of just two members who urged the caucus to keep her. He thought she might listen to him. "I don't know how this helps us, six months before an election, when we're trying to win the White House," he privately pleaded with her.

That April, just a month earlier, Jordan had told Greene he felt confident that Trump was going to win back the White House and that Republicans would take back control of the Senate. "The only thing that makes me a little nervous is, could we somehow lose the House?" he had said. "Let's don't make it a chance." Trump, meanwhile, made it clear that he was no longer in the mood for more theatrics from the House that could damage his campaign.

But being called "Moscow Marjorie" by her House Republican colleagues and the *New York Post* now just played into Greene's hand. She was back in with Steve Bannon, who gave her a full, uninterrupted forty-five minutes on *War Room* after she announced that she would move forward with her plans to oust Johnson. "It's a brilliant move," he said, commending her, arguing that she was "giving original, pure Trump."

Greene would return the favor, joining Bannon in Danbury, Connecticut, to rally support just before he headed to his minimum-security prison to serve a four-month sentence for contempt of Congress. (He had defied a subpoena to testify before the January 6 Committee because he thought the committee was a sham.) The prison sentence, which began July 1, would take Bannon off the air and out of the mix until just days before the election. To him, this was no coincidence.

His plan was to come back more powerful than ever, a possibly svelter hero to his followers, someone who had suffered personally for the cause. "I served on a Navy destroyer in my twenties in the North Arabian Sea and Persian Gulf," Bannon said. "I'm serving in prison in my seventies. Not a bad bookend."

But to remove a Speaker, Greene needed more than just a handful of Republicans to support her. She needed Democrats to also want that Speaker gone, and Democrats viewed the nascent Johnson speakership much differently than they had viewed McCarthy's.

Top Democrats like Hakeem Jeffries, Katherine Clark, and Pete Aguilar had worked to create an environment to make the hesitant Johnson jump in and bring the Ukraine bill to the floor. Some of them viewed Johnson as slow, over his head in the job, and deeply indecisive. But he had never lied to them. Jeffries and Johnson, in fact, had immediately established a rapport, in part because of their faith: Jeffries, who'd grown up in the Cornerstone Baptist Church, was also deeply religious.

Publicly, Jeffries tarred Johnson as representing the worst of House Republicans. On television, he accused Republicans of elevating an extreme MAGA election denier as their leader. Privately, as is often the case, things were friendlier.

"I thought you would go easier on me," Johnson said to Jeffries in their first meeting after he was elected Speaker.

"Mike, I didn't want to undermine your ability to get the job," Jeffries joked and said he remembered Johnson best from their shared work on the Judiciary Committee.

"Actually," Johnson replied, "I first remember you from Bible study. I remember you, and I remember the passage of Scripture you made reference to."

Jeffries was impressed. He had visited the weekly congressional Bible study group back in 2017 as a favor to one of the few Democrats who attended regularly, and chose his favorite passage of Scripture, Luke 8:23–26, to read and discuss. He had spoken about how the passage used the word *squall,* which was different from *storm,* which is preceded by warning signs. In life and in politics, Jeffries said, one had to be prepared to deal with squalls, which catch you by surprise.

Johnson felt a connection because both of them had lost their fathers. Johnson's father, a former firefighter who suffered a traumatic accident in 1984 in an explosion that left him with burns covering 80 percent of his body, died in 2016. Jeffries's father, a former substance abuse counselor, died in December 2023.

The two men had started off on the right foot and stayed there. At the

Munich Security Conference that February, Rep. Mike Turner of Ohio, the Republican chairman of the Intelligence Committee, approached Jeffries with a suggestion. Johnson wants to pass Ukraine aid, Turner said, but it would help him get there if Democrats made it clear he wouldn't lose the speakership over it.

Jeffries took the suggestion back to his leadership team, arguing that extraordinary times called for extraordinary measures.

Plus, there was the dysfunction and chaos that come from ousting a Speaker. Again. Congress was already deeply unpopular with the American public. Democrats had a number of members from purple districts who didn't want every town hall meeting back home taken over by questions about more congressional chaos.

"Of course, it hurts them more," Aguilar told his colleagues about the political calculus of a leaderless, chaotic House. "But at some point, it's just too much—devolving into this again."

On a Wednesday afternoon in early May, after weeks of dangling her threat, Greene rose to introduce her motion to oust the Speaker. The chamber erupted in boos from Democrats and Republicans alike. It was the moment she had been waiting for.

Wearing a black dress with a pair of red glasses perched on her nose, she looked like a disappointed schoolteacher as she pointed to both sides of the chamber. "This is the uniparty, for the American people watching."

Greene took her shot and failed when Democrats voted with all but 11 Republicans to quickly kill her motion, but there was no real way for her to lose. In a post on Truth Social backing Johnson and encouraging Republicans to stick together, Trump's first words were "I absolutely love Marjorie Taylor Greene." Hardly a sign that her position in the MAGA-controlled party was at risk.

Johnson now owed Democrats his speakership and would spend the next six months filling his own red meat tank, which was, once again, empty.

I hope the young women get
the justice they deserve.

—KEVIN McCARTHY

A T THE REPUBLICAN NATIONAL CONVENTION IN MILWAUKEE IN JULY 2024, McCarthy was being interviewed on the floor of the Fiserv Forum by CNN's Kaitlan Collins when Matt Gaetz burst into the middle of the live shot. The two hadn't seen each other in person in months, and the country, for the most part, had moved on to bigger matters—like the fact that Trump had been shot at a campaign rally in Butler, Pennsylvania, and Democrats were trying to push Biden to step aside. But these two seemed trauma bonded.

"What night are you speaking?" Gaetz heckled McCarthy, who did not have a speaking slot and was there mostly to schmooze with Trumpworld figures he might work with in the future and do television hits trashing Gaetz. "If you took that stage, you would get booed off of it."

Here they were at the RNC, about to nominate the man they had both supplicated themselves to as the party's presidential nominee, and they couldn't move on from their feud, which was remarkable mostly for the fact that it was still going. At this late stage, it was hard to know who was demeaning himself more by keeping the beef alive—the ousted Speaker who hadn't moved on or the rank-and-file congressman who had won but seemed to have derived no lasting satisfaction from it. They almost seemed to need each other.

"He looks very unhinged. I mean a lot of people have concerns about him," McCarthy said in a follow-up CNN hit. "I'm not sure if he was on something, but I do hope he gets the help that he needs." What really worried him, he said, wearing a somber expression, were the underage women Gaetz had allegedly had sex with. "I hope the young women get the justice they deserve when it comes to him."

McCarthy got a taste of justice when Gaetz took the stage for his five-minute speaking slot later that week looking like a Las Vegas version of himself. His always-raised eyebrows appeared even more arched and longer. His cheeks were contoured, creating a different face shape, a pear, the skin tight and shiny. His new look became an instant meme, hashtagged under "FillerQueen."

"Matt Gaetz (R-Botox)," journalist Peter Hamby tweeted.

Gaetz's bizarre appearance was so distracting that it was impossible to listen to anything he said. In a Trumpian world where appearance was everything, this counted as a mild disaster. McCarthy couldn't have come up with a better revenge if he had tried—and he had tried. Gaetz was the talk of the convention.

"He does love makeup," Lauren Boebert said when she was shown a picture of him.

"What the fuck was he thinking?" members texted one another.

"We need to find out who the makeup artist is," one McCarthy ally joked to the former Speaker.

McCarthy and Gaetz were an entertaining sideshow at this point. After Gaetz crushed his McCarthy-backed challenger in the primary, beating him by forty-five points, he noted on X that the only thing the McCarthy revenge tour had achieved was "raising my margin of victory." It was the end, for this cycle, but surely not the last time these two would tussle. McCarthy was still bent on making sure Gaetz could never rise to higher office, like governor of Florida, and that he would get justice one day through the release of the report by the House Ethics Committee, which was still investigating allegations of sexual misconduct and drug use.

While they acted out their personal feud, one of the bigger questions hanging over the Milwaukee convention, aside from whether Trump would win back the White House, was whether Republicans would be able to keep control of the House. With Democrats in despair over Biden's walking-dead candidacy, it suddenly looked possible, even probable, that Republicans could win everything: the White House, the Senate, and the long-shot House.

Johnson, who had once thought of himself as a caretaker Speaker, was now planning on staying in the job for another Congress. Trump and his transition team spoke to him often of the cabinet post of attorney general ("He doesn't know a lot of constitutional law attorneys," Johnson would tell people), but the pressure of that job sounded worse to him than the pressure he was under as Speaker, the job he now wanted to keep.

The one scenario he spent a lot of time thinking about and hoping to avoid: the position he might be in if Republicans maintained control of the House and Trump lost the election. He played it off with humor. "Of course I wouldn't help certify that election!" he joked to people—a joke that didn't always land right since he had, in fact, played a leading role in trying to overturn the election results in 2020. But on a more serious note, he said: "I have thought a lot about the potential scenarios. And I'm going to do the right thing. As you know, I've been under pressure before. I certainly hope we have an election outcome free of controversy."

Johnson ultimately never had to cross that bridge: Trump won the electoral college and the popular vote decisively. This election outcome was terrifying to many Democrats, but it was free of controversy. In a meeting at the White House a week after the election, Biden promised Trump that his administration would do "everything we can to make sure you're accommodated."

If there was one policy issue that Democrats thought would help them win control of the House in 2024, it was abortion. When abortion rights were on the ballot, Democrats had won in every election since the overturning of *Roe*. The party spent one hundred million dollars in swing districts on ads framing Republicans as abortion extremists. It was a strong card, but it was their only card.

Johnson, a true believer when it came to outlawing abortion, was politically savvy enough not to press the issue. He even joined the large chorus of Republicans who claimed they supported unrestricted in vitro fertilization, though he, like most of them, had co-sponsored legislation that could severely curtail or even outlaw aspects of the procedure.

The truth was that Republicans were stuck in a bind, struggling to reconcile their party's hard-line policies, which were grounded in conservative religious doctrine, with the reality that the vast majority of the electorate viewed the issue differently. They dealt with this by pretending to support access to contraception and IVF, introducing legislation that purported to protect those rights but that actually did nothing to expand protections. These bills were tiny fig leaves designed to protect them from their most unpopular positions, which they were stuck with because the powerful anti-abortion forces still held so much sway in their party. Republicans who were previously on the record for abortion bans hid behind placid statements about "allowing the voters to decide," hoping to disappear the issue from national elections and leave it in the hands of statehouses.

California Rep. Michelle Steel, one of the first Korean American women elected to Congress, represented the most egregious example of how Republicans were flailing on the issue that year. Steel, an immigrant who represented Orange County, was the kind of GOP recruit whom McCarthy liked to tout as the new face of the party—an Asian woman who was seen as reasonable enough to win in a district that had elected Biden in 2020. People like Steel were supposed to be the "majority makers," in McCarthy parlance, the ones who demonstrated that Republicans could win everywhere.

In 2021, like the vast majority of her colleagues, Steel had co-sponsored the Life at Conception Act, but as a vulnerable Republican up for reelection in 2024, she was notably not listed as a co-sponsor when the bill was brought up again two years later. The bill was particularly problematic for her—California voters weren't worried that their state would outlaw abortion, which made them that much more concerned about a nationwide ban like the one Steel had previously supported.

In January 2024, when we called her office requesting an explanation for her change of position for a story in *The New York Times,* Steel panicked. Worried that she would be portrayed as a flip-flopper, she impulsively added her name as a co-sponsor of the legislation just hours ahead of the story's publication. A month later, the Alabama Supreme Court ruled that frozen embryos should be considered children, putting IVF treatments in jeopardy.

In reaction to the shocking ruling, Steel was one of the vulnerable Republicans who quickly ran to social media to post her support for IVF and to note that she herself had relied on the procedure to start her own family. Her post was quickly flagged by X as fact-challenged, given her co-sponsorship of the Life at Conception Act, which could severely restrict IVF treatments.

In March, Steel surprised everyone by announcing on the House floor that she was withdrawing her name as a co-sponsor of the bill. "I'm removing myself from the bill because it could create confusion about my support for the blessings of having children through IVF," she said.

Yes, her position was confusing, but it wasn't the bill's fault. In the span of three months, Steel held three different positions on a single issue, and it all reeked of desperation. Steel would go on to lose by just a handful of votes, but it brought little solace to Democrats. With Trump at the top of the ticket making gains with almost every demographic group across the country, Republicans managed to keep control of the House with almost the identical wafer-thin majority that had made their lives so difficult for two years.

Ballot measures protecting abortion rights won in seven states, including three that Trump won. Voters still cared about it, but control of the House was ultimately determined not by an issue or how its leaders had wielded their power but by larger political winds. And those favored Trump.

House Democrats cheered themselves by noting that they had outperformed the top of the ticket by a larger margin than in any presidential election cycle since 2004. But that was a hard statistic for many people to rejoice about when Republicans had won the trifecta of the House, the Senate, and the White House.

Still, House Democrats had kept the margin low enough to assume they would win it back in two years, when they could once again act as a check on Trump. They had kept the Republican majority so small that it was likely to be as divided and dysfunctional as ever. And this time, the Republicans would not be able to blame a Democratic-controlled Senate if they failed to produce legislative wins.

You go down in American history as one of the darkest figures.

—CHUCK SCHUMER

CHUCK SCHUMER WAS SITTING IN THE FOYER OF BIDEN'S BEACH HOUSE in Rehoboth, tired and tense. He had not slept the night before, and on the four-hour drive from Brooklyn to Delaware, he had rehearsed out loud what he planned to say, reviewing his notecards as he prepared for what was perhaps the most high-stakes speech he would ever give in his career, to be delivered to an audience of one.

It was July 13, 2024, a humid summer afternoon just before four o'clock, and from the other room, Schumer could hear the president's voice.

Biden was shouting.

Schumer was told that the president was finishing up a Zoom call with a group of House Democrats. Biden had been doing calls like this one with various factions of the party who were concerned about his viability as a candidate against Trump and were challenging him to his face, and his back was up. This was exactly the kind of scenario Schumer had been hoping to avoid for the past three weeks: the famously stubborn Biden feeling cornered and digging in even more.

But here they were. By the time he greeted Schumer and led him to a screened-in porch overlooking a pond, the president's anger had faded. They were alone, as Schumer had requested when he demanded this meeting days earlier. He had debated requesting that Biden's wife, Jill, join them, but she was on the road campaigning, and he had ultimately decided what he had to say to the president that afternoon was a message best delivered one-on-one.

Biden pointed out the local landmarks and told Schumer about the work he had done to protect the wetlands surrounding the pond they looked out on from his porch.

"I know how you feel, Mr. President," Schumer said. "Whenever I can go to any little corner of New York and there's something I did for it, I feel so good about it. And you, with all your years, you must feel that twenty times over."

Biden beamed as they sat down.

Now for the hard part.

For months, Schumer had been concerned that Biden was going to lose to Trump, and in so doing, lose Democratic control of the Senate and the chance to win back the House. It wasn't that he thought Biden was not capable of the job: The two men spoke about once a week, and, sure, the president rambled, but he had always rambled; and, yeah, once in a while he would forget why he had called him, but no matter, Schumer thought. He was convinced Biden could do the job. But with the Republican messaging machine not allowing Democrats to focus on attacking Trump, Schumer thought the barrier of Biden's age was too much to overcome in an election.

Still, the Senate majority leader felt he was in a box: If he tried to do anything about it—convene a group to discuss other options, make any calls, express his discontent in any semi-private way—it would probably leak out, only weakening the president even more. So, he had chosen to do nothing.

This made Biden's disastrous debate performance on June 27 something of a gift, a forcing mechanism to start the discussions about the president's viability that Schumer had been desperate to have for months. And it had led him here, more than two long weeks later, to this difficult task of telling the president to his face that he needed to step aside.

The sole debate between Biden and Trump had fallen on the evening before the last day of votes for the House, the day before lawmakers were set to travel home for the week of the Fourth of July. In Washington, several dozen members, including Hakeem Jeffries, rented apartments in the same building, which they referred to as "the dorm," and that evening, a group of about twenty-five lawmakers had gathered in the dorm's community room for a debate watch party.

Most of them were looking forward to a festive evening, much the way excited Democrats had gathered in living rooms across the country on Election Night 2016 to witness the ascension of Hillary Clinton as the country's first woman president. Biden's campaign had pressed for the atypical pre-convention debate, and lawmakers headed into the evening feeling confident that the matchup would help a tight race open up in their favor.

All three House Democratic leaders—Jeffries, Clark, and Aguilar—attended the watch party. But the festive mood dissipated immediately after a pale and hoarse Biden shuffled onto the stage in Atlanta. This was not the capable president they had cheered on at the State of the Union address a few months earlier. Standing next to Trump onstage was a stiff old man who whispered his answers, which sometimes made no sense.

"I support *Roe v. Wade,* which had three trimesters," Biden said. "The first time is between a woman and a doctor. Second time is between a doctor and an extreme situation. A third time is between the doctor, I mean, it'd be between the women and the state."

At one point, Biden stated, inexplicably, "We finally beat Medicare."

At another point, Trump turned to the moderators to note, "I really don't know what he said at the end of that sentence. I don't think he knows what he said, either." And that was that.

Democrats at the watch party winced. It was a line Biden should have been delivering about Trump, not vice versa. The mood was grim.

"I think I might be losing my race now," one vulnerable member said to Aguilar, about ten minutes into the debate. Aguilar put his hand on his colleague's shoulder. There wasn't much to say.

"A train wreck in motion," someone else whispered.

Others simply left early.

By the end of the ninety-minute session, those who had stayed were in a full-blown panic, and they approached Jeffries to ask what could be done about what they viewed as a potentially insurmountable disaster.

Jeffries had a motto that he often shared with his caucus throughout the screwball year, "Calm is an intentional decision," and he tried to channel it that night, even as his own internal alarm bells were ringing. "We've got to process it all, see where we're at tomorrow morning, and we'll come up with a game plan," he told them.

Schumer had much the same message for the donors he happened to be with the night of the debate, when he attended a fundraiser in California. "We'll have to see," he told them vaguely. For his part, what he also wanted to see was polling in red states where Democratic senators like Jon Tester and Sherrod Brown were struggling to hold on.

But many powerful people had seen enough.

That night, Schumer's famous flip phone started ringing, and it wouldn't stop for days. Donors, members, union bosses, and even strangers were calling him, pleading with him to tell Biden to get out of the race.

"You don't remember me," said one caller who had tracked down Schumer's home phone number. "We were together in Harvard, class of seventy-one. I got your number from the book. Please, get him to step down." (At his fiftieth college reunion, Schumer had listed his home phone number in the reunion yearbook, he now remembered. No one had ever dug it up until now.)

Shawn Fain, the president of the powerful United Auto Workers union, called Schumer to vent that he had been trying to reach Biden directly, but Biden's top aides would not allow him to speak with the president. Donors started sending Schumer unsolicited ten-page plans of how an open convention would work. (Donors, bless their hearts, always seemed to have a ten-page plan at the ready with details about how to fix everything.)

Schumer had one simple message for everyone who called him. "Do not be public," he told them. "That will get his back up, and you've got to let the dust settle. But if you can, call whoever you know in the campaign, call the White House. Let them know how you feel."

Members weren't sure they agreed with his cautious approach. Some of them openly wrestled with the question of whether they had an obligation to go public and whether they would be complicit in electing Trump if they didn't force Biden out of the race. Jamie Raskin of Maryland chose at first to go the private route, sending a letter to Biden on July 6 in which he wrote, "There is no shame in taking a well-deserved bow to the overflowing appreciation of the crowd when your arm is tired out, and there is real danger for the team in ignoring statistics." Steve Ricchetti assured Raskin that the president and the First Lady had both read his letter and that Biden planned to call him. But Biden never called. "I did expect to hear from him," Raskin said. "He called me not infrequently during impeachment." After the private route didn't seem to move the needle, Raskin released his letter publicly.

Schumer saved his frank conversations for Jeffries and former President Barack Obama, who both agreed that this was a five-alarm crisis for the party. But they also agreed that doing anything publicly needed to be very carefully thought through. They were still in a box.

Publicly, Jeffries and Schumer calmly and robotically reiterated their support for Biden. "I'm with Joe" was all that Schumer would say in public, hoping that people would read between the lines and note all the enthusiasm he was *not* bringing to that terse statement. "President Biden, as I've said repeatedly, is our nominee," Jeffries asserted, sticking with the simple stating of undeniable facts. "He has a tremendous track record of success."

This was not exactly what Jeffries thought was in store for him when he took over as leader back in January 2023. "When you're in the minority, there's not much for you to do," Rep. Richard Neal of Massachusetts, the top Democrat on the Ways and Means Committee, assured Jeffries after the latter took over from Nancy Pelosi. "You'll have time to get comfortable with the job without any pressure or decision making." Neal's words rang in his ears as Jeffries looked over a calendar filling up with calls and meetings with members pressuring him to tell a president who was old enough to be his father to step aside. Over the past eighteen months, Jeffries had led House Democrats as they played a critical role in stopping government shutdowns, avoiding a catastrophic default on the national debt, saving a Republican Speaker, and aiding Ukraine. Now his members were clamoring to force the sitting president off the ticket. What else could possibly be thrown at him?

Jeffries decided to follow the advice he had given his own caucus after McCarthy was ousted. "This is just not going to get easier," he said then. "We're in a moment of extraordinary events. The only thing you can do is lean into the principle that calm is an intentional decision." In this case, he decided that rushing was not the right thing to do, and Schumer agreed.

Meanwhile, their members and the press were hyperventilating. Their concerns were based not so much on district-specific polling as on deep

reservations they had been stifling for months. The president's poor debate performance had simply hardened their views around the age question, and many members told Jeffries there was now simply no way to
overcome it.

Rep. Adam Smith of Washington state, the top Democrat on the
Armed Services Committee, pulled Aguilar aside. "Look," he said, "I'm
doing press on this. I just need to stress how important this is. This is bad.
This is a whole new level of bad."

Even some members who were publicly supportive of Biden were ad-
vocating against him behind the scenes, pressing party leaders: "What are
you going to do about this?"

Nancy Pelosi, who had been friends with Biden for fifty years, was not
originally part of the group of lawmakers who arrived at the immediate
conclusion that the president had to go. "He's got to show us a plan and
figure out how to get through this," she told members in the days after the
debate. She said she had faith that he would. She would later conclude
that Biden had to step aside for the sake of the party, but throughout, she
acted as a free agent, communicating very little with Jeffries or Schumer
about what there was for Congress to do and sharing little with either
about her plans to speak to the president, or what she planned to say to
him. She operated as a rogue agent, at one point going on *Morning Joe,*
Biden's regular morning watch, to say: "It's up to the president to decide
if he is going to run. We're all encouraging him to make that decision,
because time is running short." For Pelosi, his decision would not be final
until it was a decision she agreed with.

On June 28, the night after the debate, Jeffries was scheduled to par-
ticipate in a congressional fundraiser in New York City, where he was set
to interview Obama in a "fireside chat" setting; they would take no questions from donors. The two met for a thirty-minute dinner together
ahead of the event. "Let's address it right up at the top," Obama suggested.

Onstage, they tried to calm nervous Democrats. "President Biden had
a rough night," Jeffries said. "It's clearly a setback for his campaign. But I
grew up in a Baptist church, and we believe a setback is nothing but a
setup for a comeback. How do we come back from this?"

Obama offered a version of what he had said publicly: that bad debates happen and that this one had greatly complicated the situation moving forward, but that Democrats had to find a way to power through it.

They were, essentially, stalling for time.

Meanwhile, Jeffries spoke regularly with Ricchetti and Jeff Zients, the White House chief of staff, trying to communicate to them his view that Harris would be a superior candidate to Biden. "We don't have data at this moment," Jeffries told them. "But the most powerful narrative in American politics is change. Vice President Harris would represent change."

He laid out to them his theory of the case. "JFK was the change candidate, he wins. Jimmy Carter, one-term governor, peanut farmer, Sunday school teacher, in the middle of Watergate, change candidate, he wins. Bill Clinton, change candidate, he wins. Barack Obama, certainly a change candidate, he wins. President Biden represented change in 2020 because he represented decency, consistency, and integrity."

"I'm reporting everything you're saying to me to the president," Ricchetti assured him. But, he told Jeffries, the White House simply had a different perspective. "We can get through it," Ricchetti said. "We think our allies on the Hill are wrong." In other conversations with lawmakers, he would tell them, "We know there are people concerned, and we know there are situations where members have to take different positions because of their districts, but he's running."

On July 3, Biden called Schumer. It sounded like he was reading off a script: "I'm still in the race," he assured the Senate majority leader, who wasn't yet ready to tell him he needed to go.

"Mr. President," Schumer said, "the only way you're going to save this is to show up day in and day out, with unscripted town halls. And people will be able to smell if it's spontaneous, and it will show that this was a one-off."

Ricchetti assured Schumer that Biden was going to put doubters at ease when he participated in a press conference after the NATO summit being held in Washington the following week. But Schumer was not at ease. "That's not even close to good enough," he fumed at Ricchetti. Schumer had just found out from press reports that Biden was using a teleprompter to speak at thirty-person fundraisers. "First-term people running for Congress with no experience don't need teleprompters in the room!" he yelled at Ricchetti. "No more!"

He also told Ricchetti that Tester and Brown, two senators (from Montana and Ohio, respectively) who were the most vulnerable Democrats up for re-election, were concerned about their own races if Biden stayed in.

"I've talked to them," Ricchetti reassured him. "They're with the president."

Schumer balked. "That's not what they're telling me," he said.

Still, Schumer held back members who wanted to publicly call on Biden to step aside, even though he didn't disagree with their assessment. He called Sen. Joe Manchin of West Virginia and urged him not to publicly pressure Biden on one of the Sunday shows. He told Sen. Mark Warner of Virginia to stand down on a meeting Warner wanted to host when the Senate returned to discuss their options. He told Sen. Brian Schatz of Hawaii not to write a public letter calling on Biden to get out of the race.

"It'll just make it worse," he told all of them, "and we're not ready."

As days ticked by and it looked like Democrats were doing nothing, Obama was pushing to do more. But he was aware of how delicate the situation was, how easily any pressure from any of them, particularly him, could backfire with a stubborn Biden, and how they only had one shot to get through to him.

He told Schumer that he himself had a fragile relationship with his former vice president, who still carried a chip on his shoulder over Obama's decision to support Hillary Clinton's candidacy in 2016; Obama had urged him not to run then. Obama told Schumer that he wasn't sure if he was the best messenger to tell Biden to step aside. "You may be a better one," he said.

Still, Schumer hesitated, arguing that the president still needed more time.

On July 8, the Monday the House and the Senate both returned to Washington after the holiday break, Biden greeted them with a defiant letter telling them in clear terms that he was running and that he wanted them all to shut the hell up. "The question of how to move forward has been well-aired for over a week now," he wrote. "And it's time for it to end."

If the purpose of the letter was to close the discussion about Biden's political future, it had the opposite effect. Democrats on Capitol Hill read the letter and seethed. "Don't do letters," Schumer told them. "We've still got to let it bubble, we got to let it sink in with the president."

But the anger was becoming harder to contain. In a closed-door lunch that Tuesday, Senate Democrats stood up and accused the president of being selfish. They questioned whether he had written the letter himself or whether his staff or maybe even his son Hunter had written it for him.

That night, the first senator to break Schumer's "do nothing" edict, Pete Welch of Vermont, called him to let him know that he had an op-ed running the next morning in *The Washington Post* calling on Biden to step aside. "You shouldn't have done that," Schumer told him bluntly.

On the phone the following day, Schumer told Ricchetti he needed to send the palace guard to address the Senate caucus. "I am not asking, I am telling you. I want Mike Donilon, you, Anita Dunn, and Jen O'Malley Dillon," he said, referring to Biden's top messaging gurus and campaign manager. "If we don't have this meeting, I cannot hold my members back anymore. You're going to get half my caucus to sign a letter saying he should step down."

Schumer didn't trust Donilon, Ricchetti, or Dunn as far as he could throw them. But he viewed O'Malley Dillon as one of the few senior people on Biden's team who was actually trying to convey the truth to the president. Schumer wanted her there as a reality check on the rest of them, someone to hold the palace guard accountable.

The meeting was granted, but only after so much resistance that Schumer had to threaten that he would ask for it publicly if the White House did not comply. "If you guys can't have a meeting with your top staff, with your Democratic senators, then this is so over," he yelled.

The July 10 meeting marked a turning point in the relationship between the Biden White House and the Senate caucus, which erupted on the president's top-level aides in full force.

"I cannot support Joe Biden unless he brings two neurologists independently to issue a public report and then have a press conference where anyone can ask questions about the report," said Sen. Jack Reed of Rhode Island, a stunning statement from a West Point graduate and former paratrooper who was essentially saying he could no longer support his commander in chief.

Sen. Sheldon Whitehouse of Rhode Island rose to say he had deep reservations about how Biden's campaign was being conducted, and he stated bluntly that Harris would be a better candidate. He told the Biden aides in the room that the message the president needed to understand was that the silence from the majority of Democratic senators was not to be interpreted as any sign of tacit support. "This was respect and affection while he came to the right decision," Whitehouse said, "but it won't last forever, because they would be lying. And right now, I'm not being truthful with Rhode Island political leaders about what I think, for that reason."

One of the only people in the room who spoke up to defend Biden was John Fetterman. "We've got to be for Joe Biden," he said. Turning to his colleagues, he told them, "You have no spine."

After the meeting, Schumer pulled Fetterman aside for a rare scolding. "You can always express what you think in our caucus, but don't ever tell our members they have no spine," he said. "It's not effective for you and not fair to them."

The Biden palace guard left that day cowed by what they had heard. Donilon, Ricchetti, and O'Malley Dillon relayed the exchanges to Dunn, who had not attended the meeting.

"There was very little support for the president staying in the race within that room, although there were a lot of people who said that they were not going to say that publicly," Dunn recalled of the message sent from Senate Democrats.

Still, the president remained publicly and privately dug in.

After spending weeks simply listening to his members, Jeffries decided the time had come to request a one-on-one meeting with the president to convey their deep concerns. He had concluded that he would stop short of telling Biden, point-blank, to step aside. But the cautious new leader decided to use the word *irretrievable* to describe the state of the House of Representatives if the president decided to carry on with his re-election campaign.

Jeffries was more understanding than many of his colleagues about why Biden and his top aides would be skeptical of the mounting pressure on him from donors, lawmakers, and pundits to step aside. He didn't view it as pure selfishness or simply an inability to let go of power. If he looked at the current situation through their eyes, he saw they had a point.

Biden had been discouraged from running for president in 2016, a race that in retrospect he would have been better suited for than Clinton was. In 2018, people again told him not to run, arguing even then that he was too old. But he jumped in and, lo and behold, defeated Trump in 2020. In 2022, he was told that his unpopularity would lead to a historic red wave in the House and Senate midterm elections. Instead, Democrats defied expectations by narrowly losing the House, winning all the governorships on the ballot, and picking up a seat in the Senate.

Jeffries thought the data points were strong, and he didn't dismiss them. The challenge lay in convincing Biden and his team that this situation was different from all those others, when the elites and the political chattering class had underestimated them.

Before Jeffries's meeting with Biden, he met with his leadership team to discuss his strategy. Aguilar had a list of five points he encouraged Jeffries to make to the president. The fifth was the most dire: "It's the unanimous view of the House Democratic leadership that proceeding will be terminal to our efforts to achieve the majority.

"We will be forced to spend on safe races, previously safe districts, and our offensive targets will evaporate," Aguilar had written.

Biden and Jeffries met on Thursday night after Biden's NATO press conference. For more than an hour, they huddled together in the White House residence, alone. Jeffries walked the president through the concerns of his members and used that carefully selected word, *irretrievable,* to describe the House.

Biden listened, but he argued that he could still win. At least now the Democratic leaders in Congress knew that he had been briefed in detail on what House Democrats thought of his ongoing candidacy. But it was not clear it had had the desired effect, and pressure was rising. Sen. Patty Murray, a senior Democrat from Washington state, informed Dunn she planned to release on the following Monday a letter signed by twenty senators demanding Biden step aside.

With pressure mounting, Schumer was up next to try his luck with Biden.

Two days after Jeffries's meeting, on the screened-in porch in Rehoboth Beach, Delaware, as the two got down to business, Schumer delivered to Biden the detailed blow-by-blow of what every senator had said in the meeting with the president's top staff.

The president was wide-eyed, leading Schumer to believe that those top aides had never debriefed him themselves.

"If there's a secret ballot, Mr. President," Schumer told him, "my guess is you at most get five yeses."

"Really?" Biden responded.

"I know my caucus," Schumer told him. "You know I know my caucus."

Biden nodded.

Now, the speech he had been preparing himself for. "Mr. President, some people go into politics for the wrong motivation: to make money and have power. And some people go in for the right reasons: They want to leave a legacy," he said. "You're certainly one of those, and I hope I'm one of those.

"We've done so many things together," he told Biden. "We did the assault weapons ban and the Brady Law when I was in the House and you were higher up than me, but we were a team. We did the Violence Against Women Act. And in the Senate, we did even more.

"When you were president, we had the best session in thirty or forty years. This is what we've done together."

Biden nodded.

"Mr. President," Schumer said, "if I had to leave politics tomorrow for whatever reason, I would say to myself, *All the shit we take in this job was worth it for making the world a better place.* And your legacy is twenty times mine."

He went on: "If you run, and you lose to Trump, and we lose the Senate, and we don't get back the House, that fifty years of amazing, beautiful work goes out the window, but worse—you go down in American history as one of the darkest figures."

Biden was only listening, allowing him to go on.

As he watched the president's body language, Schumer convinced himself that Biden had *wanted* someone to tell him this, that he *knew* it all in his bones, but that he had been badly served by some of his staff.

"If you had a fifty percent chance of winning, I'd run if I were you," Schumer said. "Fifty-fifty, to do this, to stay here, it's worth it. But, Mr. President, you're not getting the information as to what the chances are. Your three pollsters, have they talked to you?"

Biden shook his head.

"Well, I have talked to them," Schumer told him, "because they're my pollsters, too. And I think I understand polling. My guess is you have about a five percent chance. None of your pollsters disagree with me."

He ended with the ask that no one had yet made as bluntly to Biden's face. "If I were you," Schumer said, "I wouldn't run, and I'm urging you not to run."

Only twice during his speech did Biden ask him a question, and twice it was the same question. "Do you really think Kamala can win?" he asked him.

"I don't know if she can win, but she has a lot better chance than you do," Schumer told him.

Biden revealed little of his own thinking. But he did not argue with Schumer, and he did not shout. "I need a week," was all he said.

After about forty-five minutes, Biden led Schumer back out of the house through a small elevator. In its cramped car, he put his hands on Schumer's shoulders. "You've got bigger balls than anyone I've ever met," he said.

The two embraced as Schumer headed back to his car, where he broke down in tears as he spoke to his top staff about what had just transpired. He didn't know what Biden would end up doing, he told them, but he felt he had gotten through to him.

Schumer was still in the car being driven back to Brooklyn at 6:11 P.M., when Trump was shot in the ear in an assassination attempt at a rally in Butler, Pennsylvania. For days, the attention shifted away from Schumer's much-anticipated meeting with the president and Biden's decision-making process. At their convention, Republicans rallied around Trump, feeling confident the White House was his again and that he had been saved by God. Trump selected as his running mate the far-right senator from Ohio JD Vance, who did nothing to help Trump expand his appeal beyond his base of bought-in supporters. Trump and his team just assumed Biden would stay in the race, in part because they couldn't fathom what was then taking place within the Democratic Party: an organized effort to push out their leader. They couldn't fathom it, in part, because something like it simply would never happen in the modern-day GOP.

Eight days after Schumer's meeting with him in Rehoboth, Biden dropped out.

On Sunday, July 21, Jeffries was getting ready to attend a church celebration in Brooklyn for the ninetieth birthday of former Rep. Ed Towns when his oldest son burst into the room to tell him that Biden had dropped out of the race.

"Wow," Jeffries responded, pulling out his phone to read the letter Biden had posted on social media.

The news was a shock to many lawmakers who assumed, by then, that Biden was not going anywhere, that the moment had passed, and that they needed to lean on their own networks to win their local races and forget all about the White House. When Biden's post appeared, many of them weren't sure if it was real.

Five minutes later, Biden called Jeffries to let him know that it was.

"Mr. President," Jeffries said, "it was an incredibly selfless decision that you made. I'm looking forward to working together over the next six months as you finish strong."

He hung up and breathed a sigh of relief. Biden had also quickly endorsed Harris, and Jeffries thought there was still a chance to win back the House.

At the Democratic National Convention a month later, where the party officially named Harris its presidential nominee, Schumer danced onto the stage. On his way out, he fist-bumped O'Malley Dillon, one of the few figures in Bidenworld he thought had acted like an honest and realistic broker throughout.

"We did this," he told her. But Schumer wasn't dancing or fist-bumping at the Democratic Senatorial Campaign Committee offices on Election Night as he watched everything fall apart. Sherrod Brown, the last standing Democrat to hold statewide office in Ohio, was defeated by former car salesman Bernie Moreno. In the red state of Montana, Jon Tester was defeated by another wealthy businessman and political novice, Tim Sheehy. In Pennsylvania, Sen. Bob Casey, a Democratic mainstay, was defeated by David McCormick, the former chief executive of Bridgewater, one of the world's largest hedge funds.

Schumer's Senate majority was gone, and, of course, so was the White

House. Trump was back in power, lifting with him Republican lawmakers in the House and Senate who would help enact his agenda. Jeffries was not going to be the next Speaker of the House. The drubbing of Democrats was so all-encompassing that there was little Monday-morning quarterbacking about any of the Harris campaign's tactical errors. There was no equivalent of bemoaning Hillary Clinton's decision not to visit Wisconsin during the 2016 campaign, or complaining that if only Harris had chosen Pennsylvania governor Josh Shapiro, the fate of the world would have been different. Sure, Trump won Pennsylvania—because he won all seven of the swing states. The country had spoken unequivocally, electing MAGA and Trump.

For all the Democratic recriminations, few spent any time second-guessing the decision to push Biden out of the race. The only part of that decision that drew scrutiny was why it had taken Schumer and the Democrats so long to get there.

32

When the Republican Party expels the turd of Donald Trump, it will go back to being the old Republican Party.

—CHUCK SCHUMER

NOBODY THINKS THAT DONALD TRUMP'S BRAND OF FEVERISH POPU-
lism and revenge politics was born in 2016, fully formed like Athena. The
downward spiral had taken root in the party long before Trump descended
that golden escalator.

Some see a direct link tying Trump to Sarah Palin, John McCain's
fringe-y running mate in 2008, who also played on a politics of resentment
and fear that was more about style than substance. Some blame the Tea
Party—with its nativist leanings and anti-establishment impulses, which
sprouted up in reaction to Barack Obama's presidency—for the current
crop of tear-it-all-down rabble-rousers wearing congressional pins today.
In trying to make sense of what happened to the GOP, some reach all the
way back to the 1950s, when Republican politicians began mining fear,
prejudice, and grievance to enliven the party's more extreme forces.

For Chuck Schumer, it all clicked during a 2013 dinner he had at the
Palm, a see-and-be-seen steakhouse in Northwest Washington. The meet-
ing held there would exemplify for him just how much the Republican
Party was being driven from the bottom up.

That year, Schumer and McCain, the Arizona senator who would die
in 2018, were pitching a bipartisan immigration reform bill. The plan
offered a pathway to citizenship for undocumented immigrants and a
"common-sense" approach to the 11 million undocumented immigrants
who already lived in America.

In trying to gin up Republican support for the bill, Schumer had asked

New York City mayor Mike Bloomberg to help set up a meeting for him with Rupert Murdoch at News Corporation headquarters in Midtown Manhattan. If he could get Fox News to support the bill, he thought, it would pass.

Roger Ailes, the former chairman of Fox News, attended the meeting and was more skeptical of the plan than Murdoch was. "I know what you want to do," Ailes told Schumer. "You want these eleven million people to be legalized so they all vote Democratic."

Schumer told him that under the plan, it would take some fifteen years for the first person to become a U.S. citizen. "Mr. Ailes," he said, "if Republicans haven't straightened out your problems with Hispanics by then, you've got a bigger problem."

Ailes wasn't convinced, but Murdoch liked the plan, so he kept his mouth shut. A few days after the meeting, Murdoch's team contacted Schumer's office and asked him to set up a meeting with some Republican senators supporting the bill, this time in Washington.

When Schumer, along with Lindsey Graham of South Carolina, arrived at the Palm, where caricatures of its most famous patrons line the walls, he found that Murdoch had also brought along a guest: Rush Limbaugh, the right-wing radio star with more than 15 million devoted listeners. Schumer sat on the side of Limbaugh's good ear and pitched the plan. Limbaugh said he would think on it.

The dispiriting but not wholly unsurprising answer came back a few days later: Limbaugh's "dittoheads," as the radio host called his hardcore fan base, would never go for his touting a pro-immigration bill after years of hearing him rail against immigrants and call them all criminals.

Without Limbaugh on board, Murdoch backed off. Fox News was not going to endorse a deal if Limbaugh was on the airwaves campaigning against it.

For Schumer, it was a sign of how the right operated. The dittoheads were a "no," so Limbaugh was a "no," so Murdoch was a "no," so the majority of the Republicans on Capitol Hill were a "no." The party was being led by the listeners who had fully bought into the baseless claims and toxic rumors peddled by Limbaugh, who felt he couldn't forsake his brand on the issue of immigration reform and, thereby, jeopardize his credibility and livelihood.

The dinner, and the subsequent failure of the immigration push, has haunted Schumer ever since. It all still resonates with him when he thinks about how we got here today.

"If you're a steelworker, and you lost your job and you're now flipping hamburgers, I get why you're angry," Schumer said, sitting with his shoes off in his Senate office one night in June 2023. It was a pleasant evening by Washington summer standards, following a day of judicial confirmations on the Senate floor, and the Senate majority leader was noshing on gluten-free crackers and serving what he called his "special white wine," one he later conceded he didn't know much about: It had been picked out by his wife. Trump had just been indicted for the second time, this time by the Justice Department over his handling of classified documents. Schumer didn't think it would matter one bit in the presidential election. On this point, he would be proven correct.

"Why is the New York City firefighter so fucking angry? He makes a hundred twenty-six thousand dollars; has a great pension, no healthcare costs; he lives on the South Shore of Long Island, has a nice house, safe neighborhood, nice schools. And he probably has a little bungalow in the Poconos where he can take his kid. Why is he so fucking mad?"

There was no good answer, Schumer conceded, but he had come up with one that satisfied him. "The world is changing because this techno-logical revolution is happening so damn fast, he doesn't know how to get a grip on it. His kids are drifting away from him. The old roots of family, community, religion are much less grounding. They don't want their kids to go to college, because they'll drift away from them."

He added: "Trump, who's an evil sorcerer, comes in, he says, 'I can get that old world back. I'm the only one who will stand up to them.' It's a working-class party, and all the indictments aren't going to matter."

Don Beyer, a Virginia Democrat who served as ambassador to Switzer-land and Liechtenstein during the Obama administration, had a similar assessment of the hardening of the right in politics, which he shared a year before the election. "When you get to the high school or less education level, people who have been completely displaced by globalization and technology, who feel very threatened by immigrants and people of color, and women, you have a lot of lost men," he said. "Men who have not figured out how to belong."

Beyer is a white guy in his seventies who gets along with Republicans—
or at least he used to. "I keep an Excel spreadsheet of my Republican
friends," he said in July 2023. "I have eighty-three right now." He also
keeps a list of former Republican friends, many moderates, who have left
Congress either because they lost their primaries to more extreme candidates or they didn't like the direction the party was heading; their names
had to be removed from the spreadsheet (Fred Upton, John Katko, Charlie
Dent, Scott Rigell, Jaime Herrera Beutler, and Liz Cheney, among others).
Then there are those who have stayed but undergone personality metamor-
phoses since Trump took over the party (Elise Stefanik, Tom Emmer).

"My greatest disappointment is Elise Stefanik, who should know better," Beyer said. "She was always a person I could talk to. I tried a number
of times to do bills with her. Then she went off the deep end."

It might feel inexplicable to watch Stefanik's transformation, but Beyer
is also clear-eyed about how hard it is to vary from either party line in a
media environment where cable news simply exaggerates the partisan split
and outside organizations punish lawmakers who stray. "When I presided
over the state Senate in Virginia, we had lots of Democrats who were pro-
gun and lots of Republicans who were anti-gun. And similarly on choice,"
he said. "Right now, we have one pro-life, anti-choice Democrat, Henry
Cuellar from Texas. There's been a real hardening of the positions on the
important things." (Cuellar was indicted in May 2024 on bribery and corruption charges.)

Beyer believes that the hardening of the right is much deeper than
Trump and that it predates him. And Beyer is far from alone in believing
that the problem in politics and in the country is bigger than one figure.
"There's something kind of rotten in the country today, a crisis of meaning, purpose, and identity," said Chris Murphy, the progressive Democrat
from Connecticut. "I don't think that's going away. It lends itself to dem-
agogic movements, to division, to destruction. I worry if we don't address
some of the unhealthy fundamentals in our culture and economy, it
doesn't go away."

Murphy was willing to entertain the Schumer theory of the case: that
the party would revert to its old self after Trump exited the political
scene. But he didn't buy it himself. "There are plenty of examples of so-
cieties captured by a singularly unique individual demagogue and that get

healthy after that person disappears," he said. "I don't know. I'm not as optimistic as he is. I worry there's a rot at the core of the country that will continue to be exposed politically."

Murphy was concerned by the new Republican senators who were coming in, the Josh Hawleys, the JD Vances, the young breed of MAGA. And his read on the electorate proved to be more aligned with reality than Schumer's, which proved to be blindly optimistic. The new Republican senators who arrived for orientation the week after the 2024 election were loyal to Trump. Democrats found themselves deep in the political wilderness as Trump tested his strength by selecting unqualified loyalists for top cabinet positions: Matt Gaetz for attorney general, and for defense secretary, Pete Hegseth, a *Fox & Friends* host who believed that women in the military should not serve in combat roles and who was accused of sexually assaulting a woman. (Hegseth insisted the interaction was consensual.)

If Schumer had seen any of it coming, he had not wanted to face it. "Here's my hope," he said that summer night. "After this election, when the Republican Party expels the turd of Donald Trump, it will go back to being the old Republican Party."

But the old Republican Party was leaving, and the new MAGA guard was staying—and that was happening with or without Trump. In January 2024, seeking an easier race, Lauren Boebert moved to a new district in the Colorado Plains, one that had gone for Trump in 2020 by double the margin of her old district. She managed to squeak by in a crowded Republican primary thanks in large part to her name recognition and that uncharacteristic decision to keep her powder dry on the vote to oust McCarthy. Having a rival could be motivating, and Boebert and Greene would have each other to kick around for another Congress. When she declared victory on Election Night, Boebert said that Republicans needed to "rally behind President Trump to secure his third term."

Marjorie Taylor Greene, for her part, wasn't going anywhere but up: Untouchable in her bloodred district, she knew she basically had tenure in the House. The idea of serving in Congress as a conduit to a Trump White House appealed to her. But there were some important statewide races back home coming up in 2026 that she was quietly keeping an eye on. "I don't know, I honestly don't know," she said about what came next. "I want to go somewhere where I can do a good job. I don't know what that is right now." She was rewarded with the chairmanship of a new subcommittee whose goal was to cut the federal government.

Ever since he lost the speakership, Jim Jordan had been in friend-making mode, campaigning and raising money for Republicans outside the Freedom Caucus, even for House Republicans who had opposed him, positioning himself for another run at the crown. With Republicans keeping control of the House, he didn't challenge Johnson for the top job right away. But he was lying in wait if an opportunity arose: Republican Speakers, after all, never lasted that long. James Comer, for his part, would land a deal for a book about his efforts to investigate alleged corruption in the Biden family.

Gaetz still had a serious ethics investigation trailing him. But he got around that problem after the election when Trump said he would nominate him as attorney general, an announcement that shocked Washington and had Gaetz's long list of detractors trying to assure one another that there was no way he could get confirmed. After the appointment, Gaetz promptly resigned from Congress—two days before the House Ethics Committee was set to vote on whether to release its damning report. His resignation put an end to both the investigation and any potential public release of the report. Senators were still demanding to see it as they considered whether or not they could vote to confirm Gaetz. But Johnson then did what McCarthy had long refused to do—he intervened to try to make sure the material on Gaetz never saw the light of day. Claiming that it was against the rules to release a report on a former member of Congress, Johnson "strongly requested" that the report never be released. He knew he could not stay on as Speaker without being in lockstep with Trump.

Most Republicans could not picture Gaetz actually serving as the nation's top law enforcement official. They assumed he was playing a face-saving game, using the attorney general nomination as an excuse to resign and thus put the ethics investigation to bed for good. They expected that his nomination would be withdrawn or that he would not get the votes necessary for confirmation, and then he could rail against the RINOs and the deep state that had blocked him while mounting a run for Florida governor—the job people assumed he actually wanted. They were right:

The day after meeting with Republican senators about his nomination, Gaetz posted online that he was withdrawing because he was becoming a "distraction." In search of a new platform from which he could monetize and proselytize, he promptly signed up for Cameo, like George Santos had before him, and then joined One America News Network as an anchor. For Gaetz, a platform was a platform was a platform.

Bannon was released from prison two days before Halloween, exactly one week before the election. He reported straight from prison in Connecticut to the Loews Regency hotel in Manhattan for a press conference, where he told reporters he had spoken that morning with Trump. "Nancy Pelosi thought a federal prison was going to break me," he said, looking tanner and slightly trimmer. "Well, it empowered me. I am more empowered today, more focused today, sharper today, in better shape today than I've ever been in my entire life. So, Nancy Pelosi, suck on that."

The future looked less rosy for the more mainstream Republicans. Garret Graves, once the right-hand man to the Speaker of the House, found he had no path to re-election after a new congressional map dismantled his district by making it majority Black. (Privately, Graves blamed Steve Scalise for playing a role in the re-drawing of the districts, but he couldn't prove it.) Graves had harbored ambitions to become the Natural Resources Committee chair, but now he was unceremoniously out of a job altogether—in part because of the enemies he made when he aligned with McCarthy. "On a personal note, I never would have been elected Speaker without @RepGarretGraves," McCarthy wrote on X after Graves announced his decision not to run. At least he had made a good friend.

Shortly after the House elected Johnson as Speaker in 2023, Patrick McHenry announced that his time in that body was done. As Financial Services chairman, he had moved a crypto regulation bill through the House and helped on the debt ceiling. He had gotten a taste of the speakership and decided that was enough for him. His season in Congress was over. "I don't look back at this place with any bitterness," he said. "I feel good about it." Privately, McHenry admitted that there were terrible actors in his party. But he tried to sound an optimistic note on his way out. "Evolutions are often lumpy and disjointed, but at each stage, new leaders emerge," he said. "I'm confident the House is in good hands."

Despite all facts to the contrary, it was a core belief of Schumer's that politics in America would recalibrate after Trump exited the stage. Driving through Brooklyn months before the shattering election cycle, Schumer repeated the sentiment. He was concerned about the vote for foreign assistance to Ukraine, which had passed the Senate 79–18 with 15 Republicans voting against it. "There are four or five who voted for it out of conviction," he said. "There are about fifteen who are Trumpies all the way. The other twenty-five in the middle, they basically agreed it's the right thing but were scared of Trump, and secondarily, they thought it would help Biden. Those people, if Trump is gone, will go back."

Schumer was bullish on everything, especially after Biden's dramatic exit from the race. He liked telling people that Robert Caro, the famed biographer of President Lyndon B. Johnson, had referred to him, Schumer, as the "Jewish LBJ." So, he let himself fantasize about Democrats winning everything—the White House, the Senate, and the dysfunctional House—and steamrolling through progressive legislation that would have him live up to the moniker. "The one thing I'd really like to do is immigration reform," he said. He was still thinking about the 2013 failure at the hands of the dittoheads. "If that bill had passed," he said, "the country would be a different place."

But it was never going to be that simple, because nothing ever is.

ACKNOWLEDGMENTS

———

*T*HE *NEW YORK TIMES* SOMETIMES HAS THE REPUTATION OF BEING A competitive snakepit. That has not been our experience of working with our deeply supportive congressional team. All reporting is a team sport, especially covering something as unwieldy as this Congress, and we could not have written this book without the revolving cast of players that we have been lucky to overlap with over the past few years: Catie Edmondson, Carl Hulse, Karoun Demirjian, Kayla Guo, Robert Jimison, Emily Cochrane, Nick Fandos, Jonathan Weisman, Jonathan Swan, Maya Miller, and our fearless leader, Julie Davis (much more on her to come).

Our project had the support from the top echelons of the paper: We thank A. G. Sulzberger, Sam Dolnick, Joe Kahn, and Carolyn Ryan for allowing us to explore our story in a book project. And of course our indomitable Washington bureau chief, Elisabeth Bumiller, who brought us both to *The New York Times* and has always encouraged any pursuit of a good story.

At Random House, we have been so lucky to work with Ben Greenberg, an editor who immediately shared our sensibility for what we wanted this book to be and who pushed us through edits to make it better. Thank you to Loren Noveck, the production editor; Claire Leonard, for vetting the book for us; and Leila Tejani, for her patience in dealing with all of our confusion about using Word. Thank you also to Mark Warren, who originally acquired our book.

It was a pleasure to work with Julie Tate, our stellar fact-checker. And a big thank you to Javelin's Matt Latimer and Keith Urbahn for pushing us up the hill to pursue this project, even when the idea of taking on another load on top of day jobs and kids seemed daunting. We are so, so happy we did.

ANNIE: Julie Davis is what a reporter wants in an editor: someone with a strong point of view who knows what she wants, but who is also open to and excited by ideas that aren't her own. Her daily insights and edits over the past three years have deeply informed this book. I would be willing to cover almost any beat that Julie was editing.

I've been lucky to enjoy the support and friendship from all-star colleagues, current and former, who inspire me and were generous in sharing book writing and general advice along the way: Katie Rogers, Maggie Haberman, Susan Glasser, Peter Baker, Mark Leibovich, Jake Sherman, Robert Draper, Carlos Lozada, Carl Hulse, Elizabeth Dias, Mark Mazzetti, Josh Dawsey, Mike Grynbaum, Erica Green, and Elizabeth Green.

Formative editors to thank for making me (for better or worse) the journalist I am today: Jerry Lippman, Seth Lipsky, Ira Stoll, Margi Conklin, Paul McPolin, Joel Siegel, and Susan Glasser. Bill Hamilton, Elisabeth Bumiller, and Carolyn Ryan are the editors responsible for bringing me to the *Times,* my longtime dream. Thank you for doing so, and for the ongoing support.

I'm so lucky to have worked on this project with someone as stellar as Luke Broadwater! Luke is the most easygoing yet rigorous colleague one could hope to collaborate with. I'm honored to have shared this project with him.

I'm also lucky to have the most encouraging friends to rely on. Specifically, Alexis Swerdloff, Audrey Gelman, and Jonathan Boschetto, thank you for the many years of friendship and always rooting for me.

My parents, Barbara and Adi Karni, have always encouraged my writing ambitions. Even when they had to discuss my Page Six stories with their mathematician friends at Thanksgiving dinner, they did so with gusto. They also provided hours of babysitting every weekend of the past two years, which made the actual writing of this book possible. My aunt and uncle, Carrie Shapiro and Peter Frey, have been a great support to me, as has my sister, Anat Karni; I wish we could see more of each other. In

Robin Mann, I truly won the mother-in-law lottery. My grandmother Arlene would have been so proud to read this book. My grandfather Sid Shapiro has always been my most discerning reader, and my kids are lucky to know their great-grandfather.

Which brings me to Caleb and Lila, aka the naked butts: You all delight me and will always be the main event. As is Ted, whose love and support I am lucky to rely on, always.

LUKE: Congress is such a revealing beat about the American political system because nearly anyone will tell you their views on nearly anything if you're fortunate enough to catch them alone for a few minutes in the hallway. This book would not have been possible without the many, many lawmakers and aides who spent many, many hours with us recounting their experiences in the madhouse that was the 118th Congress. Thank you to all who sat for on-the-record (and off-the-record) sessions with us.

The Capitol Hill press corps is a competitive group, on top of every twist and turn that goes down in the legislative branch, but the job is done with a spirit of camaraderie. Thank you to all the excellent reporters who make roaming the halls of the Capitol more fun, including Jake Sherman, John Bresnahan, and the crew at *Punchbowl News*.

On a personal note, thank you to everyone who has fostered my love of writing and journalism over the years: my parents, Daniel and Katherine Broadwater; my high school English teachers, Ms. Deegan and Mr. Van Meter; my editors at various reporting stops, including Steve Kelly, Paul Milton, Elizabeth Eck, Jack Gibbons, Frank Keegan, Tim Maier, Laura Smitherman, Eileen Canzian, Amanda Kell, Mary Corey, Trif Alatzas, Sam Davis, and many others; my friends and co-workers in journalism who have inspired me with their commitment to the craft over the years, including Erica Green, Erin Cox, Yvonne Wenger, Scott Dance, Talia Richman, Justin Fenton, Pamela Wood, Jaime Lennon, and Stephen Janis.

At *The New York Times,* no one has been more important to me than Julie Davis, my editor, whom I trust wholeheartedly and who encouraged this project. Thank you to my reporting partners beyond the Congress team, particularly after the January 6 attack on the Capitol: Maggie Haberman, Mike Schmidt, Alan Feuer, and editor Richard Stevenson, who has often shepherded my stories through the paper. My biggest thanks go out to Annie, who was an amazing partner throughout the process of writing this book and had the storytelling vision and writer's voice to pull it off.

Finally, thank you to my wife, Jennifer, for your feedback, support, and love, and my kids, Dani and Will, for being my reason for everything I do in this life.

NOTES

NOTE TO THE READER: UNLESS OTHERWISE INDICATED, THE MATERIAL in this book comes from interviews conducted by the authors.

INTRODUCTION

ix   **"It's just going to be the same stupid clown car"**: Annie Karni, "House Dysfunction by the Numbers: 724 Votes, Only 27 Laws Enacted," *New York Times,* December 19, 2023.

ix   **"Nobody in this country"**: "Another Border Compromise," *The Morning Show with Preston Scott,* January 19, 2024.

x   **"What we've done in our politics"**: John Wagner, "Liz Cheney on What's Wrong with Politics: 'We're Electing Idiots,'" *Washington Post,* June 27, 2023.

xi   **But barely right is still right**: "U.S. House Election Results: Republicans Win," *New York Times,* November 8, 2022.

xii   **In 1856, Rep. Preston Brooks**: "The Caning of Senator Charles Sumner," United States Senate, www.senate.gov/artandhistory/history/minute/The_Caning_of_Senator_Charles_Sumner.htm.

CHAPTER 1

3   **But at the Capitol**: Elena Schneider, "McCarthy Rumors Follow Ellmers to North Carolina," *Politico,* October 18, 2015.

4   **The sunny demeanor was the Kevin McCarthy**: Lisa Mascaro, "From Bakersfield to DC, McCarthy's Unlikely Rise in GOP," Associated Press, May 7, 2018.

5   **That, in and of itself, was historically**: Gillian Brockell, "The Last Time a House Speaker Wasn't Elected on the First Ballot," *Washington Post,* January 3, 2023.

6   **"You must act without hesitation"**: Nancy Pelosi, *The Art of Power* (Simon & Schuster, 2024), p. 46.

7   **On January 2, the day before**: Elise Hammond et al., "Latest on the New Congress and House Speaker Vote," CNN, January 3, 2023.

8   **"Because it took this long"**: John L. Dorman, "Kevin McCarthy Says Republi-

cans 'Learned How to Govern' and Will 'Be More Effective' After the Party's In-fighting to Select a Speaker," *Business Insider,* January 7, 2023.

CHAPTER 2

11   **Boebert, who had squeaked by**: Scott Wong and Sahil Kapur, "Rep. Lauren Boe-bert Won by Only 546 Votes Last Year. She Isn't Changing Her Ways," NBC News, July 17, 2023.

11   **"I love President Trump"**: Maggie Haberman and Michael C. Bender, "In House Speaker Fight, Trump Struggles to Play Kingmaker," *New York Times,* January 5, 2023.

12   **Now he was in Congress**: Annie Karni, " 'I Might Wind Up in the Broom Closet': Why Eli Crane Defied Kevin McCarthy," *New York Times,* January 13, 2023.

12   **"I didn't want anything"**: Karni, " 'I Might Wind Up in the Broom Closet.' "

14   **Gaetz told her that McCarthy**: Aila Slisco, "Everything We Know About AOC's Talks with Gosar and Gaetz," *Newsweek,* January 4, 2023.

15   **The reading clerk took her place**: Video of the proceedings can be found on C-SPAN, January 3, 2023.

15   **"I'm staying until we win"**: Catie Edmondson, "House G.O.P. Paralyzed on Day 1 as Right Wing Blocks McCarthy Speakership," *New York Times,* January 3, 2023.

15   **Ahead of that day of failure**: Charles P. Pierce, "Boy, Kevin McCarthy Will Look Dumb If He Has to Move His Stuff Out of the Speaker's Office Again," *Esquire,* January 4, 2023.

18   **McCarthy stuck to inspirational bromides**: Isaac Arnsdorf et al., "How Kevin McCarthy Survived the GOP Revolt to Become House Speaker," *Washington Post,* January 8, 2023.

19   **the tide finally turned**: Allison McCartney et al., "Vote Count: McCarthy Elected House Speaker After 15 Ballots," *New York Times,* January 6, 2023.

19   **Gaetz went on Fox News**: Aila Slisco, "Matt Gaetz Says He 'Ran Out of Stuff to Ask For' from McCarthy," *Newsweek,* January 7, 2023.

20   **Ahead of what was expected**: *Carolina Journal* Staff, "McHenry Nominates McCarthy for U.S. House Speaker in 14th Round of Voting," *Carolina Journal,* January 7, 2023.

20   **The Speaker-in-waiting had corralled**: Susan Rinkunas, "Republican Men Abandoned Ailing Wives, Babies in the Hospital to Vote for Kevin McCarthy," *Jezebel,* January 9, 2023.

20   **McHenry was considered the best vote counter**: Zachary Warmbrodt, "Who Is Patrick McHenry? A Crash Course on the Temporary Speaker," *Politico,* October 19, 2023.

21   **Trump phoned Gaetz personally**: Maggie Haberman, "After Dramatic 14th Vote, Trump Calls Holdouts Who Refused to Back McCarthy," *New York Times,* January 7, 2023.

CHAPTER 3

23   **Kevin McCarthy lived in a rented bedroom**: Glenn Kessler, "Kevin McCarthy Says He Rented a 'Room'—in a 7,000-Square-Foot Penthouse," *Washington Post,* May 5, 2021.

23 **In 2021, McCarthy's rented room**: Ben Terris, "Frank Luntz Can't Quit," *New York,* May 17, 2023.

24 **McCarthy said at the time**: Kessler, "Kevin McCarthy Says He Rented a 'Room'—in a 7,000-Square-Foot Penthouse."

24 **Many members slept on their couches**: Barbara Sprunt, "Pandemic Revives Calls to Ban Lawmakers from Bunking in Their Offices," NPR, May 13, 2020.

25 **This act of personal kindness**: McCartney et al., "Vote Count: McCarthy Elected House Speaker After 15 Ballots."

25 **His own origin story**: Mark Leibovich, "Kevin McCarthy, Four Months After Jan. 6, Still on Defensive over Trump," *New York Times,* April 25, 2021.

25 **He once said of Pelosi**: Aaron Rupar (@atrupar), "'She will go at no elms to break the rules'—Kevin McCarthy on Pelosi (does anybody understand this?)," Twitter (now X), July 29, 2021, x.com/atrupar/status/1420760252631371777.

25 **In a 2015 address**: "House Majority Leader McCarthy on Foreign Policy," C-SPAN, September 29, 2015, www.c-span.org/video/?c4553471/user-clip-kevin -McCarthy-visits-hungria.

25 **he had groveled before Trump**: Josh Dawsey and Robert Costa, "Kevin McCarthy Relishes Role as Trump's Fixer, Friend and Candy Man," *Washington Post,* January 15, 2018.

26 **With his visit to Mar-a-Lago**: Maggie Haberman, "McCarthy to Meet Trump After Rift over His Assertion That the Former President 'Bears Responsibility' for the Capitol Attack," *New York Times,* January 27, 2021.

26 **A highlight of the spring 2023 Republican retreat**: Annie Karni, "At House Republican Retreat, the Focus, Once Again, Is on Trump," *New York Times,* March 21, 2023; Scott Wong and Ali Vitali, "Trump–DeSantis Drama Casts a Shadow over House GOP Retreat in Florida," NBC News, March 19, 2023.

27 **wild, conspiratorial, and bigoted statements**: Jonathan Swan and Catie Edmondson, "How Kevin McCarthy Forged an Ironclad Bond with Marjorie Taylor Greene," *New York Times,* January 23, 2023.

29 **Elon Musk visited him**: Melanie Zanona, Manu Raju, and Kevin Liptak, "Elon Musk Meets with House Speaker Kevin McCarthy and Hakeem Jeffries," CNN, January 27, 2023.

CHAPTER 4

30 **A onetime Trump campaign staffer**: Natalie Allison, "The New Trump Acolyte No One Saw Coming: Nancy Mace," *Politico,* June 21, 2023.

30 **Mace constantly criticized**: Tal Axelrod, "Republicans Will 'Lose Huge' Without Finding 'Middle Ground' on Abortion, Nancy Mace Says," ABC News, April 23, 2023.

30 **She was a high school dropout**: Daniel Wu, "S.C. Rep Says She Was 'Shamed' as Rape Victim When Asked About Support for Trump," *Washington Post,* March 11, 2024; "Rep. Nancy Mace Speaks at 2024 Republican National Convention," PBS News, July 17, 2024; C-SPAN, "Rep. Nancy Mace at Washington Press Club Foundation Dinner," YouTube video, February 10, 2023.

31 **Gaetz had been under investigation**: Ryan Nobles et al., "DOJ Tells Matt Gaetz That He Won't Be Charged in Sex Trafficking Probe, His Lawyers Say," NBC News, February 15, 2023.

36 **That evening, McCarthy passed the bill**: Mychael Schnell, "These Four House Republicans Voted Against the GOP Debt Limit Bill," *The Hill,* April 26, 2023.

CHAPTER 5

38   **Vought was also helping**: "Russell Vought, a Project 2025 Architect, Likely in Line for High-Ranking Post If Trump Wins 2nd Term," Associated Press, August 5, 2024.

38   **He wanted two trillion dollars in cuts**: Jeff Stein, Josh Dawsey, and Isaac Arnsdorf, "The Former Trump Aide Crafting the House GOP's Debt Ceiling Playbook," *Washington Post,* February 19, 2023.

39   **He was staunchly opposed**: Russ Vought (@russvought), "You are not an apologist for Putin if you oppose funding the war in Ukraine and deepening America's involvement in a distraction to our national interests," Twitter (now X), February 25, 2023, x.com/russvought/status/1629320138385235971.

39   **Vought had a particularly close relationship**: Stein, Dawsey, and Arnsdorf, "The Former Trump Aide Crafting the House GOP's Debt Ceiling Playbook."

39   **After the January 6 attack on the Capitol**: "Republican Rep. Chip Roy: Trump Committed 'Impeachable Conduct,' but Will Vote Against Impeachment as Drafted," NBC News, January 13, 2021.

39   **In 2023, he made an early**: Julia Forrest, "Texas' U.S. Rep. Chip Roy Says Florida Gov. Ron DeSantis Should Be President," *Texas Tribune,* March 15, 2023.

40   **the roadblock to the transformational change**: Thomas Massie (@RepThomas Massie), "Merry Christmas! ps. Santa, please bring ammo," Twitter (now X), December 4, 2021, x.com/RepThomasMassie/status/1467197523127422979.

41   **Massie was one of three**: Andrew Solender and Stef W. Kight, "GOP Hardliners Score Spots on Powerful House Rules Committee," *Axios,* January 23, 2023.

CHAPTER 6

43   **Biden officials consider the debt ceiling**: Jim Tankersley, "Biden's Debt Deal Strategy: Win in the Fine Print," *New York Times,* June 3, 2023.

45   **he had voted against both**: "Here's How Louisiana's Congressmen Voted on President Trump's Second Impeachment," BRProud.com, January 13, 2021; Paul Braun, "5 Louisiana Congressmen Voted to Overturn Biden's Presidential Win. Here's What They Had to Say," New Orleans Public Radio, January 8, 2021; Lazaro Gamio and Alicia Parlapiano, "How Every House Member Voted on the Infrastructure Bill," *New York Times,* November 5, 2021.

46   **opening a T-shirt stand**: John Wogan, "President Obama's Dream T-Shirt Shack in Hawaii," *T: New York Times Style Magazine,* January 10, 2017.

47   **told people he found him ineffective**: Rachael Bade, "Kevin McCarthy's Blame Game Sweeps Capitol Hill," *Politico,* April 7, 2023.

47   **The first Black woman**: Emily Cochrane, "Shalanda Young Confirmed to Head Biden's Budget Office," *New York Times,* March 15, 2022.

49   **McHenry had a chance of getting roped back**: Annie Karni, "Patrick McHenry, Former Interim Speaker, Will Leave Congress," *New York Times,* December 5, 2023.

50   **Republicans had passed the bill**: Catie Edmondson and Carl Hulse, "The Federal Debt Limit: House Passes Debt Limit Bill, Courting a Showdown," *New York Times,* April 26, 2023.

51   **stylistically, things had changed**: Annie Linskey, "A Look Inside Biden's Oval Office," *Washington Post,* January 20, 2021.

51   **"Will you take default off the table?"**: "Schumer Says McCarthy Refused to Take Default Off the Table," Bloomberg Television, May 9, 2023.

56 **Republicans insisted on imposing new**: Tami Luhby, "Republicans Use Debt Ceiling Bill to Push Work Requirements for Millions Receiving Medicaid and Food Stamps," CNN, April 26, 2023.

57 **It helped sell the cuts**: Congressional Budget Office, Letter to Rep. Kevin McCarthy, pdf, May 30, 2023, www.cbo.gov/system/files/2023-05/hr3746_Letter_McCarthy.pdf.

57 **"A disappointment across the board"**: Lindsey McPherson, "Meet the House Members Who Voted Against the Debt Limit Deal," *Roll Call,* June 1, 2023; Olivia Beavers and Sarah Ferris, "House Conservatives Threaten Push to Oust McCarthy over Debt Deal," *Politico,* May 30, 2023.

CHAPTER 7

59 **"Who cares?"**: Carl Hulse, "G.O.P. Rebels Are Breaking the Rule on Rules, Upending How the House Works," *New York Times,* June 13, 2023.

61 **"We're going to force him"**: The Recount (@therecount), "Rep. Matt Gaetz (R-FL) says he will force Speaker McCarthy into a 'monogamous relationship' with either the Freedom Caucus or House Democrats: 'What we're not gonna do is hang out with him for five months and then watch him go jump in the back seat with Hakeem Jeffries,'" Twitter (now X), June 7, 2023, x.com/therecount/status/1666469601943646209.

62 **On May 31, just days before**: Sarah Ewall-Wice and Kathryn Watson, "Debt Ceiling Deadline Is Now June 5, Janet Yellen Says," CBS News, May 26, 2023.

62 **they got word that Rep. Ken Buck**: David Choi, "Republican Lawmaker Dares Democrats to 'Come and Take' His Non-Functioning AR-15 Rifle," *Business Insider,* March 6, 2020.

63 **When the measure finally passed**: Brian Porter, "Rep. Buck: 'I Refuse to Be Complicit in This Bipartisan Bankruptcy,'" *Fort Morgan Times,* June 5, 2023.

63 **Mace, for her part**: Rep. Nancy Mace (@RepNancyMace), "Washington is broken. Republicans got outsmarted by a President who can't find his pants. I'm voting NO on the debt ceiling debacle because playing the DC game isn't worth selling out our kids and grandkids," Twitter (now X), May 30, 2023, x.com/RepNancyMace/status/1663510647190040578?lang=en.

64 **They voted against the rule**: Ellis Kim and Scott MacFarlane, "House GOP Rules Vote on Gas Stoves Goes Up in Flames," CBS News, June 6, 2023.

64 **"We're not going to live in the era"**: Matt Gaetz (@RepMattGaetz), "The era of the Imperial Speakership is OVER! I'm done with their failure theater," Twitter (now X), June 6, 2023, x.com/RepMattGaetz/status/1666207017550094336.

CHAPTER 8

65 **"A bathroom door locks"**: MSNBC, "'A Bathroom Door Locks': McCarthy Responds to Question About Handling of Documents," YouTube video, June 13, 2023.

66 **It was a stance that was enraging**: Filip Timotija, "Pro-Haley Account Shares Mace's Past Praise of Her as 'Great Leader' After Criticism," *The Hill,* February 2, 2024.

67 **At a prayer breakfast**: Brianna Herlihy, "Nancy Mace's Naughty Prayer Breakfast Speech Has Commenters All Worked Up: 'I'm a Sinner,'" Fox News, July 28, 2023.

CHAPTER 9

69   **Back in 2021, Democrats took**: Catie Edmondson, Nicholas Fandos, and Thomas
      Kaplan, "The House Votes to Strip Marjorie Taylor Greene of Her Committee As-
      signments," *New York Times,* February 4, 2021.

69   **That same year, Democrats also censured**: Donie O'Sullivan, "Republican Con-
      gressman Posts Video Depicting Violence Against Ocasio-Cortez and Biden,"
      CNN, November 10, 2021.

69   **Democrats also voted to strip Gosar**: Annie Grayer and Clare Foran, "House
      Votes to Censure and Remove Gosar from Committees over Violent Video Target-
      ing AOC and Biden," CNN, November 17, 2021.

70   **McCarthy also blocked**: Catie Edmondson and Karoun Demirjian, "McCarthy
      Ejects Schiff and Swalwell from Intelligence Committee," *New York Times,* Janu-
      ary 24, 2023.

72   **the war between Israel and Hamas**: Mychael Schnell, "Greene Moves to Force
      Vote on Tlaib Censure for 'Antisemitic Activity,'" *The Hill,* October 26, 2023.

72   **Tlaib was a complicated figure**: Susan J. Demas, "Tlaib Renews Her 'Impeach the
      MF'er' Call Against Trump," pdf, Advance Notice Brief, Congress.gov, July 14,
      2019, www.congress.gov/118/meeting/house/117001/documents/HHRG-118
      -GO00-20240320-SD014.pdf.

73   **So, just one week after Greene's censure**: Nicholas Wu and Daniella Diaz, "House
      Moves to Censure Tlaib over Israel Rhetoric," *Politico,* November 7, 2023.

74   **drafted a resolution to formally rebuke**: Annie Karni, "House Republican Drafts
      Censure of Omar for 'Pro-Genocide' Remark," *New York Times,* April 30, 2024.

75   **"Censure all of us!"**: Mary Clare Jalonick, "In Rowdy Scene, House Censures
      Rep. Adam Schiff over Trump-Russia Investigations," Associated Press, June 21,
      2023.

CHAPTER 10

76   **"When they go low"**: Michelle Obama, "Remarks by the First Lady at the Demo-
      cratic National Convention," The White House, Office of the First Lady, July 25,
      2016.

78   **An evangelical Christian, Jordan**: Luke Broadwater, "How Jim Jordan, a Fighter
      Aligned with Trump, Wrestled His Way to Power," *New York Times,* April 16,
      2023.

78   **The only major scandal**: Catie Edmondson, "Jim Jordan Is Defiant as Allegations
      Mount, and Supporters Point to 'Deep State,'" *New York Times,* July 6, 2018.

78   **Jordan had been a mainstay**: Broadwater, "How Jim Jordan, a Fighter Aligned
      with Trump, Wrestled His Way to Power."

80   **Jeffries described his thinking**: Broadwater, "How Jim Jordan, a Fighter Aligned
      with Trump, Wrestled His Way to Power."

81   **As a lead Republican investigator**: Broadwater, "How Jim Jordan, a Fighter
      Aligned with Trump, Wrestled His Way to Power."

81   **He promised fantastical connections**: Jonathan Swan and Luke Broadwater,
      "Comer, Republicans' Investigative Chief, Embraces Role of Biden Antagonist,"
      New York Times, March 21, 2023.

82   **fifty-one former intelligence officers wrote a letter**: Natasha Bertrand, "Hunter
      Biden Story Is Russian Disinfo, Dozens of Former Intel Officials Say," *Politico,*
      October 19, 2020.

83 **"The FBI warned us"**: House Judiciary GOP (@JudiciaryGOP), "Mark Zucker-berg just admitted three things: 1. Biden-Harris Admin 'pressured' Facebook to censor Americans. 2. Facebook censored Americans. 3. Facebook throttled the Hunter Biden laptop story. Big win for free speech," X, August 26, 2024, x.com/JudiciaryGOP/status/1828201780544504064.

CHAPTER 11

89 **"We have made astonishing progress"**: James Comer, Press Conference, May 10, 2023.

90 **"Did they sweep it under the rug"**: Luke Broadwater and Glenn Thrush, "Ignor-ing Warnings, G.O.P. Trumpeted Now-Discredited Allegation Against Biden," *New York Times,* February 23, 2024.

91 **"Either IMPEACH the BUM"**: Donald J. Trump (@realDonaldTrump), "The Republicans in Congress, though well meaning, keep talking about an Impeach-ment 'Inquiry' on Crooked Joe Biden. Look, the guy got bribed, he paid people off, and he wouldn't give One Billion Dollars to Ukraine unless they 'got rid of the Prosecutor.' . . . ," Truth Social, August 27, 2023, truthsocial.com/@realDonald Trump/posts/110963746628215974.

91 **Foster knew how to maneuver**: Luke Broadwater, "Former Republican Aides Shepherd Whistle-Blowers Through Congress," *New York Times,* July 23, 2023.

92 **worked with a group called the Congressional Integrity Project**: Kenneth P. Vogel, Katie Rogers, and Glenn Thrush, "Republicans Lay Out Biden Investiga-tions, but Democrat-Aligned Groups Promise Counteroffensive," *New York Times,* November 17, 2022.

92 **"Nothing spells 'INTIMIDATION' more than Biden's"**: James Comer (@James Comer), "1) Nothing spells 'INTIMIDATION' more than Biden's dark money PAC paying a plane to fly over #KentuckyDerby to attack me for simply investigat-ing public corruption," Twitter (now X), May 6, 2023, x.com/JamesComer/status/1654921137019670528.

93 **"I was out of my mind"**: Hunter Biden Deposition, House Oversight Committee, February 28, 2024.

93 **"Should we be displaying this in the committee?"**: Luke Broadwater, "I.R.S. Whistle-Blowers Allege Political Bias in Hunter Biden Investigation," *New York Times,* July 19, 2023.

CHAPTER 12

95 **Marjorie Taylor Greene had introduced articles of impeachment**: "Impeaching Joseph R. Biden, President of the United States, for Abuse of Power by Enabling Bribery and Other High Crimes and Misdemeanors," H.Res. 57, 117th Cong. (2021–2022).

96 **"I've donated to you"**: Sam Brodey and Zachary Petrizzo, "Marjorie Taylor Greene Calls Boebert a 'Little Bitch' on the House Floor," *Daily Beast,* June 21, 2023.

99 **This was a woman who had grown up**: Ben Terris, "Lauren Boebert Doesn't Want to Lose the House," *Washington Post,* March 3, 2024.

100 **"So, what happened that night?"**: *Jesse Watters Primetime,* Fox News, Septem-ber 22, 2023.

101 **"What about you in that theater?"**: Mark Leibovich, "House Republicans Showed Up at a Campus Protest. Of Course." *Atlantic,* May 3, 2024.

104   **"I rise today to serve notice, Mr. Speaker"**: Carl Hulse, Luke Broadwater, and Annie Karni, "McCarthy, Facing an Ouster and a Shutdown, Orders an Impeachment Inquiry," *New York Times,* September 12, 2023.

106   **"I think that Kevin McCarthy just wants the specter of impeachment"**: Katherine Doyle, "During an Online Fundraiser, Matt Gaetz Denounced the Biden Impeachment Effort as Unserious," NBC News, October 6, 2023.

107   **"I did one cable news hit"**: Glenn Thrush, "Matt Gaetz Is a Congressman Liberals Love to Loathe. It's All Part of the Plan," *New York Times,* March 30, 2019.

108   **"I view the Trump presidency"**: Abigail Tracy, "'The President's Big into Buddy Checks': In the MAGA Circus with Matt Gaetz, Trump's Ultimate Protégé," *Vanity Fair,* March 3, 2020.

109   **"Spot the difference"**: Ginger Gaetz (@GingerLGaetz), "Spot the difference," X, June 19, 2024, x.com/GingerLGaetz/status/1803432507796341119.

CHAPTER 13

114   **"vaping groping Lauren Boebert"**: Marjorie Taylor Greene (@RepMTG), "You voted to kick me out of the freedom caucus, but keep CNN wannabe Ken Buck and vaping groping Lauren Boebert and you voted with the Democrats to protect Terrorist Tlaib. You hate Trump, certified Biden's election, and could care less about J6 defendants being persecuted," X, November 2, 2023, x.com/RepMTG/status/1720050983596642492.

116   **"I don't want to go to any more meetings"**: Jim Jordan, *Do What You Said You Would Do: Fighting for Freedom in the Swamp* (Post Hill Press, 2021).

118   **"stab you in the back like he did me"**: Annie Karni, "Bob Good Trails in Battle for His Virginia Seat, but Primary Remains Too Close to Call," *New York Times,* June 20, 2024.

119   **" 'They're so extreme' "**: Annie Karni, Robert Draper, and Luke Broadwater, "As Spending Fights Loom, Freedom Caucus Is at a Crossroads," *New York Times,* July 25, 2023.

CHAPTER 14

121   **"They're immovable"**: Annie Karni, "With House Hurtling Toward a Shutdown, Gaetz Is Leading the Resistance," *New York Times,* September 22, 2023.

121   **Members were given about an hour**: Annie Karni, "Inside McCarthy's Shutdown Turnabout That Left His Speakership at Risk," *New York Times,* October 1, 2023.

123   **the "Nazi members"**: Marisa Iati, "Rep. Jamaal Bowman's Office Cites 'Nazi' Republicans in Talking Point," *Washington Post,* October 2, 2023.

123   **"I'm a type of conservative who wants to get things done"**: Karni, "Inside McCarthy's Shutdown Turnabout That Left His Speakership at Risk."

125   **"Just did"**: Matt Gaetz (@mattgaetz), "Just did," X, October 2, 2023, x.com/mattgaetz/status/1708991508458639420?lang=en

CHAPTER 15

127   **"The Democrats tried to do everything they can"**: *Face the Nation,* CBS, October 1, 2023.

CHAPTER 16

130 **"We need a Speaker"**: Catie Edmondson, "McCarthy Is Ousted as Speaker, Leaving the House in Chaos," *New York Times,* October 3, 2023.

130 **"this Republican majority has exceeded all expectations"**: Mark Leibovich, "Kevin McCarthy Got What He Wanted," *Atlantic,* October 5, 2023.

130 **"the greatest Speaker in modern history"**: Leibovich, "Kevin McCarthy Got What He Wanted."

132 **"I don't regret standing up for choosing governance over grievance"**: Edmondson, "McCarthy Is Ousted as Speaker, Leaving the House in Chaos."

133 **"This eviction is a sharp departure from tradition"**: Andrew Solender, "Interim GOP Speaker Orders Pelosi and Hoyer Out of Capitol Offices," *Axios,* October 4, 2023.

CHAPTER 17

136 **"I'm just going to see how it develops"**: Annie Karni, "From a Capitol Hill Basement, Bannon Stokes the Republican Party Meltdown" *New York Times,* October 4, 2023.

136 **After participating, with reservations**: Karni, "With House Hurtling Toward a Shutdown, Gaetz Is Leading the Resistance."

137 **"Want to go meet with any of them today, together?"**: Karni, "From a Capitol Hill Basement, Bannon Stokes the Republican Party Meltdown."

CHAPTER 18

141 **She went on NBC's *Meet the Press***: *Meet the Press,* NBC, January 7, 2024.

141 **She deleted all old press releases**: Sara Boboltz, "Elise Stefanik's Press Release Archive Vanishes After Liz Cheney Jab," *HuffPost,* January 27, 2024.

141 **"We will see if this is a legal and valid election"**: *Meet the Press,* NBC, January 7, 2024.

141 **Ryan described her in a 2019 *Time* magazine**: Paul Ryan, "Elise Stefanik," *Time,* 2019.

142 **"One of my killers"**: Annie Karni, "Elise Stefanik, Reinvented in Trump's Image, Embodies a Changed G.O.P.," *New York Times,* March 27, 2022.

CHAPTER 19

145 **"if she hadn't been a woman"**: "Calif.'s Pelosi Chosen as House Democratic Whip," *Baltimore Sun,* October 1, 2001.

145 **"I think Nancy is the best Speaker we've had"**: Annie Karni, "How Steny Hoyer, Pelosi's No. 2, Decided It Was Time to Step Aside," *New York Times,* December 2, 2022.

145 **after *The New York Times* reported on their mounting tensions**: Jonathan Swan and Annie Karni, "Staring Down a Debt Crisis, McCarthy Toils to Navigate G.O.P. Divisions," *New York Times,* April 6, 2023.

148 **Trump, who endorsed Jordan**: Luke Broadwater, Catie Edmondson, and Karoun Demirjian, "Scalise Withdraws as Speaker Candidate, Leaving G.O.P. in Chaos," *New York Times,* October 18, 2023.

149 **"I personally cannot"**: *The Lead with Jake Tapper,* CNN, October 11, 2023.

150 **"like David Duke without the baggage"**: Jeremy Alford, "Much of David Duke's '91 Campaign Is Now in Louisiana Mainstream," *New York Times,* December 31, 2014.

CHAPTER 20

159 **"call out all the electoral votes"**: Luke Broadwater, "Jim Jordan Refuses to Cooperate with Jan. 6 Panel," *New York Times,* January 9, 2022.

159 **They started a public pressure campaign**: Karoun Demirjian, "Jordan Activates Right-Wing Pressure Campaign in Push to Win Speakership," *New York Times,* October 14, 2023.

160 **"few sensitive little snowflakes in Congress"**: Sarah Ellison and Will Sommer, "How Hannity, Bannon and Others on the Right Helped Fuel GOP Speaker Chaos," *Washington Post,* October 17, 2023.

166 **"The most popular Republican in the United States Congress"**: John L. Dorman, "Matt Gaetz Blasts the House GOP Secret Ballot Process That Knocked Off Jim Jordan as the Party's Speaker Nominee: 'It's as Swampy as Swamp Gets,'" *Business Insider,* October 21, 2023.

CHAPTER 21

168 **"bipartisan bridge to the future"**: Cathy Wurzer and Gracie Stockton, "Rep. Dean Phillips Weighs in on House Speaker Vote," MPR News, October 12, 2023.

171 **"Globalist RINO"**: Luke Broadwater, Catie Edmondson, and Kayla Guo, "G.O.P. Nominates Mike Johnson for Speaker After Spurning Emmer," *New York Times,* October 24, 2023.

172 **"They always bend the knee"**: Jonathan Swan, Shane Goldmacher, and Maggie Haberman, "How Trump Has Used Fear and Favor to Win Republican Endorsements," *New York Times,* January 4, 2024.

172 **"Complete and Total Endorsement!"**: Donald Trump (@therealdonaldtrump), "Tom Emmer is a fantastic Representative of Minnesota's 6th Congressional District, and is doing an incredible job as the Majority Whip of the U.S. House of Representatives . . .", Truth Social, August 13, 2024.

CHAPTER 22

173 **"We're playing with fire"**: Sarah Fortinsky, "McCaul on Speakership Fight: 'Our Adversaries Are Watching Us,'" *The Hill,* October 12, 2023.

CHAPTER 23

178 **"I have never before aspired to the office"**: Mike Johnson (@SpeakerJohnson), "I'm in!," X, October 21, 2023, x.com/SpeakerJohnson/status/17157539855402 39776.

180 **Hern of Oklahoma, who had made a fortune owning McDonald's franchises**: Sarah Ferris, "Kevin Hern Is Making a Special Pitch in his House Majority Leader Bid—McGriddles Delivered to GOP Offices," *Politico,* October 12, 2023.

182 **"The Bible is very clear that God is the one"**: Andrew Whitehead and Samuel L. Perry, "The Christian Nationalism of Speaker Mike Johnson," *Time,* October 27, 2023.

183 **"for those weeks of not knowing what's going to happen in terms of funding"**:

Jeff Mason, "Biden Apologizes to Zelenskiy for Congressional Delays to US Aid," Reuters, June 7, 2024.

184 **Johnson recruited Republicans to sign the legal brief**: Luke Broadwater and Steve Eder, "Johnson Played Leading Role in Effort to Overturn 2020 Election," *New York Times,* October 25, 2023.

184 **"He's going to do a great job"**: Catie Edmondson, "House Elects Mike Johnson as Speaker, Embracing a Hard-Right Conservative," *New York Times,* October 25, 2023.

CHAPTER 24

185 **"The Swamp won, and the Speaker needs to know that"**: Carl Hulse and Catie Edmondson, "Senate Sends Biden Stopgap Funding Bill, Averting a Government Shutdown," *New York Times,* November 15, 2023.

185 **"The Swamp is on the run"**: Aaron Rupar (@atrupar), "Matt Gaetz to Steve Bannon: 'If you don't think that moving from Kevin McCarthy to MAGA Mike Johnson shows the ascendance of this movement and where the power in the Republican Party truly lies, then you're not paying attention,'" October 25, 2023, x.com/atrupar/status/1717198721178357949.

188 **"a fireside chat with Speaker McCarthy"**: The Harry Walker Agency, www.harrywalker.com/speakers/kevin-mccarthy.

188 **"wanted me to stop an ethics complaint"**: Aubrie Spady and Kyle Morris, "McCarthy Blames Ouster on Lawmaker Who Wanted to Stop Ethics Complaint That He 'Slept with a 17-Year-Old,'" FoxNews.com, April 12, 2024.

188 **"I just traveled to your district"**: Annie Karni, "McCarthy's Revenge Tour Rolls On, with Mixed Results," *New York Times,* July 7, 2024.

189 **"We don't need a Speaker that's Paul Ryan with a Bible"**: Citizens for Renewing America (@amrenewcitizen), "CRA President @RussVought says @SpeakerJohnson's NDAA is DC Cartel governance. 'We don't need a speaker that's Paul Ryan with a Bible,'" X, December 14, 2023. x.com/amrenewcitizen/status/1735426104876208454.

CHAPTER 25

192 **They were simply charging that he had breached the public trust**: Karoun Demirjian, "House Republicans Impeach Mayorkas for Border Policies," *New York Times,* February 13, 2024.

192 **Congress had not impeached a sitting cabinet secretary**: Luke Broadwater, "Senate Dismisses Impeachment Charges Against Mayorkas Without a Trial," *New York Times,* April 17, 2024.

193 **They hadn't counted on the presence of Rep. Al Green**: Kayla Guo, "Al Green, in Hospital Garb, Delivers Vote to Kill Mayorkas Impeachment," *New York Times,* February 6, 2024.

193 **"They hid one of their members"**: Guo, "Al Green, in Hospital Garb, Delivers Vote to Kill Mayorkas Impeachment."

194 **"You have trafficked in innuendo"**: Luke Broadwater, "In Long-Awaited Testimony, Hunter Biden Assails G.O.P. Impeachment Inquiry," *New York Times,* February 28, 2024.

194 **"Mr. Gaetz, look me in the eye"**: Farnoush Amiri and Lisa Mascaro, "Takeaways from Hunter Biden's Combative Deposition with Republican Lawmakers," Associated Press, March 1, 2024.

195 **The indictment alleged that the longtime informant**: Glenn Thrush, "Ex-F.B.I. Informant Is Charged with Lying over Bidens' Role in Ukraine Business," *New York Times,* February 15, 2024.

197 **They would accuse Attorney General Merrick Garland of contempt**: Luke Broadwater, "Republicans Push Through Contempt of Congress Citation Against Garland," *New York Times,* June 12, 2024.

CHAPTER 26

198 **The committee had gaveled in so late**: Annie Karni, "Republicans Flock to Trump's Trial, Risking Control of the House Floor," *New York Times,* May 16, 2024.

198 **Boebert was greeted with a *Playbill* from *Beetlejuice***: @TGLNYC, "Asked Lauren Boebert to autograph a Beetle The Musical Playbill," Instagram, May 18, 2024, www.instagram.com/tglnyc/reel/C7HpKbNuWBj/.

199 **"Please tell me what that has to do with Merrick Garland"**: Mychael Schnell, "Chaos Erupts in Hearing as Greene, Ocasio-Cortez Clash over 'Fake Eyelashes' Jibe at Crockett," *The Hill,* May 16, 2024.

199 **"Well, then you're not striking your words"**: Luke Broadwater, "'Oversight After Dark': Lawmakers Hurl Insults at Session," *New York Times,* May 17, 2024.

200 **"She ain't worth it, bro"**: Nicholas Fandos, "Jamaal Bowman Finds His Voice. Some Republicans Don't Like the Sound," *New York Times,* May 19, 2023.

201 **"In the past, I've described the U.S. House"**: John Fetterman (@SenFettermanPA), "In the past, I've described the U.S. House as The Jerry Springer Show. Today, I'm apologizing to The Jerry Springer Show," X, May 17, 2024, x.com/SenFetterman PA/status/1791471678137966855.

202 **The Biden campaign later relied on her**: Katie Rogers, "Offstage, a Band of Biden Defenders Braves a Sea of Trump Swagger," *New York Times,* June 28, 2024.

202 **She later posted a photo of herself in a bikini**: Marjorie Taylor Greene (@mtgreenee), "Today I turned 50! Many people go into their 50th birthday thinking it's a bad thing, but I truly feel it's wonderful and I'm so excited and grateful God let me live 50 years and do so many things . . . ," X, May 27, 2024, x.com/ mtgreenee/status/1795123134695113124.

203 **"The major problem was that we allowed pornography"**: Broadwater, "'Oversight After Dark.'"

CHAPTER 27

207 **"This place is horrible"**: Annie Karni, "For One Democrat, the Price of Bucking Her Party Is a Flood of Bad Reviews," *New York Times,* July 22, 2023.

207 **"See my favorite big-booty Latina, AOC!"**: Rebecca Shabad, "Rep. Ocasio-Cortez Shares Video of Man Who Harassed Her on Steps of U.S. Capitol," NBCNews.com, July 14, 2022.

210 **he was also in court testifying on Trump's behalf**: Shaun Boyd, "Congressman Ken Buck Testifies at Trial Aimed at Keeping Trump off the Colorado Ballot," CBSNews.com, November 3, 2023.

211 **"This place keeps going downhill"**: Scott Wong, Sahil Kapur, and Ben Kamisar, "Republican Rep. Ken Buck Is Exiting Congress Early, Further Eroding GOP Majority," NBCNews.com, March 12, 2024.

211 **she "shouldn't have a place in Congress"**: Ally Mutnick and Melanie Zanona,

"House Republican Leaders Condemn GOP Candidate Who Made Racist Videos," *Politico,* June 18, 2020.

214 **"You don't belong here"**: Annie Karni, "Romney–Santos Confrontation Reflects a Broader Clash Within the G.O.P.," *New York Times,* February 8, 2023.

215 **Botox, Sephora, OnlyFans**: Nicholas Fandos, "How Santos Spent Donors' Money: Ferragamo, OnlyFans and Botox," *New York Times,* November 16, 2023.

216 **"Go on the website!"**: Annie Karni, "Santos Relishes the Limelight Even as His Show Looks Likely to Close," *New York Times,* November 30, 2023.

218 **"To hell with this place"**: Michael Gold and Grace Ashford, "George Santos Is Kicked Out of Congress in a Historic Vote," *New York Times,* December 1, 2023.

CHAPTER 28

219 **"truly remarkable individual"**: David Catanese, "Truly Remarkable Trailblazer': Kentucky Sen. McConnell Mourns Dianne Feinstein," *McClatchy DC,* September 29, 2023.

221 **"sweaty and rat-like"**: Tucker Carlson, quoted in Steve MacDonald, "Tucker on Twitter, Ep. 1," Grok!, June 6, 2023.

221 **"aggressive centrism"**: Michelle Goldberg, "Kyrsten Sinema Is Right. This Is Who She's Always Been," *New York Times,* December 9, 2022.

222 **praised her as a true "dealmaker"**: Isabella Murray, "McConnell Calls Democrat Kyrsten Sinema 'the Most Effective First-Term Senator,'" ABC News, September 26, 2022.

225 **"erases our borders"**: Sarah Fortinsky, "Border Deal Meets Immediate Blowback from Conservatives, Trump Allies in Congress," *The Hill,* February 4, 2024.

225 **"Joe Biden/Chuck Schumer Open Border Bill"**: Fortinsky, "Border Deal Meets Immediate Blowback from Conservatives, Trump Allies in Congress."

225 **"We're concocting some sort of deal"**: Rachel Scott et al., "Without Seeing All Border Deal Details, Speaker Mike Johnson Says It Is a 'Nonstarter,'" ABC News, January 31, 2024.

226 **"questions and serious concerns"**: Matthew Choi, "Texas Democrats and Republicans Split on Border Proposal —Not Necessarily on Party Lines," *Texas Tribune,* February 5, 2024.

CHAPTER 29

232 **"I can make a selfish decision"**: Annie Grayer, Melanie Zanona, and Manu Raju, "How Johnson Came to Embrace Ukraine Aid and Defy His Right Flank," CNN .com, April 21, 2024.

234 **"I don't know how this helps us, six months before an election"**: Annie Karni, "In Bid to Oust Johnson, Greene Tries to Reclaim a Powerful Perch on the Fringe," *New York Times,* May 1, 2024.

234 **"I served on a Navy destroyer"**: Annie Karni, "Weeks Before Prison, a Defiant Bannon Is Still Rallying MAGA World," *New York Times,* June 7, 2024.

CHAPTER 30

240 **In January 2024, when we called her office**: Annie Karni, "With Roe Gone, Some House Republicans Back Away from National Abortion Ban," *New York Times,* January 12, 2024.

241   **"I'm removing myself from the bill because"**: Sahil Kapur and Rebecca Kaplan, "GOP Rep. Michelle Steel Rescinds Her Co-Sponsorship of the Life at Conception Act After Winning Her Primary," NBC News, March 7, 2024.

CHAPTER 31

245   **"There is no shame"**: Reid J. Epstein, "Jamie Raskin, a Key Democrat, Urged Biden to Reconsider Campaign," *New York Times,* July 18, 2024.

249   **"The question of how to move forward"**: President Joseph R. Biden, "Read Biden's Letter to Congressional Democrats," *New York Times,* July 8, 2024.

CHAPTER 32

257   **In trying to make sense of what happened**: David Corn, "It Didn't Start with Trump: The Decades-Long Saga of How the GOP Went Crazy," *Mother Jones,* September and October 2022.

263   **"Evolutions are often lumpy and disjointed"**: Annie Karni, "Patrick McHenry, Former Interim Speaker, Will Leave Congress," *New York Times,* December 5, 2023.

INDEX

———

ANNIE KARNI is a congressional correspondent for *The New York Times*. She joined the paper in 2018 and was previously a White House correspondent, covering both the Trump and Biden administrations. Before that, she worked for *Politico,* where she covered the 2016 presidential election; and the *New York Post* and the New York *Daily News,* covering local politics. She frequently appears on MSNBC, where she was a paid contributor during the first Trump administration, and has also written for *Vogue* and *New York* magazines.

X: @anniekarni

LUKE BROADWATER is a congressional correspondent for *The New York Times,* where he has profiled congressional leaders, investigated federal spending, and played a key role in the paper's coverage of the January 6 attack on the U.S. Capitol, for which the *Times* was named a finalist for a Pulitzer Prize. Prior to joining the *Times,* Broadwater worked for nearly a decade at *The Baltimore Sun,* where he was the lead reporter on a series of investigative articles that won the 2020 Pulitzer Prize for Local Reporting and a George Polk Award for political reporting. He frequently appears on television and radio programs for interviews.

X: @lukebroadwater

ABOUT THE TYPE

This book was set in Bembo, a typeface based on an old-style Roman face that was used for Cardinal Pietro Bembo's tract *De Aetna* in 1495. Bembo was cut by Francesco Griffo (1450–1518) in the early sixteenth century for Italian Renaissance printer and publisher Aldus Manutius (1449–1515). The Lanston Monotype Company of Philadelphia brought the well-proportioned letterforms of Bembo to the United States in the 1930s.